The Complete Book of Deer Hunting

The Complete Book of Deer Hunting

BYRON W. DALRYMPLE

STOEGER PUBLISHING COMPANY

Published by Stoeger Publishing Company
55 Ruta Court,
South Hackensack, New Jersey 07606

This Stoeger Sportsman's Library edition is published by
arrangement with Winchester Press
Eighth printing, May 1987

Distributed to the book trade and to the sporting goods trade
by Stoeger Industries, 55 Ruta Court, South Hackensack,
New Jersey 07606

In Canada, distributed to the book trade and to the sporting
goods trade by Stoeger Canada, Ltd., 169 Idema Road,
Markham, Ontario L3R 1A9

Printed in the United States of America

ISBN 0-88317-050-7

To T.D.,

whose unique hunting method
on a certain seven-pointer
taught me the full importance
of ingenuity!

Contents

CHAPTER ONE

Deer
of the
North American
Continent

Of all the larger animals of North America, deer are by all odds the most popular among both hunters and nonhunters. Greeting cards, calendars, paintings, books honor the grace and agility of these animals. Wildlife observers and photographers become ecstatic over a fleeting glimpse of a buck bounding through the forest or standing silhouetted on a ridge. Hunters by millions eagerly await the open season. They plan, and reconnoiter their hunting ground when possible, for months prior, and after the season their stories are told and endlessly retold throughout the remainder of the year—the trophy that got away, and the one that fell to a masterful scheme plotted by the teller of the tale. The deer is a wise and wily creature, adept at remaining unseen and at escaping when seen. It is a handsome, exciting, and therefore most desirable trophy. And venison is excellent table fare.

In addition, there are two practical reasons why deer are held in such high esteem and are so eagerly hunted: they are the most abundant big-game animals on this continent, and their range encompasses most of it. The plain fact is that without deer there would be only a meager amount of big-game hunting in America. Many states would have none.

Elk, to be sure, are reasonably abundant in a few Western states and several Canadian provinces. But the entire continental elk harvest in peak years does not reach above 80,000 animals. The deer harvest in several individual states consistently tops 100,000, and in one it annually crowds 300,000.

Moose are restricted to a range across the colder northern wilderness regions. The annual continental bag is about the same as for elk. Prong-horns also have a restricted range and are taken in similar numbers. Sheep and goats are numerically even less important. The black bear originally ranged over much of the continent, but it is abundant in only a few states today, and a total season take of 25,000 is considered excellent. In a recent year, approximately that many deer were authenticated as killed by automobiles on the highways of Pennsylvania alone—an unhappy statistic, but at least it points up the abundance of deer.

Because of this abundance over larger areas, the hunter has a far better chance of success with deer than with any other large game animal. Whereas the proportion of successful elk license holders usually averages from 10 percent to a high in a few special areas of around 25 percent, scores of deer ranges turn up success percentages each season of anywhere from 40 percent to a full 100 percent. Of course, in some states success has dropped simply because there are so many hunters. In Michigan, for example, many hunters presently grouse about a dearth of deer. The fact remains, however, that for some years the annual harvest has been somewhere near 100,000, while license buyers have climbed to as high as 600,000! It would obviously be impossible to so manage the Michigan deer population that success might be assured for every hunter. There would be no deer left at all, for meanwhile habitat is constantly shrinking.

Regardless of whether success is 10 percent or 100 percent in a given locality, the fact remains that deer are accessible to almost every hunter, either in his own county or state or nearby. That is the most important consideration. Deer, and especially whitetail deer, anciently developed a fantastic capacity for adjusting to different ranges.

So the deer hunter can find his prey in a variety of terrains and climates. I can recall the dense forest of northern Maine where I hunted

The whitetail hunter who travels must learn to hunt in every conceivable type of terrain. This buck is in a Louisiana swamp.

in bitter weather. I can vividly see the big ten-point rack of a real trophy whitetail exactly as it looked when I sighted it above the cactus and thornbush of South Texas near the Mexican border on a hot November dawn. There was the excellent buck I photographed in a Florida swamp as it trotted off, splashing water and looking over its shoulder at me. And the one in a South Dakota cornfield so fat it could barely waddle. And the dapper little fantail up in the grass, oak, and juniper zone of the mountains in southeastern Arizona, the big buck high up in the pines of eastern Washington, the buck racing through dense woods and vines behind the levee in Mississippi, the many deer trails in snow in Michigan's north woods.

Although the whitetail range in North America extends into many Western strongholds of the mule deer, because of habitat barriers mule deer have never been able to colonize eastward. Nonetheless, their own range from north to south is astonishing, reaching, with the type species and one or another subspecies, from the deserts and mountain slopes of interior Mexico to the southeastern coastal forests of Alaska. I have hunted mule deer in the United States literally from border to border, from the Montana timber to the all but treeless portions of northeastern Wyoming, from a snowed-in camp in the Colorado high country to the sweltering deserts of southern Arizona and the Big Bend country of western Texas.

Thus, deer are available almost everywhere. It is an amazing commentary on the ability of deer to adapt to man's settlement that as I write this, in the coming fall every one of the forty-nine continental states and most of the Canadian provinces will have a deer season. Not only have deer been able to adjust their life patterns to the vast desecration of their original habitats by man's civilization, but they have been able to survive in astonishing numbers. They are extremely prolific, able under optimum conditions to double their numbers each year. Of course, the great increase in knowledge of game management techniques in the past few decades has been one of the most important influences in retaining deer in abundance and deer hunting throughout their entire range on the continent.

No one really knows how many deer existed in North America before the coming of white men. Authoritative estimates have placed the total, counting both whitetails and mule deer, as high as 50 million. Occasionally someone claims that there are more deer today than there were originally. This is by no means true. What is true is that deer were brought to an endangered status over much of the continent toward the end of the last century and the beginning of this one, by vast commercial overkill. Probably at the turn of the century there were not more than 500,000 deer within U.S. boundaries, and possibly there were even fewer. Fortunately, settlement of the land, up to the point which was occurring during that period, formed great expanses of habitat better than much of the original land had been. This resulted from cutting of timber, forming "edges" and openings and allowing huge areas of new forage growth to rise. At this same time, too, the scarcity of deer, and the profound interest in them among people everywhere, prompted a move toward stricter game laws and the research that developed into the present-day science of deer management. The reestablishment of deer, their "comeback"—for today they are again numbered in millions and indeed occupy virtually all suitable range on the continent and are even in some places too plentiful—is probably the greatest conservation success story of the century, and the most brilliant accomplishment to date in the field of wildlife management.

Few people, hunters or nonhunters, realize fully how important deer have been, and are, to North American civilization. While the buffalo was of greater importance to Plains Indians, deer were more important over the entire continent. And they were by far more important to the colonists and all early pioneers. In fact, the value of deer in North America during the time of early settlement and exploration was far greater than that of cattle and domestic animals of all kinds. Curiously, even today and for many years past deer have had a value second only to domestic meat animals! State after state, studying the economic value of its individual deer herd on the basis of the amount hunters spend in that single state annually, has come up with figures close to or above a billion dollars per year!

American deer have up to the present served four basic types of hunters. The first group were those who hunted totally out of need—Indians, then whites and Indians together. Both utilized deer as a most important food source. Both used deer hides for clothing and shelter. Indians also utilized sinew and bone for thread, lashings, and tools.

As white settlement advanced, there came a period of frenzied activity, mostly among whites, in market hunting, the commercial harvest of deer for sale of both meat and hides. Many of these hunters were also "need" hunters; but whatever venison and hides they did not use themselves they sold.

Present-day readers probably have little idea of the scale of early market hunting for deer. For example, by the middle of the eighteenth century an average of 30,000 to 40,000 deer hides (whitetails) were being shipped to England and Europe each year from each of several different Southern ports. Since transport by land was then slow and difficult, probably most of these deer came from areas not too distant from those ports. Altogether, several hundred thousand hides undoubtedly were shipped each year from various Southern ports. The same thing was occurring far to the north, in eastern Canada. Tons of venison also were being sold and shipped, hams and saddles in barrels.

Market hunting continued on through the nineteenth century, and an astonishing number of deer were killed commercially for meat and hides. This occurred not just in the East, but throughout what is now the United States. In Minnesota, in California, and elsewhere tens of thousands of deer were slaughtered, some only for hides. There are records of parties of three or four hide hunters taking a thousand or more mule deer in a single area where they operated, in Montana, in only a few weeks. Railroad shipping statistics show one Midwestern city receiving venison in a two-month period that obviously totaled, according to number of hams and saddles, at least 6,000 deer.

Some years ago an old man in Michigan, a man who had lived during the time of heavy market hunting and was a historian of sorts, told me that at least 100,000 whitetails from that state went to market in a two-year period in the late 1800s. Several hunters in Great Lakes states boasted of killing as many as two to three thousand deer in a single season! Identical slaughter was also going on in the frontier Southwest, in Texas and Arizona. And throughout most of the heyday of commercial hunting, venison sold for as little as a nickel a pound and seldom more than ten to twenty cents a pound.

Market hunting tapered off and ended for very simple reasons: the deer were finally too scarce to make it worthwhile, and restrictive laws were enacted and enforced. The third group of hunters now came into being. These were the sport hunters. To be sure, white men from the beginning of settlement and Indians before them had derived some sporting pleasure from their "need" hunting and market hunting. But now there began to grow a legion of deer hunters of varying motives—some, of course, still wanted the meat and to some extent the hides—but chiefly after excitement within the framework of law.

Much of the sport hunting during the early decades of this century was by no means as good as it is today. There were, to be sure, fewer hunters, but in a great many places deer were scarce. However, conservation attitudes were growing. Seasons and bag limits were more severely drawn, and enforcement became a stern matter. The concept of managing this resource had evolved, and new techniques were used. For example, deer were trapped in counties where they existed in fair numbers and transplanted to counties or habitats from which they had been removed. Quota systems finally arrived.

And so today the fourth group of hunters, numbering in millions, are on the scene—the sport hunters whose activity is carefully regulated by law and who seldom hunt out of need, even though they use the venison or give it away to friends. Deer herds are kept well stabilized almost everywhere by enlightened management—and deer have a greater monetary value in our economy, if we must measure it that way, than they have ever previously achieved. It runs into billions of dollars each hunting season. This does not count, of course, money spent by nonhunting tourists and wildlife observers. But we must note here with heavy emphasis that it is the *hunter*—in this era of so much misguided anti-hunting sentiment—who foots the entire bill for managing deer herds, conducting further research projects, and enforcing game laws. In short, the hunter keeps deer present in abundance over all suitable ranges in North America.

Differences Between Whitetails and Mule Deer

As most hunters know, there are two groups of deer on the continent: the whitetails, which are predominantly Eastern but are also distributed over large areas of the West; and the mule deer, which are Western deer. Mule deer are commonly called blacktails. However, this confuses them with the Columbian blacktail. That deer, and the Sitka deer, were once presumed to be distinct species. But it was later decided that they are simply subspecies of the mule deer. All of these deer of North America belong to a single family and genus, and there are only two given full species status, the Virginia whitetail and the Rocky Mountain mule deer. All others are presently classified as subspecies of these two.

There are many physical differences between whitetails and mule deer. Some of them are too technical to be of interest to the hunter. Hunters need recognize only a few of the distinctive and easily noted characteristics of each group in order to differentiate them. Whitetails are

Whitetail buck. Many hunters have the impression that whitetails belong in snow country, but actually more are taken in warm climes.

Mule deer buck. Posed among piñon and juniper, he is offering the hunter a perfect shot.

animals of forest edges, brush, and heavy cover. Mule deer inhabit mountain areas and foothills, with open forest, rugged terrain of varying kinds, and eroded brushlands. They are commonly able to cope with far more open expanses than whitetails, but in general they avoid dense coniferous timber and brushless grasslands. There are some exceptions—the Columbian blacktail and Sitka deer are animals of humid coastal forests where both brush and big timber combine. We will touch terrain in greater detail in later chapters.

The whitetail has a general outline more slender, graceful, and "dainty" than the blocky build of the mule deer. Whitetail antlers are single-branched—that is, the points or tines rise from a single main beam on either antler. An occasional whitetail rack may be multibranched, but the normal rack has a single branch. The antlers of a mule deer are double-branched. A fork may appear at the end of each main beam, and tines rising from the main beam also fork. Whitetail antlers are inclined to curve around in an inward arc above the head. Mule deer antlers usually rise more or spread wide without much incurving. Columbian blacktail antler formation is basically similar to that of other mule deer. Both whitetail and mule deer bear brow tines, but it is not uncommon for them to be missing, especially in young mule deer. Some mule deer antlers do not branch in the normal double bifurcate manner. I have a set on my wall, from a Desert mule deer, that many visitors have thought to be from an unusual whitetail.

An examination of the metatarsal gland on the lower hind leg will easily distinguish whitetail from mule deer. In the former it is usually surrounded by light or white hair and is seldom much over an inch in length. In mule deer it is much longer, at least two inches, and outlined with brown hair.

Probably the tails of these deer are their best identification tags. The whitetail has a long tail, almost a foot long. It is wide at the base and most of the way to the end, and is some shade of brown to blackish on top with a fringe of white as the tail is seen in the down position. When the deer runs in alarm the tail is raised high and shows as a white flag, for the hairs are held erect. As the deer bounds the tail is waved from one side to the other. The mule deer has a short "string" tail not more than two-thirds as long as the whitetail's. It has a black tip that goes clear around the end. Subspecies of mule deer show varying amounts of black. The Columbian blacktail has a somewhat broader tail, but it is still short. It has black from the base down the center of the top and much more black across and around the tip. When a mule deer runs, it seldom raises its tail, and if it does hold it out at all, it never lifts to quite a horizontal position. The Columbian blacktail and the Sitka deer, however, are sometimes exceptions to this rule; they may, or may not, raise the tail clear up to "flag" position. But it is not waved.

Mule deer ears are much longer than whitetail ears—at least eleven inches long, and in some races longer. Whitetail ears are usually only seven or eight inches long. The Columbian blacktail ear is not quite as long as those of the other mule deer, but it is still longer than the whitetail ear.

Mule deer and whitetails also have different gaits. The gait of an alarmed whitetail is a bounding run with an occasional high leap over an obstacle. A mule deer has several odd gaits. When first startled it com-

A mule deer bounds for cover with the characteristic stiff-legged hopping gait.

monly bounds with what might be termed a "pogo-stick" motion, stiff-legged, in short hops. Then it may trot momentarily almost like a pacer, and finally when going all-out it bounds in long leaps with all four feet striking the ground at once and pushing backward.

With deer so plentiful and popular, it is surprising that there is such lack of knowledge, and also confusion, among hunters about how many species and subspecies there are, and where each ranges. Some of this knowledge, of course, is merely a matter of interest to the hunter, but it can also be important to him. The knowledgeable hunter can plan interesting hunts and will know what to expect in deer habits, what variations in appearance there may be from place to place, and what is or is not a trophy.

A good example concerns mule deer. The majority of mule deer hunters have had experience with the so-called "type" species, the Rocky Mountain mule deer. (The type species of an animal is the variety considered the standard, from which any subspecies derive.) This, as noted, is a deer in general of mountain forest edges and slopes. It is large, and a good trophy would have an antler spread of at least 28 to 30 inches. But the Desert mule deer is quite different. It has a far smaller range, and is a smaller animal but very blocky and handsome. Hunting it is a most interesting endeavor. The terrain is very different, as a rule, from that in which Rocky Mountain mule deer are hunted. And a specimen would be considered a good one with an antler spread of, say, 25 or 26 inches.

Another classic example of the importance of knowing the species and subspecies concerns the very small whitetail known as the Carmen Mountains whitetail. These deer, called "flagtails" in West Texas, are surprisingly abundant in isolated small mountain ranges of Texas' Big Bend country, and similar nearby ranges in Mexico. I've made several hunts for them, and was very surprised to learn that no Texas hunter I ever spoke to about them had correctly identified them. Most believed them to be Coues deer, the Arizona whitetail. The Carmen Mountains subspecies does indeed superficially resemble the Coues subspecies of whitetail, colloquially called the "fantail." It is small, and has a tight little rack and a large flag of a tail. But it is a totally different subspecies, isolated geographically from any contact with the Arizona deer.

It should be noted that the reason the Coues deer is given status in official records is that in its small U.S. range it is totally isolated from contact with any other whitetail subspecies. Thus there cannot be intergrades or mixtures. Conversely, the Carmen Mountains deer interbreeds fairly commonly on fringes of its small range with a much larger whitetail subspecies, the Texas whitetail. Such intergrades occur, or may occur, among most subspecies of both whitetail and mule deer.

Except for those with a small and semi-isolated range, such as Coues deer, the various subspecies have been so heavily managed by transplanting and their ranges have so much overlapped, that in many instances pure strains of a subspecies are difficult if not impossible to find. Subspecies of limited range or in some cases broad range may already have been all but swallowed up by interbreeding with more abundant subspecies on all sides of their range. This has happened, for example, with the once abundant and wide-ranging Kansas whitetail. Nonetheless, avid deer hunters can find much to intrigue them by making hunts for pure or nearly pure strains of the various whitetail subspecies. In some, for instance, the skull is narrow and the antlers likely to be narrow also in spread. They are quite different from, for example, the big, broad-antlered Northern Woodland whitetail.

Whitetail Subspecies

At the present time among North American white-tailed deer there are the type species (the Virginia whitetail) and sixteen subspecies within U.S. and Canadian borders. Another thirteen occur down across interior and southern Mexico and Central America. It is the Canadian, U.S., and northern Mexico whitetails with which we are concerned—the seventeen varied deer. Technical measurements and descriptions of each would serve no good purpose here. But at least we can give a brief idea of original ranges of each, general size, and a few characteristics. In most instances the fringes of range of each contain such complicated intergradation with one or more others that a change from one to another is not always noticeable.

This is especially true—of all species, not just deer—where terrain and climate and forage change gradually, as from northern Florida into Georgia or from western Louisiana into eastern Texas. Where there is total isolation, as on islands, characteristics are distinct. And where there is an abrupt change, as from the lower deserts of the Big Bend country in Texas to the highest mountains of that region, where piñon and madrona grow, the change in a subspecies is also distinct. For example, the Carmen Mountains whitetail is easily distinguished from the larger Texas whitetail found at lower elevations in some of these same mountains. And even some of the intergrades between the two are quite noticeable and distinctive.

The type species of whitetail is the Virginia white-tailed deer (*Odocoileus virginianus virginianus*). The repetition of the scientific species name indicates, as in all species, that this is the one from which all subspecies or geographical races derive. Presumably this deer was selected as the chief representative of North American white-tailed deer because it was the first deer seen and known by the colonists. Jamestown was the first permanent English settlement on these shores, founded by Captain John Smith and his men. Their first taste of New World venison came from this Virginia deer.

The Virginia deer ranges along the Atlantic Coast roughly from the Potomac River south to about Savannah, Georgia. The northern range boundary inland is the Ohio River, and on the west the Mississippi River. Parts of southeastern Mississippi, southern Alabama, and southern Georgia are the domain of a subspecies. The Virginia whitetail is a husky deer standing about 3½ feet at the shoulder and with typically heavy antlers of substantial spread. The top of the tail is rusty and the outsides of the legs are brown. The winter coat is grizzled but with a distinct brownish cast.

Along the Atlantic Coast are several islands on which whitetails, undoubtedly stocked anciently, and naturally, from the type species, evolved into distinct subspecies because of isolation. These are the Bulls

Island whitetail (*Odocoileus virginianus taurinsulae*), a bit smaller and darker in color than the Virginia deer; the Hunting Island whitetail (*O.v. venatorius*), also smaller and with color generally buff and dark brown; the Hilton Head Island whitetail (*O.v. hiltonensis*), about the same size as the other two subspecies, with winter coat a cinnamon cast; and the Blackbeard Island whitetail (*O.v. nigribarbis*), a medium-sized deer which is found on this and some other islands along coastal Georgia, brownish to cinnamon in general color with ears and face very dark. These are interesting specimens because of their differences from the mainland deer.

To the south, Florida has several whitetail subspecies. Probably the best known nowadays is the one not hunted, the smallest of the whitetails: the tiny Key deer, *O.v. clavium*. Once these diminutive deer ranged over the southern Keys but were brought near to extinction as settlement continued. In the late 1940s there were less than fifty left. A small refuge was established on Big Pine Key, and the deer were thus saved, but not in huntable numbers. These little deer are not much over 20 inches at the shoulder. The winter coat has a generally tawny-grizzled appearance.

On the Florida mainland throughout the peninsula and reaching up into southern Georgia on the east is found the large Florida whitetail (*O.v. seminolus*). This deer in typical specimens has antlers less spreading and narrower than the Virginia deer, and the skull is not as broad. The winter coat is short and grizzled but distinctly tan to tawny. Another subspecies, the Florida Coastal whitetail (*O.v. osceola*), ranges along the west coast of Florida, beginning roughly in the Clearwater region and ranging north and west across into southern Alabama and southeastern Mississippi in all of the lowland coastal areas. This deer is much like the type, the Virginia deer, but smaller and paler and with a narrower skull, like the Florida whitetail.

Still farther west there is a lowland subspecies, the Avery Island whitetail (*O.v. mcilhennyi*). The range begins about at the Mississippi-Louisiana border and runs west across the lowland coastal region of Louisiana and into coastal Texas well down past Houston. This is a large deer colored rather like the Florida Coastal whitetail. Its skull is usually broader, and typically the main beam of the antlers curves well around above the face or head.

All of these deer show intergrades with the Virginia deer wherever the ranges meet. They also show intermediate specimens where their own ranges meet or overlap, and on the north and west the Avery Island deer intergrades with the Kansas and Texas whitetails, which will be described shortly. Thus it is readily obvious that a subspecies of small restricted range surrounded by ranges of other subspecies can be diluted until often a pure specimen is difficult to find.

The Virginia deer's fairly large expanse of range allows it to remain reasonably pure except in localities where transplants of subspecies may have been made. Though it touches the ranges of some of the subspecies so far noted, its northern and western boundaries are rather well defined by rivers, and it can come in contact naturally with only two other subspecies, one of which, to the north, has the largest distribution of any of the whitetails. This is the Northern Woodland whitetail (*O.v. borealis*). This is the deer with winter coat of grizzled brown known to a vast number of hunters, for it blankets the entire area throughout Maine and all of New England, New York, and Pennsylvania, reaches across Ohio, Indiana, Illinois, and throughout the Great Lakes area, and across southern Canada

A big whitetail buck in Michigan.

from western Ontario eastward. The boundaries on the west are drawn by the Mississippi River and the Red River. The Ohio and the Potomac define the southern reach.

This is one of the largest whitetails. Although many specimens are of average size where range may be less than optimum, in Maine whitetails of 300 pounds show up annually in fair numbers. I've seen several Michigan and Wisconsin deer that topped 200 pounds field-dressed. There are astonishing records from Wisconsin, one of 481 pounds, one of 491. There is also a near-unbelievable record from Minnesota of 511 pounds! Of course the Northern Woodland whitetail averages far less than that. In many places a buck of 120 to 140 pounds field-dressed is a good one. But it is well known that the largest whitetails in general come from the Northeast, and from the Northern Woodland subspecies. Southern whitetails on the average are smaller. Range conditions and changes in land use have distinct bearing. As an example, some very large whitetails have been taken in recent years in farm country of the Midwest. Forage is excellent and deer numbers are not large.

In the northwestern part of its range the Northern Woodland whitetail borders the range of the Dakota whitetail (*O.v. dacotensis*). The Dakota deer is also very large, in some instances larger than *borealis*. Across much of its range the Dakota deer does not have the broad forest expanses that are found eastward. But river valleys with their margins of timber form one of its chief habitat types. The range is large, encompassing southern portions of the Prairie Provinces of Canada (parts of Manitoba, Saskatchewan, Alberta), all of the Dakotas, eastern Montana and Wyoming east of the Rockies, portions of northeastern Colorado, and all of Nebraska north of the Platte River. The winter coat is often dark brown but may be paler than that of the Northern Woodland deer. The antlers are sturdy and often look even more so because tines are likely to be short.

To the southeast this deer borders on the northern range of the big Kansas whitetail (*O.v. macrourus*). The Kansas deer range is sandwiched in among those of the Northern Woodland deer on the north and northeast, the Virginia deer on the southeast, and the Texas deer on the west (to be noted shortly). It also touches the Avery Island lowlands deer on the south. The Kansas deer is a heavy-antlered, dark animal, usually a bit smaller than the bulky Dakota deer but nonetheless large. The original range of this deer covered portions of northeastern Texas and northern Louisiana, all of Arkansas and the eastern half of Oklahoma, eastern Kansas, all of Missouri, and most of Iowa. But intergrades on every border have diluted it, transplants of other deer have been made often within its range, farming has destroyed some of its habitats, and it is thought that most of the pure Kansas whitetails are now gone.

The Texas whitetail (*O.v. texanus*) ranges across western Kansas and Oklahoma, eastern and southern Colorado, eastern New Mexico, all of Texas except the east, and well down below the border into Mexico along the entire length of the border with Texas. To deer hunters living in Texas—which has a deer herd of several million, an estimated one-fifth of the entire national deer herd, and an annual bag of about 300,000—this is a puzzling subspecies, differing drastically in size and also in coloration from place to place, probably because the range is large and the terrain so different every few miles. For example, the whitetails of the Edwards Plateau or hill country are small. My own ranch has scores of them, and it is not uncommon to take an eight-point buck of only 75 pounds field-dressed weight. The South Texas brush country has large, heavy-antlered whitetails, mature bucks weighing, field-dressed, from 140 to 200 pounds. My largest to date was 185. In West Texas bucks are of fair size.

This whitetail is a real trophy. Note that the antlers spread well outside the ears.

I hunted hard for this fine specimen of the diminutive Carmen Mountains whitetail.

Color variations, as noted, are wide. But typically the Texas whitetail is grayish in winter coat. The color of the top of the tail shows wide variation but is typically blackish to very dark brown. Antlers on the average spread wide but are fairly slender. Tines are usually long, including brow tines. Eight and ten points are common.

Earlier I mentioned the small Carmen Mountains whitetail (*O.v. carminis*). This small deer—mature bucks usually weigh much less than 100 pounds field-dressed—is found in West Texas in several small individual mountain ranges of the Big Bend country, such as the Chisos in Big Bend National Park and other high areas north of the park on private ranches. It is named for the Sierra del Carmen in Coahuila, Mexico, and is found in other ranges south of the border along and below the Big Bend of the Rio Grande. It is a grizzled gray color in winter coat. The top of the tail is reddish brown to brownish black. Good racks are handsome, tightly curved but not quite so much so as in the Arizona whitetail. This is a most desirable trophy.

The Coues or Arizona whitetail (*O.v. couesi*) is small, with a grayish winter coat. It has rather large ears, and in good specimens a handsome, compact rack, the beams coming into a tight curve frontally. It occurs in the oak and grass zone as a rule, above the desert floor with its cactus and ocotillo and below the pine zone. The range begins in the west about at the Colorado River and spreads eastward; the deer is found only in mountain areas. Southeastern Arizona with its several ranges is the dominant and best part of the range within U.S. borders. It runs northward about to the Mogollon Rim and over into southwestern New Mexico, with the prime range there chiefly southwest of Lordsburg in the Animas and Peloncillo Mountains. This deer does not extend past the Rio Grande in New Mexico. The range in Mexico is much larger, running far south along the Sierra Madre.

The other whitetails are found way up in the northwestern United States. The prominent variety is the Northwest whitetail (*O.v. ochrourus*), a large deer chiefly of the west slope of the Rockies from lower British Columbia and Alberta south through western Montana and parts of western Wyoming, into eastern Washington and Oregon and much of Idaho. At one time this deer was also distributed south into northeast California and across into Nevada, but for some time no authenticated reports of it have surfaced. This big light-colored but grizzled whitetail usually has wide-spreading antlers and is a good trophy. It has long been overshadowed in popularity by the more abundant and more easily bagged mule deer of the same region. In some instances this whitetail has become so abundant and so little hunted that licenses allowing two deer require that at least one be a whitetail.

The last whitetail subspecies to be noted within U.S. borders is really an endangered, nonhunted variety. This is the Columbian whitetail (*O.v. leucurus*). Originally it was distributed throughout much of the Pacific coastal forest from northern Oregon into southwestern Washington. But it has been unable to adapt to the press of civilization. There is presently a small pure-strain herd along the lower Columbia River, a few still hanging on near Roseburg, and possibly a few more in the Mount Hood region. This is a fairly large deer, grizzled in winter coat, with a cinnamon tail top and a wide flare of white when the tail is raised in flight.

There are a number of other whitetail subspecies in interior and southern Mexico and on down through Central America. Because of their general obscurity and the lack of opportunity for American hunters to bag them or even to identify them, we will not cover them here. However, for hunters eager to try for these under Mexico's rather complicated laws, there are ample deer present. The whitetail is in fact widely distributed over Mexico in one or another race, and undoubtedly it is the most important Mexican game species. A hunter planning a trip there can consult references in large libraries to learn about the subspecies and their distribution.

Mule Deer Subspecies

The whitetail from ancient times onward developed numerous races almost everywhere in its vast range. The mule deer, which is believed to have migrated from Asia in primitive form hundreds of thousands of years ago, was not able to spread its range as far as the whitetail, but did thrust southward astonishingly, well into Mexico. However, over approximately 70 percent of its domain it has kept its same form, and this is the so-called type species, the Rocky Mountain mule deer (*Odocoileus hemionus hemionus*). Only along the coastal ranges of the Pacific, throughout California, Baja, and parts of the U.S. Southwest, and north-central Mexico has it developed geographic races.

I mentioned earlier that the Columbian blacktail and the Sitka deer were once considered true species, then reclassified after longer study as simply subspecies of the Rocky Mountain mule deer. A most interesting point has been made by some scientists, however. They believe that the Columbian blacktail and Sitka, though not yet different enough from the type mule deer to be given species status, are nonetheless on their way to that state through progressive evolution, brought about no doubt by the influences of the specialized habitats to which they have adapted. Another point to be made regarding mule deer is that their range extends much farther north than that of the whitetail, yet they have also found it possible to adapt to desert conditions far south.

Readers must bear in mind that biologists are constantly making changes in scientific nomenclature. It is possible that new subspecies of both whitetail and mule deer may be named even before this ink is dry. But at present mule deer are classified into ten subspecies plus the type species. Only three of these deer are of pronounced importance to hunters—the Rocky Mountain mule deer, the Desert mule deer, and the Columbian blacktail—so we will look at those first.

The Rocky Mountain deer is far and away the most important simply because its range brings the greatest number of hunters into contact with it. Distribution begins far up in Canada roughly at the 60th parallel. On the west, very generally speaking, the Coast Ranges in British Columbia are the border line, and this boundary continues southward down through Washington, Oregon, and California. Eastward the deer is found in portions of the Prairie Provinces, but progressively farther south, across to western Manitoba. Within the United States the range extends from the Pacific coastal mountains eastward to the western Dakotas and western Nebraska, on down through the western two-thirds of Colorado, into extreme western Oklahoma and a bit of Panhandle Texas, thence westward across the northern half of New Mexico and Arizona and all but the southern triangle of Nevada, and then into the counties of northeastern California.

As most readers know, this is a large deer, very blocky and with large, heavy antlers in the best specimens. Rocky Mountain mule deer bucks above 200 pounds are rather common, and they go much larger. However, an average mature buck is probably around 140 to 150 pounds, field-dressed. Winter color may differ a good deal from place to place, but in general is a grizzled gray. Looking straight into the face of a mule deer with ears up, one has the impression of the large expanses inside the ears as mostly whitish, but black-rimmed. Across the top of the head between and forward of the antlers there is a wide patch of hair darker than the face and nose but usually grizzled gray-brown, set off by whitish above the eyes and a dark area between the eyes and running back in lines toward the antlers. The nose and cheeks are gray, with a ring above the upper muzzle very pale and set off against the black, shiny muzzle.

Probably the most striking identification marking of the mule deer is the large patch of white or extremely pale grayish-white covering the rump. It runs up to the tail base and in the type species and several subspecies clear around above it, almost heart-shaped, and then runs on down the inside of each hind leg. Each subspecies has slight distinctive differences in the size of the patch. In several it is smaller, with some black at the tail base, running down the top of the tail and wider at the end of the tail. In the Rocky Mountain deer only the tip of the tail is black and the tail is generally quite slender.

The Desert mule deer (*O.h. crooki*) has a small but important range within the U.S. It is found in southeastern Arizona, southern New Mexico, and the region west of the Pecos River in Texas. However, the range extends far down into central Mexico. This mule deer is smaller than the type, and usually paler gray, and seldom if ever with antlers at maximum as large. The white rump patch may be smaller, and in some of these deer there is a line of black down from the tail base. However, of the several dozen I have taken in Texas I've never seen this, nor have I seen it in Arizona. Within the U.S. range, and apparently also in Mexico, the Desert mule deer sticks to the foothills and open desert mountains and even the scrub of flat desert. It is not found except casually as one goes higher into the mountains, into the forest zone. I have seen mule deer up in piñon in the Big Bend of Texas, but the whitetails are dominant. There are intergrades of this deer and the Rocky Mountain deer in both New Mexico and Arizona, but it is doubtful that any are present in Texas.

The Columbian blacktail deer (*O.h. columbianus*) is sometimes called the "coast deer." The range extends from the mid-California coastal slope on north to the central British Columbia coast. The range extends inland up the west slope of the Coast Ranges in British Columbia and from the top of the Cascades in Washington and Oregon west to the Pacific. In California there has been a substantial amount of interbreeding with the Rocky Mountain deer and to a lesser extent farther north. The blacktail is smaller than the Rocky Mountain deer, and in winter coat darker. The tail has a broad base and is reminiscent in shape of that of the whitetail, but it is not as long. The top of the tail is black, with as a rule some white showing along the upper outer edges. Antlers are inclined to be smaller and sometimes the branches have fewer forks. This deer is extremely important to coastal hunters and in much of its range is very plentiful.

Closely allied with the Columbian blacktail but distributed farther north is the Sitka deer (*O.h. sitkensis*), found along the coast and coastal islands of northern British Columbia and southeastern Alaska. This deer, rather small, is in winter coat a richer brown than the blacktail, and has much of the outer surface of the tail brown. The skull of the buck is broader. It has been transplanted to a modest extent outside its original range in Alaska. Although natives hunt the Sitka deer for meat, there has to date been little interest in it by visiting sport hunters. This is unfortunate, for it is often abundant, bag limits are high, and it makes an interesting and unusual trophy.

The California mule deer (*O.h. californicus*) is important to a substantial number of hunters within its modest range. This deer looks much like the Rocky Mountain deer, and may also be confused in some instances with the blacktail. The rump patch is smaller and the tail shows a dark streak down the top. The range is in general between Los Angeles and halfway to San Francisco on the coast and inland, and a bit farther north as one progresses eastward. South of the range of this deer is the Southern mule deer (*O.h. fuliginatus*), a dark variety with much of the top of the tail black. The range runs from below Los Angeles on down into Mexico. It is not especially plentiful in this populous region.

A subspecies that probably interbreeds with this one is the Inyo mule deer (*O.h. inyoensis*), chiefly from its namesake county in southern California. This deer appears to be a kind of transition race between the type species and the California deer. One other subspecies is found in extreme southeastern California, extreme southwestern Arizona, and a short distance into Mexico. This is the Burro deer (*O.h. eremicus*), a large, pale deer of low elevations chiefly along the Colorado River in its range.

Three other mule deer races are known presently in western Mexico. Two are restricted to islands, Tiburón and Cedros. The third is the Peninsula mule deer found in southern Lower California.

CHAPTER TWO

Where the Deer Are

When I first began deer hunting many years ago, I made several hunts in an expanse of state forest in the Great Lakes region simply because it was near where I lived. In fact, I could drive from my home into good deer cover in ten minutes. The area certainly did have a substantial number of deer, but they were still hard to come by. Many people who hunted the territory considered success about average if they brought in a buck every other season. Some went three or four years without a deer.

A friend of mine who lived in the same town seldom hunted where I did. He drove some 200 miles north and west. I had great admiration for him because every season he brought home a good buck. But the season lasted only about two weeks, so it was handy for me to have a place to hunt close by. I could run out any time I wished. Make no mistake, I enjoyed just being out. Hunting deer is a wonderful pastime regardless of whether or not one is successful. Nonetheless, as a renowned politician has said, winning may not be everything but losing isn't anything. Knowing your chances are excellent certainly makes the hunt more exciting. Anticipation and optimism grow in proportion to the narrowing of odds.

For several years that successful friend had me believing it was his prowess that brought him success. Then one year I happened to read a set of state harvest statistics from a study that had been done in the region where he was hunting. The buck kill was something like four per square mile, and hunter success a full 40 percent when related to the number of hunters. I started checking on the success where I was hunting. I discovered it was averaging only about 10 percent, with a per-section (square mile) average which matched the other proportionately almost perfectly: roughly one deer per square mile. Pretty darned low!

Slowly it began to dawn on me that the hunters in that 40-percent expanse couldn't all be wily experts. They had to be a cross section, as anywhere. But they were doing four times as well as in my area. It was very obvious that they were hunting where there were more deer. Such a simple and obvious fact! Yet it had never occurred to me previously simply because, well, it was handy to hunt near home, and that's where I had started. I loved that woods. That didn't mean it was any deer bonanza. Why not, I then began reasoning, take a few days and go to that better region? If I connected, fine. If not, I could still make the near-home hunts.

The reasoning is so ridiculously elementary that it would seem hardly worthwhile telling it. However, it is surprising that in today's modern world of deer hunting, when almost everybody can and does make an annual foray after deer, vast numbers fail to research their hunting destination thoroughly enough, and thus deny themselves better chances of success. It certainly does pay to "hunt where the deer are," but you have to *know* where they are, and that is the purpose of this chapter. Obviously we cannot review here every square mile of territory in the United States. But it is possible to chart where some of the top deer ranges and populations are in each state.

Surprisingly, many hunters are not fully aware of deer distribution even within their home states. A portion of success depends, of course, on the craft of the individual hunter. Certainly an experienced hunter who knows every foot of his hunting ground may do well each season even if the deer population is low. He has compensated for thinly spread deer by studying the terrain and knowing where those few are and how best to outwit them. But hunters in strange territories don't have such knowledge. Hunters planning trips to other states seldom do.

Most game departments keep quite accurate annual records of their deer harvests. Some do the surveys by "Hunt Units" into which the state is divided by the game department analysts. Some use county tallies. A very few go even finer, to townships. It's necessary that they make such careful studies because deer management nowadays is a rather exact science and each part of deer range in any state must be managed to cut down excess animals or give low populations a chance to recover from natural debacles such as hard winters.

Surveys are usually made, as accurately as possible, long before a season opens. Fawn production is checked in each unit in spring. If there is a maximum fawn drop, and later in summer indication that fawn survival has been high, estimates must be made of gross numbers of deer, how many antlerless and antlered deer may be taken, what age groups are most likely to be bagged by various systems, which age groups need to be harvested. Then after the season the kill figures are correlated with the pre-season studies to discover how accurate the early surveys and regulations were. Post-season counts are also made, and often spring adult counts to make sure what occurred during winter.

Thus it can be said that deer biologists know a great deal about what is happening to their charges. Occasionally they make errors, because many factors can upset their estimates. But their records are excellent over a number of years. And so when you see kill figures for a state, a fine perusal of them will usually give you a very accurate picture of where the *most* deer are and what your chances will be in any given area. Success will obviously vary from season to season. There are many reasons why this may occur. A carefully planned harvest may be upset by severe, or too warm, weather. A late-summer drought in desert country may cause a die-off of thousands of deer and thus a light kill, which does not reflect what the true conditions were. In other words, the deer were there but Nature beat the hunter to the draw.

Nonetheless—and mark this well—over a period of years the *prime deer ranges* will remain reasonably stable, and they will *always* have the most deer. If a light kill should occur for unforeseen reasons, and a deluge of deer wreak havoc on its winter range, then a heavy kill must be arranged if possible for the next season to forestall further decimation of the winter range. A hunter who knows all such facts can very scientifically plot his hunt. Of course he must keep up with what is happening. Right now, for example, in northern Michigan the best deer hunting in the counties of the northern Lower Peninsula is shifting a bit to the west. One of the reasons is the misuse of prime parts of the range by oil and other interests.

Many such shifts can occur. But they do not occur instantly. If you know where the most deer are—that is, the best deer ranges—and you make annual checks to see what is happening, what the kill figures were for the previous two or three seasons and the conditions obtaining during those seasons, then you have a surefire charting as to where to plan your hunt. There may be minor trends or shifts, or population ups and downs. But poor deer range in our time is not likely to be rehabilitated quickly, although isolated instances can occur.

There may be other variables in different hunting areas, too. For example, in my adopted home state of Texas I can kill a deer any day—almost—on my place in the hill country, if I want to take either sex, big or little. Down in the brush country of South Texas, deer are much less abundant but also much larger. Many are real trophy whitetails. Offhand I am not sure as I write this which South Texas county has the most deer. What I do know is that a number of true trophies have come from two or three of the counties. So, this too is valuable. If I wished to hunt for a trophy deer, long odds, I'd go to one of those counties, and the heck with success percentages. In fact, I've hunted those counties and I know what is there and it excites me. I spent parts of seven seasons before I killed my first one. I could have killed a so-so deer every one of those seasons, I'm fairly sure, although I had no great number of opportunities for shots. It's tough cactus-country hunting, just possibly the toughest whitetail hunting on this continent. But I was after a trophy and I finally got it. Conversely, surveys show that several other brush country counties have a higher success ratio but smaller deer. And again, the hill country success, where my ranch is, shows so close to 100 percent that the small percentage of hunters who don't succeed were probably asleep, or looking for big deer, which these aren't.

Thus, the material I offer in the following pages, tediously and carefully gathered, is only basic and has to be sensibly applied by the hunter. It will give you a broad look at where the most deer are, and thus serve as a basic guide. You must check current regulations. If you are willing to take any deer, hunt an area where there are any-deer permits or where either sex is legal, in a spot where high kills and high success are shown. If you want a trophy, then you have to do a bit more checking on your own. Trophy areas change over a few years. Seldom can you find true trophies where heavy kills occur, with a deluge of hunters participating. The deer just do not have a chance to become mature, prime specimens, five to eight years old, although the herd may, overall, be supremely healthy and abundant and in balance with its range conditions.

So, in our computer age, be thorough enough to form a kind of mathematical plot for your deer hunt and there is no question that your chances of success will be enhanced. In the following briefing, because left to right reading is usual and because of a kind of personal perverseness about always having to begin a coverage of anything in the United States with New England, I have started at the upper left, in the Northwest. For easy geographic reference, regional portions of the U.S. are blocked out in groups of states. Following the state-by-state rundown of the U.S. "Lower 48," there is a section dealing with Canada and northern Mexico.

Northwestern U.S.

WASHINGTON

Herd estimate, 500,000, almost half blacktails, a third mule deer, approximately an eighth whitetails. Columbian blacktails range from crown of Cascades to Pacific. Mule deer blanket eastern Washington, with whitetails in some forested eastern counties. Buck kill is usually high, total hunter success at least 30 percent, in some Units much higher. The insular counties—Kitsap, Island, San Juan—often have overpopulation of blacktails, kills above five per square mile. Other good blacktail counties: Grays Harbor, Mason, Thurston, Pacific, Wahkiakum, Cowlitz, Clark. Most of blacktail range outside heavily populated districts offers fair to excellent opportunity. For mule deer, Stevens in the northeast, Okanogan in the north, Chelan, Kittitas, Klickitat are excellent on slopes. The Blue Mountains in the southeast also show fair success. This does not mean other counties are poor. Excepting the Columbia Basin region northeast, east, and southeast from Wenatchee, the state has quality deer hunting throughout. Public lands are vast.

OREGON

A top deer state, with harvests often 100,000 to near 150,000, two-thirds bucks, with hunter success as high as 50 percent overall most seasons. Columbian blacktails range from the top of the Cascades to the Pacific, in a few places in the north (Mount Hood National Forest) cross onto east slope of Cascades. From the Cascades summit eastward all is mule deer range. The Columbian whitetail, an endangered species, is not now hunted. Mule deer are the most numerous and make up half again as much of the harvest as blacktails. Among the best blacktail counties are the central-western ones of Lane and Linn, in the northwest Tillamook, the southwest Douglas, Coos, Jackson. Mule deer are spread fairly evenly east of the Cascades, both in open forest and brushy foothills and flats. All the hunt Units of northeastern Oregon invariably show high hunter success, with half the hunters scoring. The southeastern Units are almost as good. Vicinities of Wagontire, Hart Mountains, Steens Mountains are prime. Though Oregon deer populations offer good hunting almost everywhere, the northeastern counties have an edge for mule deer, the southwestern counties an edge for Columbian blacktails. Public lands constitute almost half the state.

IDAHO

Mule deer are the abundant species but there are whitetails in the northern Panhandle. They're difficult, sporty, but amount to only 10 to 15 percent of the total harvest, which runs 60,000 to 70,000. The top mule deer areas are as follows: northern Adams County along the Snake River north and east to the Salmon River in Idaho County and on north and west to Lewiston; the region in general on the east side of the state along the Salmon River and U.S. 93 from Shoup to Challis and a bit south, then east to the Continental Divide; the southeastern area chiefly south of U.S. 26 and east of Idaho Falls and Blackfoot, particularly Swan Valley region. Success is often very high in these areas, from 50 to 80 or 90 percent. Whitetails and mule deer are both found in the northern and western Panhandle, with average harvest in aggregate roughly one deer per square mile. Many hunt Units everywhere in Idaho show about the same, but the areas noted as best for mule deer commonly show from three to as many as five deer bagged per square mile. Public lands total around 70 percent of the entire state acreage.

Southwestern U.S.

CALIFORNIA

There are many deer in California, mule deer and Columbian black-tails, with the latter the most abundant, but with both California and Rocky Mountain mule deer well represented. Dense human population and many hunters present difficulties, and in the past so have unstable deer populations. Harvest averages a high of around 70,000, a low of 40,000. Success probably is 10 to 12 percent, or less, overall. Coastal forests and foothills from Santa Barbara County on north to the border offer good chances at blacktails, with northern areas best. The Sierra-Cascade ranges, western slopes, in national forests down as far as the Stanislaus National Forest also have blacktails in abundance. The preponderance of all California deer are taken in the northern counties. Humboldt often is the top county, with Siskiyou, Mendocino, Trinity, and Shasta among the top five. Tehama and Plumas counties rate fairly well. So does Mono on the Nevada border. Other northern and mid-California counties in the vast expanses of national forests rate fair. There are some 20,000,000 acres of national forests plus numerous other public lands. For Rocky Mountain mule deer the Modoc National Forest and portions of the Lassen National Forest in the northeast are the places. California mule deer take over in the other forests to the south and across the middle of the state.

NEVADA

Rocky Mountain mule deer are the targets in Nevada. They range over most of the state. Harvests have fluctuated drastically over the past few years, from a high of around 50,000 down to roughly a third of that. Hunter success during good years is high—perhaps 50 percent, and in some cases much higher. Elko County, in the northeast, where parts of the Humboldt National Forest are located, is far and away the best hunting. Individual mountain ranges here—the Independence, the Ruby Range—are prime. So is the Jarbridge Wilderness near the Idaho line. Northern Washoe and Humboldt counties, northern Lander and Eureka, the national forest lands of White Pine, northern Lincoln, and northern Nye counties are all excellent. There is a good deal of all but unexplored trophy mule deer hunting in Nevada, in various small mountain ranges that are inaccessible except by pack-in. Overall, there are few hunters—hunting has been little publicized outside the state—and public lands encompass at least 80 percent of the state. A hunter willing to explore here can find a big-buck bonanza.

UTAH

This is a top Rocky Mountain mule deer state, with an annual kill averaging around 100,000, occasionally much higher, and a basic overall success percentage about 25 percent but in many hunt Units in good seasons skyrocketing up to 50 and 75 percent or more. Hunting is good almost anywhere. Here are some especially favorable locations: northeastern Morgan County, western Box Elder, northern Duchesne, northern Daggett, the long-famed Book Cliffs in eastern Utah, the Manti-LaSal National Forest block and surrounding area near Moab, the Dixie Forest north of Kanab and the mountains around Kanab, western Emery County, the country north of St. George. Southwestern Utah gets an especially heavy influx of nonresidents, however. Eastern Utah and some central and southern Units get less pressure, away from cities and the easier hunting. For example, I've checked out the rugged country around Price, from which some awesome bucks are taken. It is tough going but usually not crowded. Utah has millions of acres of public lands.

ARIZONA

This is not a high-kill state, but nonetheless wonderful hunting for serious deer enthusiasts. Arizona has been having some deer-herd difficulties, presently seriously researched, and hopefully not permanent. A good average annual harvest is around 20,000. It has been higher, and lower. In average years success statewide runs about 20 percent, but in some individual Units is much higher. Variety is interesting: the Rocky Mountain mule deer of the northern forests and rough lands; the Desert mule deer across the south, chiefly in the southeast; the Coues whitetail (Arizona whitetail or "fantail"), also chiefly of the southeast; the unusual Burro deer, a mule deer subspecies of western Pima and portions of Yuma counties. Most seasons the kill is about two-thirds Rocky Mountain deer, one-sixth Desert mule deer, and one-sixth whitetails, with an occasional Burro deer. The so-called North Zone, roughly north of an east-west line through Phoenix, contains the most productive hunting, furnishing more than two-thirds of the total kill. Also, success percentages run much higher on Rocky Mountain mule deer in the north than on either Desert mule deer or Coues deer in the south.

North Kaibab is the best location for Rocky Mountain deer, but many antlerless are in the total. The far-northwest "strip" is rugged but trophy country. Other good areas are Apache National Forest and the Williams region. For both whitetails and Desert mule deer, the individual mountain ranges of the southeast are best, the whitetails in general higher up than the mule deer. Some good ranges are the Chiricahuas, Santa Ritas, Tumacacoris, Catalinas, Santa Teresas, Grahams, and Galiuros. There is an abundance of national forest and other public land.

Continental Divide States

MONTANA

This is one of the continent's best deer-hunting locations. Deer are plentiful almost everywhere. Annual harvest averages around 100,000. Success percentage is astonishing, usually anywhere from 75 to 100 percent. There are both Rocky Mountain mule deer and whitetails. Composition of the kill usually runs about 75 percent mule deer and 25 percent whitetails, chiefly because the mule deer are easier to hunt, in more open cover. Some antlerless deer are cropped, but the buck kill reaches as high as 60 to 70 percent. It is virtually useless to attempt to pinpoint top locations. Both varieties of deer range over most of the state, and a good hunt can be had almost anywhere.

West of the Divide, the southwestern quadrant offers excellent mule deer hunting in reasonably open forest and foothill country. Some whitetails are here. The northwest is prime whitetail country because it has dense cover. Three top-rated counties here are Flathead, Lincoln, and Powell. Mule deer are also present. East of the Divide the mule deer hunting is excellent all along the east slope. Small individual mountain ranges such as the Judith Range offer fine hunting. The forest on the east slope is more open than west of the Divide. Elsewhere across eastern Montana mule deer are abundant in a variety of situations, from river bottoms to the low hills of the eastern border country where the cover is scattered pine and some brush. Over all of the east, whitetails cling mostly to the various river-bottom breaks. Thus opportunities for either deer are excellent anywhere along the streams. The Snowy Range in the Lewis & Clark National Forest, and portions of the Custer National Forest in Carter County in the southeast, furnish quality hunting, particularly for whitetails, which are dominant here. Public lands total millions of Montana acres; finding a place to hunt is no problem.

WYOMING

Both mule deer and whitetails are available in abundance in Wyoming. The annual total harvest averages around 70,000. Total success is high, at least 75 percent and in some years higher. Antlerless deer are cropped, but the buck kill runs about two-thirds of the total. Make-up of the total kill averages around 80 percent mule deer, 20 percent whitetails. Regulations are set by hunt Units. One group makes up the Black Hills region of the northeast. This is the top area of the state for whitetails and often furnishes 85 percent or more of the state's total whitetail kill. It is also good mule deer country. Total aggregate kill from the Black Hills Units amounts some seasons to better than 25 percent of the total state harvest. The southeastern and south-central counties where large tracts of the Medicine Bow National Forest are located furnish the next most important part of the state's deer harvest, usually more than 25 percent. These are almost entirely mule deer. The north-central counties, where the Big Horn National Forest is located, are another extremely important area that includes foothills, river bottoms, and open country where mule deer are abundant. Roughly 25 percent of the harvest comes from here. Thus, the regions noted furnish at least 75 percent of the state kill most seasons. There is good hunting in the mountains and forests of western Wyoming, but by no means as good as over the eastern half of the state. There are millions of acres of national forests and other public lands.

COLORADO

Long a top U.S. deer state, Colorado has recently changed its regulations drastically and consequently lowered the harvest. There have been rumors that the deer herd is in trouble. However, hunting is still excellent and current problems will undoubtedly be solved, except the swiftly growing population of this state. For many years prior to the present system the annual kill was around 100,000, sometimes higher. Success has averaged at least 50 percent and at times was nearly 90 percent. Hunting is almost entirely for mule deer, although there are a few whitetails, some from transplants, in eastern Colorado. Although a hunter who knows the country can find good opportunities in eastern Colorado, 90 percent of the harvest comes from the western two-thirds of the state. Here a number of large national forests blanket the bulk of the area, which is mostly mountainous. Foothills and slopes have a surprisingly even distribution of mule deer. It is virtually impossible to pinpoint the "hottest" locations. Practically every hunt Unit throughout the forests region, on both slopes, has in the past consistently shown at least one out of every two hunters successful. A few long-famous locations are eastern Rio Blanco County; northeastern Mesa and eastern Garfield counties; the region between Glenwood Springs and Grand Junction; eastern Moffat and western Routt counties; the Uncompahgre National Forest region; and areas around Cortez, Durango, and Pagosa Springs. However, again, so much of the mountain region is excellent that there is little choice. Obviously finding a place to hunt is no problem.

NEW MEXICO

Mule deer are the important targets in New Mexico, the Rocky Mountain deer in the north, Desert mule deer in some of the southern counties. There are also some whitetails, of two varieties: a scattering of the Texas whitetail along the eastern border, and the Coues or "fantail" found in the extreme southwest. Probably the total whitetail population does not exceed 8000 or 10,000, and the kill is low. Total deer harvest averages around 30,000 animals, possibly 10 percent of the state herd. Success percentages vary from place to place, running from 30 to as high as 50. Some hunters desire a trophy Coues. This hunt should be made preferably in Hidalgo County, where the largest population exists. Grant and Catron counties to the north also have a modest population. Some of the best locations for large mule deer are the Jicarilla Apache Indian Reservation, west of Chama; the foothill country surrounding Chama; the Divide country west of Los Alamos; the Questa–Eagle Nest region; and on up to and west of Raton, all in the Sangre de Cristo Range. There is also good hunting in the Gila National Forest of the southwest. Probably the most abundant mule deer, with fewer trophy heads, are found in central southern New Mexico, in the several tracts of the Lincoln National Forest and the Sacramento and Guadalupe Mountains. Several million acres of national forests, plus numerous state-owned tracts, make public hunting grounds practically limitless.

The Central Plains & Farm States

NORTH DAKOTA

This is a much better deer-hunting state than most hunters realize. Whitetails predominate, but the southwestern portion of the state has mule deer. Permits for mule deer are carefully apportioned to avoid overhunting. The total average annual bag of all deer runs from 20,000 to 25,000. Number of available permits for various seasons tends to limit or add to the kill. Success is very high, as much as 75 percent. In areas or seasons for bucks only, a hunter has roughly one chance in two of scoring. Where one hunts is dictated to some extent by the location of public lands. The National Grasslands in the southwest are a good bet, covering about a million acres. Lands surrounding the huge reservoirs on the Missouri River also are excellent for whitetails. There is hunting on numerous state-owned game management areas scattered over the entire state. A list can be obtained from the game department. By and large, wooded stream courses anywhere in the state furnish good whitetail hunting.

SOUTH DAKOTA

Whitetails are the chief targets in South Dakota. They are found throughout the state, some exceedingly large, fat specimens even in the farm country of the east. Although there are a few mule deer east of the Missouri River, most are west of it, and even there the whitetails are more numerous. Regulations change from time to time, but for many years hunting east of the Missouri has been for residents only. Thus the East River kill is mostly by landowners and their friends. Permits have also long been limited. Success is extremely high because hunters know their lands intimately. Total annual deer kill runs about 25,000 animals. West of the Missouri in what is called the West River Prairie region, as opposed to the Black Hills in the southwest, permits also have been limited; both whitetails and some mule deer are taken and a very high success is consistently achieved, 75 to 80 percent or more. In good years a little less than half the state kill comes from the West River Prairie hunt. There are national grasslands in the northwest, southwest, and south-central regions, and some national forest in the northwest. Stream courses and reservoir borders are good hunting. The Black Hills region usually has unlimited licenses, with nonresidents allowed; good whitetail hunting, a few mule deer, success in bucks-only seasons around 50 percent or a bit more. East of the Black Hills proper, in counties south of the Cheyenne River, north of the White, and west of the Missouri, some good trophy deer are taken.

NEBRASKA

Mule deer are predominant over most of western Nebraska, whitetails over the eastern half, but there is intermingling almost everywhere. The harvest is dictated by number of permits issued, which is usually 20,000 or more. Hunters can expect success percentages anywhere from one chance out of two to two out of three. As a rule about 65 percent of the take are mule deer. There are four chief hunting grounds that may be tagged as among the best in Nebraska: the Pine Ridge country of the extreme northwest, with mostly mule deer taken each season; the Sand Hills country of Cherry County and southward, where some 65 percent of the deer are mule deer; the northern counties east of the Sand Hills, where the ratio is much closer to 50–50; and the southeastern border counties. Generally speaking, river courses throughout the entire state offer excellent hunting. There are some national grasslands and national forests, but most hunting here is on privately owned lands, by permission or with guides.

KANSAS

Once abundant, deer were considered extinct in Kansas forty years ago. Today there is a substantial herd, mostly whitetails over much of eastern Kansas, a few mule deer in the northwest. Presently hunting since it began again has been for residents only, with a specified number of permits and a kill somewhere between 1000 and 2000 as a rule. Throughout the state, the courses of all the streams, where wooded, are where most of the deer are found. Brushy creek bottoms form cover for the mule deer of the northwest. Public hunting grounds include state-owned game management areas, lands around the reservoirs. Most hunting is on private lands.

IOWA

Although regulations can change, this has for some time been a state where only residents can hunt, and only with bow, shotgun, or primitive weapons. Permits are limited, and harvest runs around 10,000 or so, with about a third of hunters successful. The counties along both east and west borders—that is, along the Mississippi and Missouri rivers—have good deer populations. Another substantial herd is in a swath of country west of Des Moines and then south to the border. Some of the best counties, as a rule, are Allamakee, extreme northeast; counties straight south of Des Moines on and just above the southern border; the counties on the Missouri between Sioux City and Council Bluffs; and Guthrie County west of Des Moines. This is, of course, whitetail hunting. River and creek bottoms anywhere in the state and brushy draws or woodlots in the corn belt make good locations. Some extremely large deer have come out of the farm country. State forest lands and numerous state public hunting areas furnish public hunting, but most is on privately owned land.

MISSOURI

The abundant whitetails pioneers knew were all but wiped out in Missouri early in this century. Transplants and management have worked wonders. Today all of Missouri has deer and the annual kill crowds 30,000 in good seasons, with as high as 75 percent bucks. Hunter success overall runs 12 to 15 percent. The country below the Missouri River is best, the Ozarks region usually with highest deer population. The blocks of the several national forests in southern Missouri furnish excellent hunting. Texas County in the south edge of the Clark National Forest shows high production, as does Ozark County on the southern border in the Mark Twain National Forest. Other national forest counties with good kills are Carter, Taney, Pulaski, Wayne, and Howell. Benton County, not in a national forest area, also is a top-rated location, and so are several counties on the Missouri River, such as Ste. Genevieve.

The Mid-South

OKLAHOMA

Good management has changed the deer picture in Oklahoma from a debacle of some years ago to a sizable herd today, with fair hunting and probably better still to come. There are deer throughout the state. These are all whitetails except for some mule deer in the extreme northwest in the last county of the Panhandle, Cimarron. For some seasons the total deer kill ran around 5000 annually, but the trend is upward as the herd grows. Presently the best hunting is in eastern Oklahoma. The southeastern Ozarks counties are among the best—McCurtain, Le Flore, Atoka, Pushmataha, Pittsburg. On the eastern border highly rated counties are Delaware, Cherokee, and Sequoyah. In the north, Osage County along the Arkansas River rates well. Along all of the main river courses chances are fair to good. This is an expanding situation and areas surrounding the top counties will undoubtedly get better as the deer spread range and the herd grows. There is some national forest land in the southeast, numerous state-owned lands well scattered elsewhere. The U.S. Naval Ammunition Depot at McAlester has a prime hunt each season to crop a meticulously managed herd. Success is high.

ARKANSAS

This is another state in which deer were almost gone some years ago, but transplants and enlightened management have done a fine restoration job. Nowadays the state herd is probably above 300,000 and an average annual kill of 20,000 or more is normal. This is all whitetail hunting. Lately the high areas of success have consistently been in the southeastern and southern counties—Clark, Nevada, Union, Dallas, Ouachita, Calhoun, Cleveland, Bradley, Ashley, Arkansas, Desha, Drew, and Chicot. To visitors this may seem surprising, since Arkansas has some large expanses of national forests in the northwest and central west. There is indeed fair to good deer hunting in the forests, but it is doubtful that presently they furnish more than 20 percent of the total deer kill. There are a number of state-owned public hunting areas in the best counties and also in the national forests and elsewhere. There are also spots, like the White River National Wildlife Refuge, that have annual hunts, in some of the best deer range available.

LOUISIANA

Deer have had many problems in Louisiana for many years. At one time they were actually an endangered species hunted mainly by club owners on private lands. Nowadays things are better. Most of the state has deer hunting on public as well as private lands. For some reason poaching is still a perplexing problem. However, the annual sports harvest averages around 30,000 animals and deer are in good shape generally—all whitetails of course—throughout Louisiana. Over the past few years the buck kill has been extremely high, but that may have to level off as management stabilizes the herds. Presently the counties south of Monroe and above Catahoula Lake and then east to the Mississippi River have the highest deer populations. However, northwestern Louisiana and the counties containing national forest lands in the east-central portion of the state stack up well. The next decade will undoubtedly see shifting deer populations, a spreading out of existing concentrations. Presently the northern half of the state records the preponderance of the kill. Nonetheless, southern Louisiana has many deer and in some instances along coastal areas more than food can support. Currently regions rate as follows: the east-central and northeast counties are first, with about a third of the kill tabulated from these; the north-central counties are second, furnishing possibly a fifth of the bag; west-central counties come next, and the northwest follows, the two together furnishing a bit less than a third of the total bag. Again, population shifts may be expected in the future. A number of public lands add to national forest acreage for public hunting.

TEXAS

Texas has the largest number of deer of any state, probably somewhere between 3,000,000 and 4,000,000, with an annual harvest of around 300,000. In some counties more deer should be harvested. Most of the deer are whitetails, with the Texas whitetail the most abundant but with several other subspecies present in the east and the Carmen Mountains whitetail in parts of the Big Bend region. Desert mule deer are found in West Texas and a modest number of Rocky Mountain mule deer in the Panhandle. Hunter success throughout Texas is extremely high, in many locations 100 percent. But hunting is unlike that in other states, for there is almost no public land. Deer hunting is almost entirely by hunting lease on private lands, by fee hunting by the day, or by so-called "package" hunts on private lands. In other words, it is totally commercialized. This makes it fairly expensive, but also accounts for the high success. Fair to good deer hunting is found throughout most of the state. North Texas, the Panhandle, and East Texas fall into this category. Three regions, however, hold the heavy concentrations. First is the hill country or Edwards Plateau northwest and west from San Antonio roughly to Devil's River, Sonora and Junction, Mason, Llano and Burnet. The deer are whitetails. In the central counties of the area they are small. In such counties as Val Verde and in the so-called Divide area from Mountain Home to Rocksprings they are somewhat larger. The brush country of cactus and thornbrush south of San Antonio to the Mexican border, with cities such as Eagle Pass, Laredo, Uvalde, Cotulla, and George West, contains large whitetails. They are not as plentiful as hill country deer, but many are real trophies, with heavy, dark antlers. There is much day hunting and package hunting in the hill country. Most of the brush country is taken up by long-term leases of hunter groups. For mule deer, the prime locale is in the Big Bend country of West Texas and other counties west of the Pecos River. Probably Brewster County has the heaviest deer concentration here. The season is shorter than for whitetails and most hunting is by groups who book "package hunts" on the large ranches. By diligence one can also collect, in the small high ranges here, a flagtail or Carmen Mountains whitetail.

The Great Lakes Region

MINNESOTA

This is an excellent whitetail state. Though deer have periodic problems throughout the Great Lakes region, this herd is in good shape, numbering somewhere between 500,000 and 750,000. Annual kills have averaged up around 100,000, about half bucks, with hunter success around 35 percent. Best of the deer range is in the northern half of the state, with the exception of the northwest. The bulk of public lands—national and state forests and management areas—are here. Some counties with consistently good success are St. Louis, Cass, Itasca, Aitkin, Koochiching, and Beltrami. In the east, Pine County also rates high. Many large deer come out of the agricultural counties to the south and southwest, but deer are far less abundant here. By and large the forested north and east furnish the preponderance of the kill.

WISCONSIN

This state has long had a high annual kill, sometimes far above 100,-000. But success has waned to some extent as hunter numbers have skyrocketed. Most seasons a good many antlerless deer are cropped. Overall success may run up to 25 percent. On bucks it is less. There is good hunting scattered all over the state. Bayfield County in the far northwest is excellent. So are Oneida, north-central, and Marinette, northeast. In central Wisconsin, Jackson, Wood, Waushara, and Waupaca counties all show outstanding kills. So do Marathon and Shawano just to the north of the others. Price County in the north-central area also rates well. There are, of course, many other excellent counties. Southern Wisconsin has the lowest kill, in the farm country. Generally the northwest and northeast districts rate near the top, with west-central and east-central next. Among the national and state forests and state-owned public lands several million acres are open to hunting.

MICHIGAN

Michigan deer hunters nowadays have one chief problem—too many people. The high population eats away at deer habitat and puts so many hunters afield that success is not as high as it once was. There is still a good deer herd, with harvests crowding 100,000 annually. Success has been running around 12 percent, since there are hundreds of thousands of hunters competing. For some years the heaviest kill has been spread over the northern counties of the Lower Peninsula. A typical season has shown more than half the total state bag from here. Next in importance is the Upper Peninsula, with western and southwestern counties especially important, and a total kill of somewhat less than one-third. Southern Michigan farm lands have a fair number of deer, many of them large. One-eighth or less of the total harvest comes from here. Public lands are abundant throughout Michigan in national and state forests and other state-owned lands open to hunting.

ILLINOIS

Obviously this cannot be a high-harvest state. It is too populous. Nonetheless, whitetails have done extremely well in adapting to human encroachment. Hunting is by limited permit, with types of weapons also limited. Surprisingly, some seasons success has run as high as in better deer states—about 12 percent of the permits filled. In a few counties the success is higher, to 25 percent. The kill over past years has run from 5000 to 7000. Some extremely large whitetails turn up annually. Counties in and bordering the Shawnee National Forest in the south usually show high kills. However, success is in general better in a number of counties bordering the Mississippi. These reach all the way from the extreme northwestern counties to the west-central river-border counties. Public lands are not abundant.

INDIANA

Types of weapons are limited in this densely populated state, but deer are generally spread over most counties in modest numbers and the annual harvest amounts to 4000 or 5000. A substantial number of deer are found in the northeastern counties, and a lesser number in counties below South Bend and La Porte. The southeastern counties also have a good deer population, and a few south-central counties just above and within the Hoosier National Forest match these. Below the forest, in the central counties bordering the Ohio River, there is another concentration area. The forest and a few of the state-owned forests and game areas offer public hunting. However, the best of this—by permit system—is found on the several large expanses of military-installation lands in the southern part of the state. Probably 50 percent of the annual harvest is furnished by these.

OHIO

A fair number of deer still hang on in Ohio. In some past seasons the harvest has amounted to slightly under 2000, with a 10 to 12 percent success. Hunting is by limited permit. A few counties in extreme northwestern Ohio show fair populations. Best hunting is generally in the east, and along the Ohio in the southeast, where Wayne National Forest lands are found. The several state forests have in the past provided good success among the public lands. Locations of these and other tracts of public lands can be obtained from the game department.

The Appalachian States

KENTUCKY

Once the Virginia whitetail was abundant in Kentucky, but today few if any pure strains remain. The deer were near extinction years ago. Other whitetails, particularly the Northern Woodland strain, were brought in. Deer are now reestablished in much of the suitable habitat. Annual harvests average 7500 to 10,000, with success around 30 percent. Probably distribution of deer will change in Kentucky over coming years. Currently the central part of the state, in counties south of Louisville, sustain the best concentrations. Some prime areas are Meade, Hart, Hardin, and Edmonson counties. Some western counties such as Livingston and Ohio, and to the south, Christian, also have good herds. A few northern counties northwest from Lexington also show substantial numbers. The eastern national forest lands are quite good but are in some places hard to get into. There are ample public lands in both state and national forests and in wildlife management areas, and also some excellent hunting on the military lands such as Fort Campbell and Fort Knox and the Bluegrass Army Depot. In the west, the so-called Land Between the Lakes gets better year by year.

TENNESSEE

This state all but exterminated its deer by early in this century. Reestablishment has been successful both on private lands and in particular on state-owned wildlife management areas and military lands. Hunts for some time at Fort Campbell have furnished as much as 20 percent of the total state kill. The total state bag runs from 7,000 to 10,000. The wildlife management areas and military hunts are the important spots, with as high as 80 percent of the deer coming from these public lands. Good hunting places are scattered because the management areas are. Generally speaking, counties along the Mississippi and Tennessee rivers show the most deer. The Cumberlands and the national forests along the east closely match them. The game department can furnish lists and locations of the public hunts, and their regulations. Average success statewide runs from 15 to 20 percent. It is interesting to note that a few years ago this state began trying to establish Columbian blacktail deer by transplant. Whether or not they will flourish to huntable numbers is not yet known.

WEST VIRGINIA

This state, like Tennessee and Kentucky, had all but wiped out the whitetail long ago. Reestablishment over recent decades, however, has been very successful. There have been some harvests above 20,000, and bucks-only hunting with about half that. West Virginia deer hunting will undoubtedly fluctuate in success as the herd grows and careful management brings abundance to some areas where now there are few deer. In general at present the largest populations are in the northeastern counties and in some of the eastern counties on national forest lands. Next come northern counties east and northeast from Clarksburg. Some 80 percent of the kill recently has come from these regions. However, the southern and western counties also have deer established. Public hunting is available in the state and national forests and on state-owned public hunting areas.

PENNSYLVANIA

This is a rather astonishing deer state. Even with its tremendous human population, deer under excellent management have remained so abundant that annual harvests approaching 150,000 have been possible, and kills of around 100,000 are routine. In normal seasons bucks make up about 60 percent of the bag. By far the greatest number of deer are in the forests of north-central Pennsylvania, with Potter County often the heaviest producer and a kind of center surrounded by other excellent counties. To the west, counties in and around the Allegheny National Forest are also good producers. The northeastern region shades the northwest a bit, with Bradford County one of the consistently high-kill locations. Eastern border counties fanning out from Scranton are just about as productive. Southern Pennsylvania does not have as many deer in most counties. The populous southeast has a good many, but some hunters shy from it because it is crowded. The southwest has some excellent racks although fewer deer. South-central Pennsylvania is fair. There are no problems finding public lands. There are state forests, the one national forest, and scores of public tracts called game lands, state-owned.

The Central Atlantic States

MARYLAND

Though fairly crowded, Maryland deer hunting is quite good. The annual bag fluctuates from 7000 or 8000 to half again as many. Success is around 10 percent but in a few locations or seasons may be a bit higher. Central and southern Maryland have some deer, but the hunting here is most successful for those who own lands or know the terrain intimately. By far the greatest number of deer are found in the eastern counties, with western counties next in line. In the east, the two southeastern counties, Worcester and Dorchester, generally are top-rated. And in the west the two counties of the extreme west are the ones. Nonetheless, a few of the north-central counties and others bordering Virginia, as well as the east-shore counties across and south from Aberdeen, show fair success. Public hunting is available on state-owned management areas and state forests.

DELAWARE

Delaware is too small and too heavily settled to have any great amount of deer hunting. However, a few hundred are taken annually, by shotgun and bow hunters, and even that is rather surprising, for this state was closed to deer hunting for many decades. Now hunts keep the herd cropped to size. Most hunting is on private lands, but public hunting occurs on state forests and wildlife areas, and occasionally on refuge lands which deer have overpopulated. Hunter numbers are modest, which brings success percentage up to around 12 or 15 percent. Central Delaware furnishes at least half the bag, the south perhaps a third, the north the remainder.

VIRGINIA

It is a curious commentary on Virginia deer hunting that here, where the whitetail was first known by the colonists and where the species was named, deer hunting was first brought close to extermination. Early in the 1900s there were only a few animals left. Management has changed that. The state now has fine hunting, with an average annual harvest of 25,000 or more, and a success among hunters of roughly 25 percent. While deer now are well distributed over the entire state, a few counties of the central far west with substantial acreages of national forest lands usually show the heaviest harvest. The southeast also shows up very well, with Southampton County a hub. Residents split the state into "West of the Blue Ridge" and "East of the Blue Ridge." Comparing the two according to size, the total kill in each averages very close to equal. This illustrates how many good areas there are, although possibly the west has an edge. Public lands, in national forests and state-owned management areas and others, are abundant.

NORTH CAROLINA

There is a well-distributed deer herd in North Carolina today numbering several hundred thousand, in most locations reestablished after the near-disappearance of deer years ago. Annual harvest ranges somewhere between 30,000 and 40,000. A great deal of the hunting is on private lands, by clubs or under lease agreements or by fee payments. Thus it is difficult to state precisely where one may find the best hunting, for it is a matter of first locating a place to hunt. Public lands are fairly numerous and well scattered. Largest are in the national forests—Pisgah and Nantahala in the far west, the smaller Uwharrie in the central part of the state, and the Croatan in the east. There are also paper company lands open to hunting and a number of state-owned management areas.

SOUTH CAROLINA

This state has long had a confusing deer-hunt picture. There are deer in every county, much of this by reestablishment. There is a preponderance of club hunting and lease hunting on private lands, and no one knows just how large the annual harvest is. Undoubtedly it is at least 25,000 and it may be twice that. Hunting with dogs is traditional on private lands. The lowland region of coastal South Carolina has abundant deer, but almost all is in private lands. However, the Francis Marion National Forest has opportunity for the public. In the Piedmont region and the west, where deer are somewhat less abundant but larger, there are large blocks of the Sumter National Forest and within these a number of game management areas on which the state is bringing deer to abundance with carefully controlled still-hunting and stalking. Success presently is not especially high but probably will improve in years to come.

Southeastern Gulf & Atlantic States

MISSISSIPPI

As late as the 1930s deer were practically gone from Mississippi, because of overhunting. Now reestablishment and good management have built a state herd of several hundred thousand. The annual bag ranges from 25,000 to 30,000 or more, with the buck kill high. Overall hunter success is around 25 percent. Bucks, particularly in lowlands, are big, and deer hunting and the herd are expanding steadily. This means that shifts in population trends may occur in the future. Presently, however, the bulk of the heavy concentration, and kill, centers on counties that border the Mississippi River. Over half of the harvest usually comes from these. Club and leased lands take in much of the best of the deer range here, and this undoubtedly influences statistics. There are ample public hunting grounds, however, with abundant deer, in the half-dozen national forests well distributed throughout the state, and on state-owned wildlife management areas.

ALABAMA

The Alabama harvest runs around 25,000 annually, and some seasons is higher. Success is usually a shade less than 20 percent overall. As in much of the South, club lands account for by far the largest share of the bag, and success is higher here than on public hunts. On the average a hunter on public land has about a one in ten chance or less of getting his deer. All told it is not so much a matter of where the most deer are but where a hunter may find a place to hunt. The national forests—three of them—furnish excellent hunting. The several state wildlife management areas, with carefully managed hunts, are consistently providing more and more success. Paper company lands are also to some extent available. The game department can furnish lists of open lands and their locations.

GEORGIA

The Georgia deer herd is substantial. The harvest averages 25,000 to 30,000 or more, and usually overall success gains a high of around 25 percent. This is another state with shifting trends. Apparently the herd is growing and spreading and utilization of lands is such that deer habitat may grow in the future. Presently the central part of the state has the most deer. The counties here are in or near the blocks of the Oconee National

Forest. Counties along and near the Chattahoochee River on the western border in the general vicinity of Columbus also support a large concentration. Northern counties within the Chattahoochee National Forest also are top-rated, and so are a number along the Savannah River. Management on a number of game management areas is slanted at better and better public hunting. There are also tracts of paper company holdings open to hunters.

FLORIDA

Florida has abundant deer. In a number of instances when population was low or nonexistent, northern deer were transplanted. For some years the deer herd, under good management, has been growing. Even with the heavy influx of people it is possible it may continue to grow to double the present size, which is probably about 200,000. Conversely, constant human encroachment may upset this prediction. At any rate, current hunting is quite good, with a kill of perhaps 20,000. It is difficult to state where the heaviest deer concentrations are. Northern and northwestern Florida have the largest specimens and the most accessible hunting. Swamp portions of southern Florida have plenty of deer but are difficult for hunters. By and large, the several national forests of the northern half of the state and the numerous wildlife management areas furnish ample acreage for public hunting and substantial deer populations.

The Northeast

MAINE

Extra-large whitetails come out of Maine every season, and this is one of the best deer-hunt states in the United States. Compared to many prime Western deer states, Maine is small, but over 200,000 deer hunters roam its forests annually, and bag between 30,000 and 40,000 whitetails. Success averages around 20 percent consistently. Although northern Maine has long been highly lauded as a deer hunter's paradise, it is the southern half of the state that furnishes by far the major share of the kill—the north zone possibly one-fifth, the south zone usually close to four-fifths. The chief reason is accessibility, and the fact that edge cover is far better for heavy populations of deer than dense forests, although some extremely large deer come out of northern Maine. Southwestern counties rate highest in kill, partly because of hunter pressure. Nonetheless, the deer have to be there, although success percentage is not quite as good there as elsewhere. Northwestern Maine shows very high success, up over 40 percent, but of course this is real back-country hunting, with fewer hunters. South-eastern Maine and the coastal counties are, all told, best for the major share of hunters, and success here beats the general average. What may surprise visitors is that contrary to general opinion Maine does not have vast acreages of public wild lands. But hunters have long been accepted and there is no problem finding a place to hunt.

NEW HAMPSHIRE

This small state has fine deer hunting, with annual harvest running 9,000 to 15,000, usually about half bucks. There is no place in the state down to township level that does not offer good hunting. For some years Grafton County has furnished the highest kill. Carroll County in central New Hampshire and Coos County in the far north are also good. The northern half of the state accounts for over 50 percent of the total annual harvest. Many townships in these counties show consistent kills of three or more deer per square mile. However, the southern counties are also fair to good. There is no great problem about public lands. In the far north permission is easy to get, and in central New Hampshire the White Mountain National Forest provides prime hunting.

VERMONT

One of Vermont's problems in past years has not been how to provide enough deer but how to arrange to crop enough deer in some areas to tailor the herd to its range. Astonishing as it may seem, in past years this small state has been taking an average of more than 20,000 deer annually. Whether that can continue is questionable, but nonetheless the hunting presently is very good. East-central counties currently show highest production and bag. The national forest lands in central and southern Vermont rate very high. Hunter pressure is severe, and this brings success down to about 12 percent. Public lands, national forests and others, provide ample hunting grounds.

MASSACHUSETTS

Over recent years deer have decreased in Massachusetts, and it is possible that hunting may have to stop. If this occurs it will be a blow to resident hunters, who have long and avidly and in large numbers followed the sport. However, the careful management that the game department is giving the herd may stabilize deer numbers so that a few thousand may be cropped annually. Past seasons have shown kills of 3,000 or 4,000 and success around 5 percent. The western half of the state has most of the deer, in Berkshire, Franklin, and Worcester counties. There are public lands in state forests and wildlife management areas.

RHODE ISLAND

Deer range is exceedingly limited in this small, populous state, but on available habitat deer have done well. There has long been a modest amount of hunting, with shotgun or bow, to keep the herd trimmed. Several dozen animals are bagged each season. State forests and management areas offer public opportunity.

CONNECTICUT

There are still a few deer in this state, and token hunting. In recent years only archery hunting has been allowed in the state forests, although on private property shotguns have been legal. Probably not more than a couple dozen deer are taken.

NEW JERSEY

The deer kill here is surprisingly high for a crowded state. It averages around 5000 but rises occasionally to nearly twice that. In most seasons the buck kill is high. Hunters are numerous and this brings success down around 5 percent. The northwestern counties consistently furnish a major share of the bag. There are also fair deer populations across the state in the swath between Trenton and Camden, and even down into Cape May County in the southeast. State forests and wildlife management areas offer public hunting.

NEW YORK

New York has a large deer population. Harvests run from 60,000 to upwards of 100,000, with the buck kill well over half the total. Heaviest deer harvests and excellent deer populations are found in some of the western and central counties such as Allegany, Steuben, Yates, Ontario, Schuyler, Chemung, and Chenango. The Catskill and Adirondack areas are the other concentrations. Delaware and Sullivan counties show very high kills, but pressure is tremendous here. Farther north, Franklin, Hamilton, and St. Lawrence counties are best. There are vast public lands in the Catskills and Adirondacks, and also many state forests and other state-owned lands scattered over the entire state. In the central and western counties hunting on private lands, when permission can be obtained, is usually excellent.

Alaska & Canada

ALASKA

The Sitka deer is abundant in parts of the Panhandle and on islands, including Kodiak, where it has been stocked. It is underhunted, and only the die-offs due to particularly rough winters keep the herds anywhere near in line with food supply. Limits are as high as four per season. More hunters should avail themselves of this opportunity.

BRITISH COLUMBIA

Deer hunting here is varied: Columbian blacktails on Vancouver and the southern coast; Sitka deer along the northern coast and its islands; Rocky Mountain mule deer inland; whitetails mostly in the south and southeast. Hunting success is consistently high, averaging 75 percent or more. Much of this is due to high bag limits—several deer in some hunt Units. Success on a per-hunter basis runs much lower. The southern part of the province has the highest deer populations. Often the coastal islands become overpopulated. Not many nonresidents try B.C. deer hunting because visitors are interested chiefly in the larger species. Deer hunting, however, is excellent.

ALBERTA

There are both whitetails and mule deer, but the latter have decreased over past years. Best mule deer populations are presently in the southwest, along the foothills of the east slope. Whitetails are more numerous and their range is spreading. The southeast has a good population, as do parklands of the central south.

SASKATCHEWAN

There is quality hunting here, chiefly for whitetails. Of the total kill of around 35,000 to 45,000 only about 2000 to 4000 are mule deer.

Whitetail success is above 60 percent as a rule. The dense concentration of whitetails is in the southeast. Mule deer are found in the southwest.

MANITOBA

Whitetails have been steadily colonizing in Manitoba and pushing their range farther north following settlement and lumbering. Both the southeast and the southwest have large whitetail populations. Portions of the Interlake area north of Winnipeg also are well supplied. Hunter success in the better ranges runs above 50 percent. Mule deer, once present over much of southern Manitoba, have nearly disappeared.

ONTARIO

Whitetails are found in fair numbers in several parts of the province. Western Ontario offers good hunting in the Kenora and Rainy River regions. Most of southern and south-central Ontario have important populations. There are also fair numbers along the northern Lake Superior shore. Success varies over the deer range, from a low of about 20 percent to a high above 30 percent. As in all the extreme northern range of the whitetail, severe winters have a drastic effect on deer numbers season to season.

QUEBEC

Deer hunting is popular but the kill is not very high, nor stable. It averages somewhere well below 10,000, much of the time closer to 5,000. Most of the deer range is below the St. Lawrence. Heavy concentrations occur from time to time on Anticosti Island.

NEW BRUNSWICK

This is one of the best provinces for whitetails. The kill averages above 20,000, and chances of success run about 25 percent. Some of the best counties are Victoria, Queens, Kings, Albert, Charlotte, Sunbury, Restigouche, and York.

NOVA SCOTIA

Deer are abundant, and the average harvest is close to 25,000, with chances to score at least 35 percent. The heaviest concentration of deer occurs on Cape Breton Island. There are deer in all Nova Scotia counties. The eastern counties are slightly better than the western ones, but hunting can be rated good almost everywhere. There is a very curious situation regarding Nova Scotia deer. Though few hunters realize it, whitetail hunting here rates as good as any in North America, but originally deer were not native to the region. They were brought in late in the nineteenth century and built up to their present solid establishment and abundance.

NORTHERN MEXICO

The deer picture here is generally confusing because so little concentrated management and research has been applied in the region. The Texas whitetail range extends well down below the U.S. border from Juárez to Matamoros in a variety of terrains. However, country people here, to whom venison is food and often a real need, kill deer at every opportunity, and can hardly be blamed for it. I have hunted for other varied game over much of Tamaulipas when for days neither deer nor deer sign was seen. In small areas of the Big Bend region the Carmen Mountains whitetail is reasonably abundant. Over northwestern Mexico, but not Baja, the Coues deer or Arizona whitetail is abundant in middle altitudes, usually around 6,000 feet. Throughout all of interior Mexico south from southeast Arizona, New Mexico, and West Texas the Desert mule deer is abundant, but again, often hard pressed. Some exceptional specimens have been taken by Mexican sport hunters, however, in desert situations north of San Luis Potosí. Other mule deer subspecies are found in modest numbers in the extreme northwest and on Baja and nearby islands. Game regulations, as many readers who have tried Mexico well know, are often perplexing and enforced according to the whimsy of local authorities, and gun restrictions make hunting somewhat difficult in general. The fact is that aside from the experience of hunting in Mexico and with local people, which can be pleasant indeed, there is really very little reason to go, except perhaps for a good Coues deer. There are some excellent trophies of these, but one has to stumble upon natives who can help find them. For Texas whitetails and Desert mule deer opportunities are so excellent in the United States that it is doubtful if the average visitor will find better hunting below the border.

CHAPTER THREE

The
Whitetail
Personality

    Writers about deer and deer hunting have seldom perceived sharply enough the distinctions between the two deer groups—the whitetails and the mule deer. Certainly they may know the physical differences, but within families of animals each variety has its own individual habits and reactions, and these we can think of as aspects of their "personalities."

    A common example among small game animals is found in the squirrels. The gray squirrel, or "cat" squirrel as it is often called, is a forest creature, and the fox squirrel is a species of farm woodlots and primarily of forest edges. Pass under a tree in which a fox squirrel is feeding and it will hide and stay immobile. Walk noisily under a tree containing a gray squirrel and it will fly away through the tree tops in frenzied flight.

    Undoubtedly over many centuries personalities of animals evolve because of their specific environments. But no one is wholly certain just how these influences operate. The whitetail deer is a perfect example of the puzzle, because of its amazing ability, mentioned earlier, to colonize vast areas with very different terrains, altitudes, climates, and vegetation. The hunter who has spent a lifetime in the north woods of Wisconsin can hardly envision the whitetail as anything but an animal of northern forests and snow country. He wants a "good tracking snow" for the hunting season, and thinks he just cannot get along without this.

Conversely, the hunter in southern Louisiana thinks of the whitetail as a swamp animal, often racing across flooded swampland, splashing water to drive away hordes of biting insects. However, only a few hundred miles

This Michigan forest trail spells deer weather to many Northern hunters who feel they must have tracks to follow. Actually, when snow is heavy and forage is scarce, you don't even have to follow the tracks—just find the forage, and the deer will be there.

The Southwestern hunter expects to find his whitetail amid cactus and thorn-brush, not snow and evergreens.

west of these hunters, there are others in southern Texas who have never hunted deer elsewhere. They know positively that the whitetail lives in dry expanses of prickly pear, huajilla, and scrub mesquite, and that the viciously thorned retama with its green bark is much liked by bucks as a shrub on which to polish antlers. As a matter of fact, more whitetails by far are killed each year in warm climes than in cold ones, and as I have noted the largest whitetail herd in the nation is presently located in the rocky live oak and cedar hills and the thornbrush expanses of Texas.

How can a hunter possibly put together a basic set of hunting rules for whitetails, when the animals roam such an immense and varied domain? It's not as difficult as it seems.

The fundamental reason is that the whitetail *personality* is the same regardless of where it is found. However, you have to know how to interpret that fact. It obviously cannot mean they eat the same food everywhere, nor select the same types of hiding places, nor follow undiffering daily movements. Each is influenced by the particular habitat situation. But if you know how a whitetail behaves in northern Wisconsin, and are capable of *translating* differences in terrain as related to food, water, safety, and comfort wherever else you may hunt, you will soon discover that the deer is the same everywhere. Its reactions and habits are the same. Only the topographical, vegetative, and climatic conditions differ from place to place. The deer may seem superficially different in actions and reactions because of this, but in reality they are always typical whitetails, regardless of where they live.

The reason I include chapters on whitetail and mule deer personalities in this book is that this facet of deer hunting has never been covered thoroughly enough. Today hunters travel widely and easily. Formerly a deer hunter was either a whitetail hunter or a mule deer hunter. He seldom traveled. Now hunters from the East swarm to the West each season, and vice versa, and many hunters make trips from South to North and North to South annually. One who imagines both groups of deer are "just deer" has already created problems for himself without knowing it. They are totally different. By learning about both, the very comparisons assist one in knowing what to do, or not do, under each circumstance. I'm quite certain that when I first began hunting mule deer, after having previously had all my experience with whitetails, what I learned about mule deer helped me to be a better whitetail hunter. And I am positive that my previous experience with whitetails made successful mule deer hunting much easier. But I was also startled to observe behavior in mule deer that was completely unlike what might have been expected of whitetails under similar circumstances.

The whitetail at any time or place is an extremely nervous, intense animal. It is jumpy, excitable. It makes not the slightest difference if the deer has never previously seen a human being, or any other danger. Nervousness is a *trait*, inherited over hundreds of generations. To be sure, whitetail deer can be raised and tamed. I have a friend who feeds deer in his yard, and some of them will come up to take corn or other food from his hand. Yet the appearance of a stranger upsets them, and the slightest quick movement or unusual sound will put them wildly to flight.

Many years ago early settlers found whitetail deer exactly the same. Some of their alertness, their tenseness, may have been due to hunting by Indians, or to predation by mountain lions and other carnivores. Certainly when the colonists bore down with hunting, the deer became "wilder." But the fact is, they were already wild and flighty when first encountered by whites.

Now consider a small ranch in the region where I live. This is an area where Angora goats and sheep are raised, along with a modest number of cattle. Predators such as bobcats, lions, and coyotes have for the past hundred years been unmercifully decimated. Goat and sheep raisers simply could not tolerate their presence. Thus, the abundant deer have no natural predatory enemies. Man is the only predator, and only during hunting seasons.

On my small ranch, where no one lives, an expanse of exceedingly rough canyons and hills with plentiful water and excellent cover and food, we have too many deer most seasons. The place gets no severe hunting. My boys and I, and an occasional guest, kill less than a dozen deer in a season. Most of the time our deer are not even aware they are hunted. Nothing, as I've said, preys on them. Like other animals, their memories

Small whitetails of the Texas hill country.

are not long. They certainly do not remember for months that they have been spooked around modestly for several weeks of the year, maybe two days per week in that period, by two or three humans. Animals may be conditioned by incessant disturbance, but the memory of fear does not linger. A deer spooked while feeding runs away and immediately begins feeding again.

We do no indiscriminate shooting, and seldom have had a wounded deer. There are sounds from neighboring ranches—a chain saw, a tractor, voices. Motor-vehicle sounds are common. A friend who keeps a few horses with mine on the ranch drives through on the rough trails at least once a week. But do these deer become tame or trusting? Ha! They are wild as hawks.

Why, when nothing ever harms them and seldom legitimately frightens them? The answer is the *whitetail personality,* and if I impress upon you this fact, that a whitetail deer is practically neurotic in its imagined fears about imagined dangers as well as real ones, I will have taught the most important lesson about how to approach the art and science of hunting whitetail deer.

An indication of this inherent wildness can even be seen in the physical condition of whitetails. A whitetail deer is said to be "fat" when the entrails are well larded and there is at least a modest amount of fat under the skin. Until you have seen a truly fat mule deer it is difficult to realize what the comparison means. I've seen mule deer so fat that when the hide was taken off not a bit of red showed. Tallow completely covered the carcass, and in some cases I have measured it literally two inches thick across the rump. To be sure, some whitetails, particularly in the somewhat "artificial" environment nowadays of farm regions, become extremely fat —for whitetails. But you will never see, in a season and place of extremely good forage, an average of fat on whitetails similar to that on mule deer under like conditions. I note it because it is a definite indication of the jittery whitetail personality, which never allows them to become complacent.

On numerous occasions when not hunting I have spent hours in blinds observing whitetails. A doe and fawn may be feeding along totally unaware of the observer's presence a hundred yards distant. The doe puts her head down to grab a bite or two. She then jerks it erect. Constantly she will raise her head with this erratic, nervous movement, not in the slow manner that a placid animal has. She will stare here and there, flick her ears forward, flick one backward. Down goes her head again. But before she has a chance to grab the next bite, something—she has no idea what—alarms her. She jerks her head up again. The startled fawn jumps and stands looking at its mother.

I have watched whitetails do this until they literally tired me out with their incessant worrying. If something special has caught the animal's attention, it will shift weight from one front foot to the other, over and over, and lower its head to look from a different angle. Commonly whitetails will shift the head position from side to side. The eyesight of deer differs from that of man, and the shifting is an attempt to see in a different plane, to bring what it sees across the field of vision in a modified position.

Curiously, certain sounds do not seem to alarm whitetails, but what will or won't alarm them is not very predictable. I have often watched feeding deer when a shot was fired distantly. Usually they have no reaction at all. A close shot, of course, will disturb them. Not long ago I watched several deer as a group of turkeys moved out of the brush and past them. They took the big birds for granted, hardly glancing at them. Yet I have seen a squirrel run down a tree and send a deer hightailing. The shadow and wing sounds of a buzzard wheeling low over them will sometimes spook whitetails.

Nature writers are fond of perpetuating the old myth that a red squirrel chattering or a jay squawking tells a deer a hunter is coming, and also tells a hunter a deer is coming. Actually deer pay little attention to the sounds of squirrel or jay, or to any such small sounds of creatures among which they live their daily lives. And although these sounds may mean to a hunter that a deer is coming, most of the time they are meaningless. Jays rail at other jays and for that matter at squirrels.

I have seen deer put to flight by as small a commotion as a tiny songbird flitting noisily in a bush. This is odd, because they should be used to such sounds. But it typifies the whitetail. A sudden rustle . . . and the deer bolts, not even knowing what it heard. Curiously, however, whitetails seem to read quite accurately most sounds made by other deer, and certain small animals, and man. An armadillo rustling noisily as it grubs for worms and beetles seldom draws a glance from a nearby whitetail. The clinking of a deer walking over small loose rocks may cause another feeding deer to raise its head, but seldom puts it to flight. Yet try doing the same thing as you stalk a deer and it is instantly gone.

In fact, to a whitetail it must certainly be apparent that a walking man sounds like nothing except a walking man, regardless of how carefully he prowls. As an aside here it should be noted that a hunter sneaking along is often less successful than the one who walks naturally. I'm not speaking now of a careful stalk on a deer that is unaware, or of skilled still-hunting. But when deer are in the area, and even sometimes when they are in sight, a sneaking approach will terrify them, whereas they may be reassured by a man walking along naturally, in the open, even mumbling to himself and plotting an angled course seemingly away from the animals and never looking toward them. I've done this, and seen it done, on several occasions. The deer, apparently assuming the hunter has not spotted them, stand immobile. Occasionally a shot can be set up just this way.

Several years ago I did some experimenting, from a blind, to see what sounds and sights whitetail deer might or might not tolerate. I recall one morning sitting in the blind with full camouflage on, even to headnet and gloves. Several deer were nearby. The rancher on whose property the blind was located had been feeding them for weeks. This, of course, is an unnatural situation and gathers together groups of whitetails which would not otherwise be nearly so gregarious. At any rate, I tried making various sounds. The blind was built a couple of yards above the ground. One large window allowed me to see out. All the interior of the blind was painted a flat-finish black.

I discovered that the deer would allow me to mumble in a monotone, subdued. They would look around but did not seem to have any idea what the sound was. If I grunted as a buck in rut sometimes grunts, one or two doe deer would casually look around. The sound was not disturbing. But if I tapped on the side of the blind, or scraped a foot across the floor, they were panicked. Yet they really could not seem to tell what they had heard or exactly where the sound came from.

The most interesting incident of that session was when my camouflage headnet came loose and flapped in the breeze. I am quite certain the deer did not wind me. But the small piece of dull-colored cloth flopping in the breeze spooked them.

There is a big lesson here for hunters. Undisturbed, deer do not range over large home territories. Whitetail studies have shown on numerous occasions that given food, water, comfort, and safety many whitetails stay within a half section of land all their lives. Now deer are sharp observers, and it is obvious that any deer must come to know every stick and stone and bush in this small bailiwick it calls home.

Those deer, for example, were used to seeing the blind and its opening. They had not been disturbed as long as I hunched quietly looking out. The camouflage blended well and was just an immobile blob. But when the net flopped, this was something that didn't belong. Time after time hunters spook deer not because they have been scented, or seen as hunters, but simply because a whitetail, jumpy in the extreme to begin with, detects something that it has *not seen in that spot previously.* If you drive from your home to the office and return, two trips a day, you get so you know every house, shrub, and sign. If something new appears, it calls your attention. Nothing very astonishing about that. The whitetail is such a jittery creature that anything unnatural is presumed to be dangerous, and flight is the best way to put it out of sight and mind.

I would hope that readers as they follow this chapter and the next—which discusses the mule deer—will consciously make comparisons between the two deer. This is how you learn. As an example, consider what happens when a whitetail has made up its mind that something is amiss. It may be that the deer has not actually sighted danger. It may simply have picked up some wafted scent that is nerve-wracking, or heard some sound that isn't quickly and easily identifiable. The instant reaction is to flee.

There are some exceptions. A puzzled whitetail may take a moment to convince itself. But without even sighting the supposed danger its impulse is to get gone from that place. Conversely, as we will see in some detail later, a mule deer may put it off literally for minutes, or foolishly suppose it is hidden when it is not. And when the whitetail flees, bounding up a ridge, let's say, you can bet that not in one case out of fifty will it stop to stare back at what it presumed scared it. This deer doesn't really care what frightened it. The main thing is to put the ridge between it and danger, imagined or otherwise. Remember that when we get into the mule deer chapter.

Furthermore, there is little point in racing to the top of a ridge over which a whitetail has just bounded, although as with most rules there are exceptions. To be sure, you might get a running shot as it crosses the valley below. But you'd have to hurry, because the whitetail seldom will slow down. It may run over several ridges and through several canyons, particularly if it has actually seen you. Mule deer reactions are quite different because they are much more placid creatures.

The lack of gregariousness among whitetails is also a notable personality trait. Of course, when deer are fed, as those I spoke of near the blind, they may gang up. I have also seen numerous whitetails feeding on green feed in winter such as patches of winter oats. Where they were abundant to the point of overpopulation, I've counted as many as fifty on a small field. These are special circumstances. But if you observe closely even at such times you'll note that the animals are not very closely grouped. It is easy to pick out a doe and her nearly grown fawns here, maybe several does close together. But keep watching, and if they get too close, particularly if there are old does present, they will rear up on hind legs, ears back, striking out with front feet. Whitetails are not group animals, even though loose groups may consort to avail themselves of special forage or water.

Over the years when I lived in Michigan, I can never recall seeing a group of bucks together except on one occasion when three, all mature, crossed a trail in front of me. This was not during season. A couple of years ago I was shooting photographs of whitetails in a place where a

Whitetail does on an overpopulated range in south-central Texas.

rancher had fed them for years in winter. To reach the spot the deer had come around through a close stand of mesquite to avoid being in the open. This threw a number of deer together, and I presume they had learned, because forage was so good, to tolerate each other for short periods. In that instance I watched as many as seven bucks coming in together. But they were never friendly—some hooked at others, and when they left each went its separate way.

Of course seasonally whitetails will act in a different manner. But most of the year the doe and her fawns are a separate family, and bucks are in general loners. Whitetails do not seem to require the close company of other whitetails. They may bed down on a ridge, two here, three there, only thirty to fifty yards apart in an area where they are abundant and where there is especially suitable cover. But the need to consort closely is not strong.

In speaking of whitetails running first and wondering later what frightened them, I have probably suggested that they are not very curious animals. Again there can be exceptions. But we should not mistake puzzlement for curiosity. I have on many occasions watched a doe walk toward me when she was alerted. What she does in this instance—bucks occasionally but not as often do the same thing—is to keep her ears up, her front legs stiff. She moves one step at a time, head jerkily swinging back and forth in a brief arc. At last she may stop and stamp her foot. A hunter must be aware of what this signal means. Buck or doe, the animal is puzzled to the point of insecurity. The stamp may sometimes be intended to make the "danger" show itself.

There are other uses for this signal—which will be covered in a chapter about bucks in rut—but at this high moment of indecision and puzzlement the deer is saying that things aren't just right, and its instincts tell it to flee. Invariably the stamp of the foot precedes by a few seconds, or less, a snort of alarm. Occasionally a doe—almost never a buck—will come on step by step, stamping a foot several times over. But if you are waiting for a shot, or a photo, and you see or hear that stamped foot, it tells you you'd better hurry.

The snort says, "I'm going now." Most of the time the snort comes as the deer wheels and bounds away. But here again, a whitetail hunter must know how to interpret this signal. A deer that is at a distance and catches a disturbing scent, but is unable to see anything that is cause for alarm, may snort a number of times. In such an instance, however, "blow" is probably a better word. It's a different sound. Well I remember instances of fishing a trout stream after dark and having deer up on the bank in the woods, unable to see me, blowing out breath in a drawn-out "whoosh" time after time.

On occasion such a deer may actually be evidencing some curiosity as well as perplexity. I have watched often from a blind in a tree when, after a number of these quick wheezing breaths spaced at intervals, a deer finally walked out where I could see it and looked around. Something as an aside to bear in mind here is that a hunter on a stand actually "oozes" scent that spreads from his position slowly like smoke or fog. On a still morning a hunter takes a stand and for the first few minutes to half hour cannot be scented very far away. Much depends on how moist or dry the air. But the longer he stays, the farther the scent blanket spreads around him. There is also a great difference in individual people. Some, crude as it may sound to say it, smell far stronger than others, even when well bathed.

At any rate, the final snort of a whitetail is crisp and short and loud. When you hear that, it means the same as that loud *putt!* of an alarmed tom turkey—the deer is already in flight. Invariably this will be a bounding run that puts a lot of distance behind the deer in a hurry. Also, this sound may be made by either sex, and commonly is. However, does do more of it than bucks. Some hunters are under the impression that only bucks snort. Usually the sharp snort of alarm is followed by several lesser exhalations. If you cannot see the deer but only hear it, this series will tell you without any question that the deer is running.

Other whitetail signals are both immensely intriguing and important for hunters to recognize. They are integral parts of the whitetail personality. One that few hunters recognize is what may be termed the "all clear." Suppose you are on a stand, or stalk-hunting very slowly. You spot a deer. It may be feeding, or walking along. Suddenly it stops and stares at you, or at least in your general direction. Whatever you do, don't move a muscle. Freeze in whatever position you must. You can be certain that if the deer continues simply to stare it has not winded you. On occasion a whitetail may stare so long, utterly immobile itself, that you wonder if you can hold out. Meanwhile, however, keep your eye on its tail. Assuming it is not unduly alarmed but only wary, the tail will be down. Suddenly it will flick once from side to side. This does not mean the deer is about to run. Quite the contrary, it means the deer has decided all is okay. It will either begin feeding again or walk on in the direction in which it was headed.

This does not necessarily mean it won't stare again in a few seconds or a minute or two. You have to be ready to match immobility instantly. But again, keep your eye on the tail. Presently there is the slight flick side to side again, and the deer's attention is momentarily ended. I have hunted with only two or three deer addicts who were aware of this whitetail trait.

A standing, alerted whitetail that begins slowly to raise its tail until it is about straight out behind is a badly disturbed animal. As the tail comes up slowly, the deer may add the stamping of a front foot and a whoosh of breath. Almost certainly at this point you have a spooked deer to deal with, and if you are going to shoot you had better hurry. Remember also that almost always in this situation the deer will be facing you, which isn't the easiest shot unless you are close. As the tail raises it may momentarily be held straight out behind and then swung stiffly and slowly to the side. The deer is at that instant on the verge of bolting. There is a possibility that if it has not scented you it just may turn with head flung high and back and trot stiffly away, tail at slightly above half-mast. But usually it will wheel, throw the tail high, and bolt wildly, snorting as it goes, tail swinging from side to side like a white flag.

Bucks have another tail signal you should be able to read instantly. An incident that occurred a year ago while I was trying to help a friend get a good buck well illustrates. The rut had been rather erratic, stretched-out, not concentrated. But it was late in season and I did not expect to see any "rutty" bucks. Suddenly we saw an excellent animal, running. There was no time for a shot before it disappeared behind a thicket, and besides a shot would have been precarious.

My fellow hunter cussed in exasperation. "A real trophy, and we spooked him!"

"No," I said, "we didn't. That buck is following a doe and we may be able to get him yet."

I had seen that the buck was not bounding but running. A well-spooked whitetail bounds away. A buck in rut and pursuing a doe may bound, but often simply runs. The clinchers, however, were two sure signs: the deer had its neck stretched out and head low and mouth open, and its tail was held straight out behind. A buck following a doe may not *always* hold its tail out like that. But a running buck with a stance such as I've described almost certainly is pursuing or trailing a doe.

In this case we just sat tight. I had a hunch the doe, if caught up with, would likely circle back around the edge of the ridge. They often do, leading the buck around and around. As it happened, the gamble paid off. Within ten minutes we saw the doe. And we observed another sign that is just about surefire. She came trotting out of a thicket, paused, flopped one ear back, and turned her head halfway around. She was listening and watching behind her. In addition, her tail was held not fully down but barely raised out away from her body. She was ready to be bred. With another flick of an ear behind, she trotted off again. In seconds the buck came barreling through the thicket, so glassy-eyed with desire that he made no pause to see if danger lurked. My friend's hunt was concluded right there.

Although deer are not notably vocal animals, occasionally a buck in rut makes a sound that hunters should recognize. Vividly I recall the first time I heard it and realized what it was. On a frosty morning in northern Michigan I had left a log cabin in the woods where we were staying for our hunt and had walked as quietly as possible through a scattering of snow up from the Pigeon River and into a series of low ridges where I intended to take a stand.

There were small openings in the mixed poplar, birch, and conifers, and as I started to cross one a doe ran out from across the opening almost toward me. I stopped short, spang in the open, not moving a muscle. The doe did not look at me. She looked behind. This clued me that a buck must be following, but I could not tell where. Suddenly I heard the sound, a series of low, guttural grunts—not loud, but audible even at the distance I guessed the buck must be, possibly sixty paces. The sound was repeated and then I could see the deer, standing in brush looking at the doe. Then and there I filled my license.

You may not ever hear the sound. It is not always uttered. I have observed at close range scores of bucks in rut and heard it only a few times. But a hunter who recognizes this unusual utterance may pick off a trophy now and then that he'd not connect with otherwise.

Rather rarely a deer may bleat—or blatt. Fawns may do this when seeking the doe they are nursing. An injured or trapped deer may make such a sound. In a later chapter we will deal with sounds hunters can make to attract whitetails. But I would say overall that listening for vocal sounds of deer, except the grunt I've described, is not an important part of successful hunting. However, one should certainly always be alert for sounds made by bucks fighting during the rut. The clash of antlers carries far, hoofs sliding in gravel or rocks, crackling of brush. Even during pre-rut days, bucks polish antlers by practice-fighting on brush or saplings. Occasionally these sounds can be heard. On one occasion some years ago in Wisconsin I distinctly heard a buck tearing into a bush, walked straight to the sound, and bagged the deer.

Whitetail does are invariably more easily observed than are bucks, for several reasons which we will discuss in a later chapter. It is a good idea to get to know all you can about does. Few hunters pay enough attention to them, because most are eagerly looking for a buck and settle for a doe as a last chance. However, thorough knowledge of whitetail doe habits is of vital importance at times in getting the buck. For instance, if you have a group of does and fawns in sight, as I've noted there will be clashes between does when they get too close to each other. In almost every instance you will see that one doe, an old one, possibly without fawns, is infernally crabby. Watch this one! She will also be the most alert and experienced, and if any deer in the group is going to give you away it will likely be this one. If you are going to go on still-hunting, by all means contrive to "lose" her! Or, if you are on a stand, sometimes it may be best to sneak away and take a new one where no alert old lady can tell on you.

However, the same bossy old doe may be useful, or any does for that matter. For they may tell on a buck as quickly as on a hunter they've spotted. Always when I am observing antlerless deer I try to select the one that seems most alert or wary. This one is obviously the best observer among the group. I keep watching to see what the doe is watching. A deer that suddenly sees another deer does not act disturbed. Thus, a doe that has been jittering away every few seconds may suddenly turn her head and stare intently, but calmly. The ears will be cocked fully forward. If the deer continues to stare, I'm usually ready to bet another deer is coming, or passing by distantly. The doe may not be in heat and may have no real interest in a buck at the time. But she may well be staring at a buck. I have collected several bucks just this way, by following the gaze of an alert doe.

I also, incidentally, always watch livestock if it happens to be in view. Cattle, horses, sheep, and goats do not disturb whitetails—unless the livestock is frightened somehow and runs, which will cause deer to follow suit. But most farm animals will turn to stare at deer, and occasionally a hunter discovers their ghostly presence that way.

Because does are generally more in evidence than bucks, they can be agonizingly exasperating as well as helpful. Does have loused up many a buck hunt by noisily giving hunters away. If you see one or several,

To the buck hunter, whitetail does can be exasperating. They are always giving you away.

have a close look to ascertain if they can help you by leading a rutting buck to you or by "pointing" a buck for you. But if the rut is not on and there's a chance they may spot you, do your best to avoid them. A doe with grown fawns in fall will seldom have a buck with her. She will drive the fawns away or run away from them during the breeding period. Any time you disturb a jittery whitetail doe or group of them, and they run, they are very likely to alert a buck nearby. Never disturb any deer you don't intend to collect, if you can possibly avoid it.

The whitetail doe ready to be bred has a certain manner that can be valuable knowledge to a hunter. As she comes out of a thicket she seems to glide along. She takes mincing steps, and when she is not with a buck, but ready, she may actually trail a buck that is in rut. The reason for this is that she seeks a scrape—as will be explained in more detail in a later chapter. She may locate a buck scrape and urinate in it. The buck will visit the scrape and follow from there. The hunter who observes a doe following a buck trail to a scrape will have the location of the scrape pinpointed—and there is no better stand.

It is interesting to note well the *build* of the whitetail as compared to that of the mule deer. The build actually gives a clue to the deer personality. The whitetail is a graceful, even fragile-appearing creature.

It has a slender build, as if it were fashioned purposely to slide through brush and varied cover. Further, the very gracefulness and fine molding of its features plainly bespeak its intense nature. Of course the build of doe and buck are quite dissimilar. This observation can be invaluable to the hunter. The easiest way to describe the difference is to say that looked at from broadside a doe seems somewhat triangular from the base of the neck on back across the body, and a buck seen from the same angle looks rectangular. An experienced hunter who is a keen observer can spot a buck whitetail distantly with naked eye or glass even when antlers cannot be distinguished. It is done by noting the stance of the deer.

Scores of times when I have been assisting friends in hunting whitetails, or when I was teaching my boys to hunt, I've looked at a deer far off and said, "It stands like a buck." Most of the time I've been right. A buck looks blocky, even facing you. Also, it invariably stands with forelegs straight down and well separated. Look carefully at whitetail does and you'll see that they are extremely narrow in the shoulders and often stand almost knock-kneed, the upper forelegs seeming to sprout from very nearly the same place and then the lower legs splaying out from the knees.

All of these odds and ends added up make the whitetail a distinct animal personality. The type of cover it inhabits could also be considered part of its personality. It can be summed up in capsule form by saying that this ever-worrying, nervous creature seeks constantly to be either hidden or at least only a few bounds from a hiding place. Certainly whitetails will cross openings, and are known under special circumstances to feed in open fields. But fundamentally they are neither deep-forest creatures nor inhabitants of open country. They are *edge* animals.

The reason they are not animals of mature forests is a matter of livelihood. Mature timber overpowers understory growth and second-growth and thus destroys the forage on which the deer must survive. Most hunters know that cutting of forests enhances whitetail deer populations. Cut-over areas produce abundant new crops of food reachable by deer. The secretive whitetail insists on having food and cover in the same places or at least in such close conjunction that safety from real or imagined dangers is within mere steps. Observe the routes of travel used by whitetails that are undisturbed and you will find they invariably follow the cover, the edges, never short-cutting through expanses of open country.

Of course, over their vast domain it is not always easy to tag what an "edge" really is. But with practice and close observation, "edge" can be translated from place to place. A strong point to make, to illustrate for you where these deer consort to the highest degree, is to say that if you never hunted anywhere except along creek or river bottoms, regardless of where you were within whitetail range, you would always find deer. In Chapter Two, listing the best hunting areas in the various states, I often say that whitetail range is along "most of the state's river courses and creek bottoms." This is because both forage and the mixed cover of brush and trees and edges that these deer insist upon are always found along stream courses.

They are found elsewhere, too, of course—in fact in any place that resembles in make-up what a stream course has. But the stream course is always a magnet, and typical, anywhere. In places like the South Texas brush or the Deep South swamp, obviously you have to dope out what replaces the stream course. Swamp openings and hammocks are one example of prime coverts. In the cactus country where no streams flow the deer usually nowadays get water from ranch tanks. But the magnet here

A true trophy whitetail of the brush and "creek bottom" country near the Mexican border.

is always the dry wash or what natives call a creek bottom, even though water is there only when it rains. The reason these dry creek bottoms draw whitetails can be simply explained. Because these courses get the most of the sparse water that falls on an arid country, the heaviest vegetation always grows here. These are safety havens, comfortable, and usually with some of the best forage.

You should now have a solid idea of what kind of animal the whitetail deer is. Let me urge you again, as you read on through the next chapter, to note carefully the differences in habits and personality between whitetails and mule deer. Knowing one thoroughly helps you understand the other better.

CHAPTER FOUR

The
Mule Deer
Personality

The foregoing chapter about the whitetail indicates that it is a difficult quarry for hunters. The fact is, I personally consider the whitetail deer the most challenging and difficult big-game animal anywhere in the world, so far as the craft required of the hunter is concerned.

Mule deer are totally different animals. Sometimes they are awesomely sharp, sometimes incredibly stupid, but they are always altogether lovable. I have the highest regard for them, and for numerous reasons I have a real soft spot for them.

Some of the most interesting deer hunting I have experienced has been during forays after mule deer in open country, both with the Rocky Mountain deer and with the Desert mule deer. The chief attraction for me in this open-country hunting is that it offers one a wonderful opportunity to observe the deer, their habits and reactions.

Several years ago, I was on a trip doing a magazine assignment about mule deer hunting. I had to carry several cameras, of course, and could not do any hunting myself until I had shot a great many photos of the other hunters in action, and of deer. We were driving along a rough ranch trail in a four-wheel-drive vehicle, looking at the long, steep slopes and glassing them. I happened to spot the antler of a deer skylighted on a ridgetop quite close by. Just one antler tip showed. The deer was over the ridge. A scattering of low brush fringed the ridgetop and several Spanish bayonet plants thrust their myriad sabers against the sky.

"Hold up," I said to the driver. "That antler looks large. Let's have a look."

I climbed out and behind me came one of the hunters, beginning to get excited. He said something in a loud voice. I motioned for him to be still. My intention had been to climb the ridge and perhaps get some good telephoto shots of the deer, and maybe a hunter might bag a good trophy right here. As it turned out, there was no need for stealth. At the sound of the hunter's voice, the deer stalked up and stood silhouetted grandly on the ridge, looking down at us.

The hunter all but fell apart. "Should I take him?" he hissed.

The buck was an excellent ten-pointer. I said, "Hell, no! Just hold your gun around halfway behind you so it'll show. I want some pictures."

Meanwhile I was backing up, for I had a 300mm lens on the camera and had to get some distance so I could get part of the hunter, out of focus, in the frame, and the deer sharply focused atop the ridge. As I backed I fiddled swiftly with the camera. When I looked up again, there were *two* ten-point bucks staring down at us!

I began wildly firing the camera, backing again for a better angle. What an opportunity! The hunter was begging me to quit so he could claim a trophy—and during this interval two more ten-pointers appeared to pose with the others. Unbelievable. But not the end. Shortly before I had finished the roll of film, a fifth came into view. I "shot" the whole group, and had the hunter, his pose a natural one of astonishment, a blurred figure in the corner of the frame.

As I ended the roll all the bucks were standing perfectly calm and placid, as if wondering what all the fuss was about. At this point I really didn't want the hunter to shoot—the deer had been such disciplined actors. But I never got a chance to tell him so. As I said, "Out of film," the hunter jerked his gun around and started to load it. For reasons known only to those bucks, after all their naive foolishness they suddenly exploded into action like a flushing quail covey. In a burst of flying rocks and flailing legs, they hurtled off the ridge and disappeared. Gibbering in anguish, the hunter raced to the ridgetop. The bucks were nowhere in sight.

That incident tells a great deal about mule deer. They are odd personalities, in many respects unpredictable. Often they seem not to know what they are about to do, until they do it. Then just as you start thinking they are big dummies, some gray-faced old monster will outwit you as concisely and professionally as any whitetail.

One mule deer trait illustrated by that group is their gregariousness. They often remind me of cattle. They seem to like the company of their kind and to depend on it, to need it. Of course, there are many loner bucks. Almost without fail these are old bucks. However, I have commonly observed bucks bedded singly during the afternoon, and watched them get up along toward shadow time and presently be joined by others that had been singly bedded but not too far away, a loose association.

One recent fall I was producing a TV film in some of the finest mule deer country in West Texas, the Catto-Gage Ranch. We were shooting deer footage before the season opened, so neither deer nor our crew would be disturbed. Late one afternoon I glassed a series of ridges and counted fourteen bucks, all of very passable trophy proportions. They were strung along, two here, one there, three yonder. But they were obviously a group that consorted daily or at least I suspected that.

Later I told Jim Hayne, one of the ranch owners, about these deer and said there was one in particular I wouldn't mind having when season opened. Jim, a friend of ours named John Casey, and I went to those same ridges shortly after sunup on a crisp morning after season opening—and there were the deer, every last one, feeding placidly along!

In areas where mule deer are superbly abundant it is not at all uncommon to see groups of does and fawns, perhaps with a few spikes or forkhorns mixed in, numbering anywhere from fifteen to forty. Sometimes a big buck mingles with such a crowd, but not often. Usually groups of three to five or six bucks hang around together for months at a time. Except during the rut, neither the bucks nor the does bicker unduly among themselves. Nor do the bucks, during rut, fight as viciously as whitetails do. On occasion a pair will really get after it. But the incidence of bucks battling to the death, or interlocking antlers and dying that way, is much lower among mule deer than among whitetails.

Some mule deer buck fights are really comedy. They bluff a lot but do little serious damage. Oddly, however, when aroused a buck mule deer is an amazingly ferocious creature. Jim McLucas, who originated many of the techniques of big-game live-trapping in Montana, and has trapped elk, deer, bighorns, goats, and antelope by the thousands for Montana for many years, told me one time that the one animal he was really afraid of, in a trap corral, was a buck mule deer.

"When we trap bucks with antlers on, naturally we have to saw the antlers off so we can handle the animals for loading and transplant. Elk are easy compared to a mature mule deer. He'll stand off there in the pen and eye you, just itching to get at you and ram a tine into you."

Mule deer are not nervous, like whitetails. They're not worriers. As McLucas said, a big buck in a pen stands calmly appraising the situation. Whitetails under similar conditions are often in a frenzy. Feeding mule deer browse along with unconcern. There is no nervous head-jerking and ear-flicking. If something disturbs them, the deer will stare, flopping their large ears forward. If they decide to run, seldom is there any panic. They just go. A big buck can make tremendous time, in astonishing leaps, traveling for short distances up to possibly thirty-five miles per hour. But it is not often that mule deer flee in such a manner unless really pressed.

On dozens of occasions I have watched a "flight" routine that is quite amusing. A deer, either buck or doe, suddenly is aware of my presence, perhaps with a camera. Or perhaps there are several deer. I start to raise the camera and the deer stare. But then they suddenly realize I am too close. Almost as if in embarrassment at their folly, they turn and walk on an angle away. This walk itself is comedy. The legs are held rather stiffly, and as a front foot is placed exaggeratedly forward the head comes backward, then forward again as the other foot comes down—almost like some vaudeville dancer making an exit offstage and casting sly glances back at the audience.

If really startled, a mule deer will bounce away for a short distance, using what I like to describe as its "pogo-stick" gait. It bounds nearly straight up, but forcing itself forward in a short leap, stiffening all four legs and holding them straight as it comes down. Thus all four feet hit at once, and up the deer goes again. Whitetail hunters having a first fling at mule deer are always startled to see this. Rather often this display, which does not amount to swift retreat at all, is used when the deer is still not quite certain that real danger is present.

I've watched this act many times. The deer bounces off like this for perhaps forty or fifty yards, then comes down and turns broadside to stare back at the intruder. But finally, when the deer decides to really get gone, it gives a beautiful display of a powerfully built animal in grandly efficient motion. As I noted in Chapter One, mule deer run with a unique bounding surge. They leap high and far, and come down on all fours with all hoofs digging and shoving backward to send the animal through another great leap. A big muley can cover up to twenty-five feet in a single bound! No snorting, no flag waving as in typical whitetail flight—simply a powerhouse going through brush, over rocks, up any steep mountainside like a fast freight.

There are, of course, individual differences among animals, just as among human beings. Some mule deer are wilder than others. But none evidence the near-neurotic behavior of the whitetail. One of their most curious and typical traits is the desire to have a last look at whatever put them to flight. I cannot resist relating a wryly comic hunting incident to illustrate this habit.

I badly wanted a really good Desert mule deer for photos for a story I was doing. A Desert mule deer with ten points and a spread of 26 inches can be considered substantial. I saw such a deer go into a draw that was backed up by a steep, high slope and a rimrock. After it I went. I was carrying a .264 magnum so I could reach out if necessary. In the gun and in my pocket I had a total of five cartridges when I left the vehicle I was riding in.

Before I could spot the buck, a group of does I had not seen suddenly appeared at the base of the slope. They stared, then began trotting up the mountain. This alerted the buck, and he bounded along behind them. It was too much. He was a trophy deer. I held as carefully as I could and squeezed off. The explosion rattled off the rimrock and the bullet made a violent *splatt*. This sent all the deer flying in high gear. They ate up that slope as if it were level ground. In excitement I touched off another, and another, and finally, hands shaking, the ones from my pocket. Not a hit. By then the deer had topped out. The does slowed to a trot and disappeared. That huge buck stopped, turned, and stared down at me, fully skylighted. A long shot but actually an easy one—only not so easy without a cartridge. The big dope was still standing there when I walked away.

I won't say this will always happen. But it occurs with some regularity. I am convinced mule deer are more curious than whitetails. One should learn never to shoot at a buck running up a ridge, but to wait until it tops out. If the deer doesn't stop and look back, it may well slow down and simply walk over. Why they do this I'm uncertain, but I have witnessed it scores of times.

When mule deer run up a ridge like this, they are very likely to stop at the crest and look back. In any case they probably won't run far after they go over.

Where mule deer are hard hunted they are not so likely to act this way. And a big old trophy buck may barrel over the ridge and keep right on going at top speed over the next one. However, nine times out of ten, the moment the danger is out of sight the deer presumes itself safe and slows down. More than once I have shot at a good mule deer buck and missed, watched the deer go out of sight over a ridge, then climbed after it and discovered it feeding along unconcerned barely over the crest. This is a common trait and simply a part of the odd mule deer personality.

The mule deer build seems to me to reflect their temperament. They are blocky, husky. There is nothing fragile about them. The legs are solid and stocky. The feet are astonishingly large. Heavy old bucks in rocky country have hooves worn and splayed and unbelievably massive. Viewed broadside, even the does appear rectangular in body outline. Mule deer ears are at least a fourth longer than whitetail ears. They often appear to flop almost like mule ears, and some does seem almost ludicrous when their ears are cocked. Indeed, when forage is good and mule deer are fat and content on a range, their heavy, rounded bodies and sleek coats remind one of domestic livestock. As I have said in the preceding chapter, where food is even reasonably plentiful, mule deer are invariably fat. Under optimum conditions, even in warmer climes where they do not need so badly to store it for winter, they are utterly larded, inside the body cavity and under the hide. I am quite certain this condition stems from their placid temperament.

Although mule deer occur in a variety of terrains, these deer—except the Columbian blacktail—are creatures with a far more pronounced acceptance of open country than are whitetails. I have hunted mule deer in locations in northeastern Wyoming where there was not a tree for a hundred miles, except a few ancient cottonwoods in creek bottoms. One of the largest bucks I ever took, in fact, lived in this type of country, where deer hide in the deep gullies and treeless headers with small patches of brush. Commonly mule deer are found in abundance in sagebrush foothills where only scattered trees such as junipers, or none at all, are present. In West Texas, mule deer are abundant on the seemingly barren mountainsides of the Big Bend country, where only sotol, bayonets, lechuguilla, and a few other high-desert plants grow above inconspicuous grasses.

However, this does not give the complete picture. Throughout all of the Rockies region the deer are found in forest settings. But hunters should not interpret this to mean mule deer are truly forest animals. It is proper to say they are deer of *open* forests. Dense climax forest is no more useful to them than it is to whitetails or any other large animals, for ground-level food is lacking. A most interesting feature of mule deer terrain, regardless of the vegetation, is its invariable "slant." Mule deer seem to insist on slopes and steep mountains, and rugged badlands. Unbroken brush sweeps are not suitable. But open, seemingly rather barren land with scattered brush is often very productive of mule deer.

While it is true, as we've seen, that these deer have colonized broadly from north to south, they have not been successful in overcoming certain

vegetative and topographical obstacles that whitetails have somehow sur-
mounted. Prairies have always deterred them, except in spots where stream
courses offer some brush. It may be, however, that flatlands are one real
inhibiting factor to mule deer colonization. It is noteworthy that they are
seldom found, and never abundantly, where wooded or even brushy lands
over large areas are fairly level. Rough country is always nearby.

To me one of the most intriguing facets of the mule deer personality
is their choice of bedding places and often of hiding places. A fat deer
likes to be cool, and what is cool to man may seem too warm for the deer.
So muleys are always seeking cool spots in shade where they can bed
down—except of course in bitter weather. But they like to be able to see
out. Conversely, a whitetail buck may hide in a dense spot where it can
see but little. Its security is based on remoteness. Perhaps mule deer select
many of their resting locations simply because the see-out spots are more
common in rough terrain, and usually cooler, or warmer, as the day demands.

A large old buck will sneak into a high thicket and come out onto
an open, rocky point overlooking a valley. He can see everything below.
He is vulnerable from behind, but almost always there will be two ways
to run off the point. Hunters who know this trait glass all such points from
the valley below, and thus is many a big buck undone. These deer also
select rimrocks for resting places, in mild weather always on the shady
side, and on the sunny side if there is a freezing wind. High rimrocks
have thousands of crannies large enough to hide a deer in cool or sunny
comfort during the day, and are more complicated for a hunter to glass.
A careful search up on top, however, will jump many a mulie at extremely
close range.

But these are the usual spots. What I always marvel most at is the
way great big mature bucks will lie down in open country on a ridgeside,
usually well up toward the top, but spang in the open, using only a single
small bush for shade or cover. I have glassed and photographed deer in
this situation many times. It is, to be sure, easy to miss them even when
glassing. But still, a hunter who knows this trait won't miss all of them.
A single Spanish bayonet may offer the slim shade a buck will select. A
small juniper all alone on a slope may have a buck under it. A large rock
that has stopped water runoff and thus allowed a bit of brush to grow,
perhaps hardly enough to fill a bushel basket—this may be the place where
a trophy buck decides to lie down.

A perfect chance at a mule deer buck that was bedded under a small bush.

Others, where cover is more abundant, as on slopes where grass, juniper, and perhaps small pines grow, will scorn a dense thicket and bed down under a small piñon or juniper out in the grass. In fact, one recent season Travis Roberts and I hunted for just such a buck. Travis, well into his sixties, has lived in the Big Bend country all his life and there is not much he doesn't know about it. The day was hot and it was midday and not a deer was in sight.

"We'll jump one," Travis said.

He turned off the ranch trail and drove his old pickup along a slope where it would barely stay upright. There were a few thickets of leafy brush maybe twenty feet in diameter, and there was tall grass, and sparsely scattered there were the small junipers and piñons. Presently Travis stopped.

"You see him?"

I saw him. Lying in the spot of shade cast by a small pine, and perfectly silhouetted against the golden grass, was a really handsome ten-pointer. The thought crossed my mind that you would never, but never, catch a whitetail buck in that kind of situation. And if you did, it would be over the hill before the pickup stopped. I do not mean that whitetail bucks won't lie doggo and let a hunter pass. They often do. They often also sneak out of a bedding or feeding spot without a sound. The reason most hunters are never quite sure about this is because the deer do it so expertly they are seldom seen. A whitetail buck will literally hold its head down and all but get on its knees at times to sneak away. But this is only when it believes it has not been spotted, and it is always in heavy cover.

So here was an excellent buck, looking at us, plainly seen. What was it "thinking?" I'm convinced mule deer often believe themselves hidden when they are not. The rest of this story serves to confirm it. I took my rifle and approached the deer. I just didn't intend to shoot it that easily. Now what would the buck do when I finally jumped it? A whitetail would darned well have every bush and tree between it and me. What this mulie might do was just not predictable.

I was within forty paces before the deer decided it better leave. It wasted no time, bounded up the mountain, but right through the open, across a grassy patch. I shot. I hate to say it, but even at that close range and a target that appeared as big as a range steer, I missed it. Dirt and dust billowed. There was a brush thicket with leaves on it just a couple of bounds from the deer. Had it got behind that and plunged toward the ridgetop, where junipers and pines were thicker, I probably never would have had another chance. But no, it crashed into the thicket and stood absolutely still.

This, too, is a common muley trait. While both hunting and using a camera I have stalked mule deer on numerous occasions when one would trot off, or run off, or even just walk off, get into a small thicket, and stay there. Sometimes you can walk right up to and around the hiding place and the deer won't move. In this case, I could see the buck's head and neck. It was an excellent rack and it was also, as I had seen, an extremely fat, large animal. I collected it.

A more curious manner of hiding, perhaps, is utilized often, usually by mature bucks where there just isn't any place to hide, or they get trapped in a dead end that offers no ready escape. Vividly I recall an experience, again with Travis Roberts. We were driving along and had no idea about killing a deer. A big buck saw the pickup and went larruping up the open ridge. A few scattered sotol clumps and bayonets were here. That was all. As the truck got closer on the winding trail below, the deer dropped its head low, slowed to a trot, passed between several sotol stalks. It then turned around, still keeping its head down, and lay down. Once again, it stretched its neck out and placed its head flat on the ground.

Why didn't it go on over the ridge out of sight? Only the deer knows. I've seen mule deer, caught in a bed, use that same ruse of laying the head down flat, lower jaw right on the ground. Usually the antlers give it away. On numerous occasions I have stalked deer with a camera, using the ruse of a late-afternoon stalk to put sun in the deer's eyes. I've seen mule deer become puzzled, in an area where cover was sparse. The deer could not make out exactly what I was. So, it would lie down in the closest brush. Columbian blacktails are known to jump and run and flop down in a brush patch, too, letting a hunter race around trying to find them.

To sum up the hiding habits, in general mule deer prefer to hide rather than run, and just the opposite is true of the whitetail. This, of course, is a little too much of a generality, but it does offer a basic key to personalities. When hunting has been going on for several weeks, for example, whitetails in most habitat types are extremely wild and will be up and gone without a hunter seeing them. In a few localities—I think of a piece of country on the Mexican border cut with deep, brushy canyons—the whitetails have to be choused hard to move them. But that is a specialized situation of terrain. However, almost everywhere mule deer when hard hunted will cling to the thickets of mountain mahogany or other brushy or rocky hiding places and it becomes extremely difficult to rout them.

So far I have purposely discussed mule deer in general, but meaning chiefly the Rocky Mountain mule deer, the Desert mule, and the others of the terrain types described. The Columbian blacktail is a quite different proposition, but chiefly its habits are an expression or consequence of the dense coastal-slope vegetation in which it mainly thrives. There are thickets of understory cover in coastal rain forests so dense that a hunter cannot get through them. In California blacktail country several varieties of dry brush spread over foothills, forming barriers hunters would have to crawl through.

The blacktail lives easily in all this country, threading the canyons, following trails on the steep slopes, slipping through small openings in the brush patches, and gathering in proper season beneath oak or other trees in more open areas to feed on acorns and small browse. In this setting of heavy cover it is not easy to observe what the blacktail is doing, to pinpoint its habits. The fact is, blacktails are conditioned by their habitat to use two main methods of protecting themselves.

One is to hide. They are uncanny about it. Many a blacktail hunter crawling around in a thicket has suddenly found himself staring at a hidden buck that has been listening all the time, waiting for danger to bypass it without discovery. It is commonly very difficult to get blacktails out of their close cover. In some parts of California even the use of dogs has been allowed to move the deer. Driving by groups of hunters who work a canyon while lookouts on points along the rim keep watch for targets is a standard blacktail hunting technique. These deer have been observed jumping from a bed or resting place when all but stepped on by a hunter, then racing around a rocky outcrop up a blind canyon and dropping down into short brush to hide. The hunter, following, ponders over the disappearance of his quarry.

The other blacktail ruse is the "big sneak." On drives it requires astute coverage by the hunters to avoid having the deer double back, or drift along a small, thin piece of cover silently and unseen and go right by the waiting rifles. Thus, in some respects blacktail hunting is similar to hunting whitetails, or a cross between whitetail and mule deer hunting. Even the deer, with its broad tail, gives that illusion. The deer is a mule deer, right enough, but the cover it inhabits is probably in process of evolving it into a new species, changing its habits and the approaches a hunter must use.

In all the discussion of mule deer I may have given the impression that these deer are unintelligent. In order to show what they are like compared to whitetails, some extreme examples have been used. So before we leave them, and before you go mule deer hunting for the first time expecting easy pickings, perhaps some qualification is in order.

Many whitetail hunters have concluded that mule deer are "dumb." But the one word which in my estimation best describes the mule deer in a wholly wild state is "deliberate." It is a composed, serene creature, fashioned to its bulky, sturdy proportions by having evolved in a rugged, wild land. It is also in many ways naive simply because it is totally a wilderness creature. The whitetail has had to cope with mankind and his awesomely burgeoning population for several hundred years now. The mule deer has had some of the same problem but by no means to the same degree.

Further, the whitetail learned long ago how to cope with the problem, how to live with civilization. As I write these words I am in my office, which is a part of our home. We are about three miles from the limits of our swiftly growing small city. We have twenty-four acres here, with two small ponds. Much of our acreage is well wooded, with live oak, Texas cedar, Spanish oak, and low brush such as agarita. But all around the fringes of this small oasis there are homes with only an acre or two. So it really isn't any wilderness. Yet I can walk across the back of the property any time and jump several deer. Some mornings six or seven are bedded fifty paces from the back door. It is impossible to grow any shrubs or flowers that the deer will eat because they gobble up every one. For that matter, right in town it is common to see deer when we drive home after dark.

This is not unusual, really. Throughout the East, whitetails thrive on the closest fringes of civilization. In all of the Midwestern farm country hundreds of small woodlots and river bottoms that are cultivated right to the tree line have their quota. However—does this same situation exist with mule deer? Hardly. I cannot imagine a mule deer living in my back yard. There are times, certainly, when heavy snows drive hard-put mule deer into Western farmyards and close to town limits seeking forage. But the mule deer does not thrive near man's settlement to any degree. It requires big country. It will tolerate the ranch vehicles and horses and their riders on large ranches of the West, of course, because it has no choice, but the mule deer has never adapted to civilization and undoubtedly never will.

In fact, as our population has increased, the whitetail population has actually increased in most places right along with it. Whitetails must be severely cropped annually in many places to avoid too much increase. But unfortunately the mule deer population has had an overall decrease as human numbers have increased. At this time it is in a transition period. Mule deer are in at least mild trouble in several Western states, and in what may prove to be serious trouble in others. Biologists are not certain as yet what the trouble is. It is probably many-pronged—diminishing optimum habitat, possibly too much protection of mature forests for the good of the deer, and just maybe predation on fawns in some instances. At any rate, although mule deer and hunting are not presently in any real danger, nonetheless these deer are not increasing. It is very likely that this calm, deliberate, rather naive creature of the wilderness simply cannot learn to cope with the ever-increasing pressures of civilization and adapt to them.

There are still plenty of trophy bucks to be hunted here and there. And a mature muley buck in his own bailiwick is a rough customer to bring in. Much of the difficulty originates with the habitat, which is so expansive, and so rugged. A trophy buck is an amazingly canny animal about selecting a hiding place and keeping his private life private. Also, with growing

In many states there is a heavy kill of forkhorn deer, especially Western mule deer. They often hang around with does.

numbers of hunters, the moment the season opens the disturbance is something the old buck will not tolerate. Here again is the evidence of the wilderness personality. A trophy whitetail knows how to hide out all season in a small woodlot. The trophy mulie moves back, and back, and doesn't show if he can help it or unless someone stumbles upon him, until well after the ruckus is over.

The mule deer that fill the major share of licenses are the antlerless animals where those are legal, and the spikes and forkhorns. Statistics from nearly all mule deer states show this plainly. The reasons are simple. These young bucks run with groups of does. They are also giddy youngsters. There is probably no deer as uneducated as the forkhorn—a boy just about to form an interest in girls but with little sense about how to get along in the world.

I related earlier in this chapter how I found fourteen trophy bucks feeding on a series of low ridges and how we went back on opening morning after them. We collected two that morning. Hunters on this huge ranch are carefully regulated. As almost everywhere in Texas, there is no public hunting. The ranch owners decide how many hunters they will take, at a fee, for the season. Thus, they and the ranch hands know exactly who hunted where, what was killed, and where it was killed. That group of bucks had been photographed, then hunted for a quick flurry of action that opening morning. No other hunters were taken there. For several days we drove to this remote area, trying to find one of their number that we had wanted, to fill out for the three of us. We did not see the remaining twelve again.

One of the ranch hands told me later, "I found your twelve bucks, and that biggest one was sure a beaut."

"Where were they?" I asked.

"I was working laying a water line to pump over those back ridges for cattle," he said. "They were about a mile straight back in from where you saw them, away from every ranch trail and sign of a human."

This, then, is the mule deer. Those bucks didn't see a human more than two or three times a year. They were roughly twenty-five miles away from ranch headquarters on a spread of a quarter-million acres. But they just did not like the shooting, the disturbance of their wilderness, and so, not in panic but deliberately, they drifted as far away as they could get.

One other facet of the mule deer personality must be touched. This is the vertical migrations made in mountain country where snow is heavy. It is a natural phenomenon caused by weather, which forces the deer from their high summer range to a lower-altitude winter range. Some mule deer, of course, will stay in the foothills all summer. But the bulk of the population, and invariably all the large bucks, will be up in the cool mountains. Forage is lush there in summer, and not just in restricted areas but everywhere. Many of the deer will range from 7,000 to 9,000 feet altitude, up in the aspens and pines. I have seen big bucks higher than that a number of times, when making high-country pack trips in summer. I recall one awesome old brute that almost spooked my horse, when it bounded from low willows up around 11,000 feet.

When the snows come, the deer begin to move down. For now their food is becoming scarce and they are hampered by deep snow. Hunters often misinterpret what "bad weather" is, however, to a mule deer. They aren't panicky about a severe early-fall storm. I recall once getting trapped in 22 inches of snow in the Rockies when deer season opened. Everyone was itching to get out, to get down lower where the deer would be. But the storm was soon over and most of the snow melted. The deer had not moved. And they wouldn't until really pressed.

The migrations are interesting. Certain deer populations use the same winter range season after season, and have for who knows how long. They drift along down the mountain, often taking their time. Then if a hard blizzard hits, the migration speeds up. Hunters who know the ancestral routes, where these are especially well defined because of terrain, have an opportunity to pick off some real trophies at this time. In less rugged country where migration can spread out over large expanses of mountain slope, there is of course less concentration of the deer. The most interesting aspect of these migrations is that some of them may cover astonishing distances. Summering ground may be as much as forty or fifty miles from the winter range. In a few cases it is known to be twice that.

Perhaps my fondness for mule deer is because they really are easier to hunt, except for the physical effort involved in their often rugged domain, than the whitetail. Or it just may be that I admire their stalwart refusal to join our civilization!

CHAPTER FIVE

Bucks and Does

Do you know the difference between a buck and a doe? The question seems so ridiculous that it may sound like a joke. But it isn't. Of course every hunter knows the physical differences between the two—but very few have paid enough attention to the *mental* differences.

I believe that I was the first to point out in print, in a magazine article a few years ago, that to be a truly successful deer hunter one must learn to think of bucks and does not just as different sexes of the same species, but as radically different animals. They differ so widely in general habits, at least in the habits that are most important to a hunter, that it is almost as if they were different species.

The day-to-day routines of any mature buck are not at all like those of the doe. This is emphasized even more among whitetails than mule deer, but it is true with both. All buck deer are by far more difficult to outwit than are the does. Does may be wild, certainly, but they are not fundamentally as *secretive*. I suspect the reasons are found in a basic law of nature: the female is more in evidence because it is her function to attract; the male is much less so because he carries and protects the seed.

Also, hunters like to kid themselves about the strong-willed regal stag. Nature-faker writing has always depicted the buck deer as a fearless protector of his family, or as some indomitable sultan leading the herd. All of this is utter nonsense. The buck couldn't give less of a hoot about his "family." During breeding season he does dominate the doe to some extent, and fight with other bucks instinctively. But even then it is the doe that is the real leader, while the buck, consumed by his passion, will often pass a hunter without even seeing him because he is lured on by a coy doe. As a matter of fact, among deer of both varieties it is invariably the *old does* of the groups that are the bossy ones, and the mature bucks are the ones who keep their privacy.

How many times have you heard hunters griping—or done it yourself —because after a week in the woods you have seen does and fawns by dozens, possibly a few spikes with them, but not a single large-antlered buck. "The bucks are all shot out," they say. Or, "We need to close the season and let the bucks come back." Studies by virtually every deer state have shown time and time again that sex ratios among deer are never spread wide enough to give any credence whatever to such statements.

It is possible, obviously, to hunt so hard for mature bucks that their numbers are cut down. But seldom under present-day management does it occur, because hunting is too well controlled. The fact is that sex ratios among both whitetails and mule deer are, on the whole, fairly similar. The fawn drop for any given year will run slightly higher for males than for females. There may be some annual fluctuations, and others controlled by influences such as latitude, climate, and range quality. But by and large there will be anywhere from 102 to 120 bucks for every 100 does among newborn fawns. This is very similar to the ratio for people, and a number of other animals.

As the fawns grow the males are subject to no special natural attrition sex-wise. During hunting seasons where any deer is legal, most hunters will try for a buck, and so more bucks may be killed. But as time wanes, most will settle for an antlerless deer. There is a chance, of course, that some of these will be buck fawns. But kill statistics for many years in many states that have antlerless quotas or either-sex seasons show that the ratio of bucks to does in the bag is never high enough to remotely endanger the seed. And, as I have said earlier, kill surveys also show in most places a heavy take of young bucks. Thus, there are always enough mature bucks around. But they see to it that they are inconspicuous!

Regardless of where you live, you will hear stories every season about the monster buck that "turned up out of nowhere." Usually these bucks are said to have "wandered in" from some far-off place. That's highly doubtful. Deer are not wanderers. During the rut some bucks travel a larger area than they normally would. But if does are plentiful no buck needs to, and he stakes out—as we will see in a later chapter—a quite exact breeding ground. That old monster that "wandered in" you can just bet had been living in the area all his years, keeping his private life very private indeed.

A good example of the uncanny ability of bucks to stay out of sight is evidenced every season down on our ranch. The terrain here, as I've mentioned, is rugged. There are steep, rocky canyons, lots of dense cedar,

This good Wyoming muley may have evaded the hunter for several seasons—but he did not come out of nowhere; he was living on the same range all the time.

brushy thickets, and stands of live oak. Our rough, bulldozed roads are so laid out that the place seems much larger than it is. They wind around the ridges and overlook the canyons and the creek bottoms. Our deer season is usually six weeks long. Though my boys and I don't kill a lot of deer, we go down there as often as we can simply for the enjoyment. Everyone wants to take a big buck.

However, we can drive around those trails day after day and almost never see a mature buck. Almost any day we can count at least twenty or thirty does and fawns, and now and then a spike or a forkhorn. But we know that those few young bucks aren't producing all those fawns that keep us really oversupplied with deer. We like to prowl around, because we all feel this is the highest sport in whitetail hunting, sneaking, trying to outwit a good one. Several times we have done it, too. On one occasion the three of us, pussyfooting along the edge of a steep, rocky canyon at high noon when it was hot, were able to get up within mere feet of three big bucks we didn't know were there. They were bedded along rock ledges and practically turned wrong side out when they flushed. Terry, my younger son, has had a hard time forgiving me, for I dropped the biggest of the lot just as he was about to.

On occasion we have gone out before or after season at night with a light, just to see what we had around. And we have seen some good bucks. The odd part is that during the season, even sitting on a deer stand in our complicated terrain it is difficult to down a good buck. These mature males have their aloof habits and hideaways. We are sure we know where some of them are. But they are in such places that it is virtually impossible to surprise them.

Thus, I feel that every deer hunter should attempt to learn to be a *buck* hunter. This is a far cry from training yourself as a deer hunter, which means an any-deer hunter. But if you hunt in an area where any deer is legal, and even if you are willing to take the first deer you see, you still should hunt as though you're after a buck. If you do, you certainly won't have any trouble bagging a doe—and you just may bring in Mr. Big!

Bucks cling to cover far more than do does. They are vastly more cautious. When the rut is on, but not to a point where a buck is overwhelmed, it is always the doe that steps out first into a clearing. Sometimes the buck will skulk in cover behind her for ten minutes or more. He is not only watching for danger he can sight, but he is also watching the doe. If she evidences even the slightest nervousness or apprehension, he

This handsome trophy mule deer was bedded in a spot of shade from the small clump at left.

won't follow. An interesting observation I've made on numerous occasions is that the doe may walk calmly across a small clearing. You realize by her actions that a buck is almost certainly behind her. She disappears into the cover on the far side. Presently the buck bolts out and races across. Maybe he does this because he has lost sight of his paramour. And maybe he does it instinctively because he doesn't want to be seen. He's taking no chances.

Bucks select lie-up spots quite different from those that the does find adequate. Or rather, while does may bed down in places bucks would select, any mature buck will avoid the somewhat carelessly selected place that does ordinarily use. When I wrote in the preceding chapter about the mule deer bucks sometimes lying where we could easily see them by glassing, you shouldn't get the impression the deer is being careless. A mule deer that beds down shortly after daylight or a least by midmorning up high on a ridge under a small bush has sound reasons. From the other side of the ridge nothing can possibly know it is there. From its vantage point it can see long distances, and every movement anywhere in the valley. If it does spot danger, it will bound up and over the ridge.

Meanwhile, if it lies in shadow it is really not easily seen by the predatory hunter far across the valley. Many so-so hunters, in fact, won't even bother to look in such open places. Many others will glass the slope with a quick sweep of a binocular and will pass right over the immobile animal. Further, the deer, which lives as much by its nose as by its other senses, knows by instinct that in mountain country on most days that have any sun at all there will be updrafts—thermals—moving steadily upward from the time the sun warms the slopes and valleys until at least mid-afternoon. By then on most days the deer will get up to feed and probably move lower. Now the thermals change direction as the sun lowers, and bring scents downslope to the deer. In sharp contrast to all this, mule deer does in groups can be found at almost any time of day when they are bedded lying in grass or brush of creek bottoms, or right out in the middle of a sparsely covered creosote-brush flat.

In whitetail country the places big bucks select to hide whip many a hunter. The head of a brushy coulee that has big timber offering dappled shade overhead is typical. Fallen leaves from the large trees make approach impossible without noise. If the leaves aren't down, the brush crackles and scrapes when a hunter moves through it. Stones clink or roll. Or if a place still more remote is available, the old trophy deer will find it and use it.

I remember a fall in Michigan when I observed does and fawns lying in daytime right out in open poplars and jackpines, contentedly chewing their cuds. It exasperated me to see this because we had been hunting a week and had yet to see a buck. Somehow that day we got turned around—camp became lost! In getting oriented two of us floundered through a tamarack swamp no intelligent hunter would ever get into. Out in the middle of it we discovered an expanse of higher ground, dry, with tall grass and a tangle of alders and juneberry bushes. And right there we made our second mistake. We jumped a beautiful ten-point buck and my partner shot it. I'm sure I would have, too, except he beat me to the draw. Getting the deer out, let's just say, was also a predicament no intelligent hunter would get into. The old blighter was hidden where nobody but a fool would find him—and before we were through we were convinced two fools had!

You will never find a trophy buck in a place where he has less than two escape routes. And some form of escape is always so close that the animal can get into the obscurity of timber, or over a ridge, or into a side canyon instantly. In a dense creek bottom I have seen big whitetails pick a spot right on a sharp bend. The deer is shaded by brush and it can see each way. Whichever direction danger comes from, all it has to do is dart around the bend the opposite way and disappear into the brush.

Big bucks select places where everything they need is nearby. A long trip to water—unless it cannot be avoided—is a danger in itself. Better to find a small puddle where cover is heavy and stay there. Bucks dote on finding feeding places that are remote or well hidden. One good example I think of can be seen any year on our ranch, which I have used as a kind of observation laboratory.

There are cedar breaks where trees were trimmed at the bottom years ago. Thus they grew large and tall, and crowded out small cedar and other undergrowth. Here short grass stays green all winter long. A buck can stay inside the cedars and feed all day if he chooses to do so. There are small side headers cutting into the mesalike cedar break. At any disturbance, the animal can go any direction that is necessary and be out of sight in seconds. We have lain and watched bucks in these cedars. Does would be outside, in the open edges. But the buck would not ever show himself. There was no need. He had cool comfort, winter greens, safety, and drinking could wait until dark.

Old hands at deer hunting have a saying that the last half-hour of shooting light is when the trophies fall. How true! You may see bevies of young bucks and does almost any time of day. But when the light fails until without a scope you'd be in trouble, that's when the gray-faced old codgers begin to move, and even then ever so stealthily and warily until full dark covers them. But be aware that this last light is a tricky hunting time. When a deer has been hiding all day waiting for darkness, its first foray into the edges of cover is made with great tenseness. No telling what danger may be lurking. Conversely, the buck that has been feeding during the night and is on its way to bed down just after daylight is more vulnerable. It has not been disturbed and has thus had some hours of reassurance.

The same rule holds for deer going to water, especially if drinking places are limited. It is an axiom of wildlife lore that danger lurks at the waterhole. The meat eaters skulk here waiting for their quarry. Therefore an old, wise buck will approach water cautiously. Only when it is certain the way is clear will it put its head down to drink. Right then and for a few moments after it is also vulnerable. It has settled down and is convinced of security. However, such a deer will never remain long. Drink and leave is the rule.

I cannot possibly detail for you here every type of nook and cranny those big bucks will select for hiding places. They are legion. But with the illustrations I have given, it should be easy, after studying a block of deer country, to make your own guesses. Set a rule that where the small bucks and the antlerless deer hang out is not trophy terrain, except perhaps at rutting season. Work from that premise. Where can a big buck best keep his privacy in this area? Check the possibilities one by one. Then don't barrel into them. Figure your chances of making a sneak and where the escape routes are for the deer.

Let me offer two illustrations before leaving this part of the subject. Mike, my older son, and I were on our ranch one still afternoon several years ago. As we sat getting a cool drink from a bubbling spring on our creek, we talked about how to go about finding a good buck.

"There's a side canyon that's almost unnoticeable," Mike said. "It cuts into our lower side creek and rises steeply—do you know where I mean?"

I did. This one climbs sharply to head up near the top of a big, rough hill on which we have no vehicle trail. The ranch had had a modest amount of hunting, but no one had been on that hill so far. It was just too tough thinking about getting a deer off it. I said so.

"You're overlooking one item," Mike said. "I'm going to pretend that a big buck is lying in the small hollow at the very top of that sidedraw. It's an absolutely perfect hide. But above it everything is heavy cedar."

"So . . ."

"So there isn't much to eat, and no water. When the deer gets up, right at dusk, it will come *down* the draw."

We laughed about it and kidded along—but we also decided just for fun to assume this was a good theory. As dusk drew down he and I climbed partway up the big hill. We found a ledge screened by cedars, where the rock was flat and solid—noiseless footing. Not a hint of breeze moved. Step by step we moved along the ledge. It butted into the edge of the draw and here there was tall grass below the big Spanish oaks. We stood totally silent and immobile against the cedars that dusk had painted black.

At first I thought I heard the rustling of an armadillo. Presently the rustle changed, growing more distinct as it came closer, to a rhythmic pattern, the quiet steps of a deer tiptoeing down that draw. The deer, a handsome eight-pointer, didn't stop until it was within ten paces. I'm sure by then it could scent us, but with no air movement could not tell precisely how far we were or where. Mike raised the rifle and collected the deer. He had been *buck* hunting!

On another occasion a friend of mine showed me in hulking desert mountains a small canyon completely hidden. There was no road near it, but just outside the mouth there was a ranch tank that held some water. To get here we had to hike, because the trail left when the tank was built had long since washed away. Because of the way the huge rocks were formed on past the tank, the canyon mouth, only a few feet wide, was totally hidden. But behind those it opened up into a spacious expanse where both sun and shadow, and ample forage, were present.

He said, "There's an enormous mule deer buck living in this canyon. I've seen him twice just at dusk and he goes right back in after a drink. Tomorrow is his day!"

What he meant was that tomorrow the deer season opened. That next morning he took his wife, who had never shot a deer, into the canyon at daylight. Without any difficulty whatever they found the deer and she dropped it. Out of scores of deer taken by hunters on that property, this was the biggest buck they had ever seen. The inference should be obvious—*bucks are different!*

Earlier I touched upon the fact that the ages of bucks are a factor in their wariness. A spike is a naive little deer. But having been away from its mother only a short time it still can be jumpy, although lacking in experience and judgment. The forkhorn—of course some deer never have simple forked antlers but go from spike to six, etc.—has come to attain some craftiness and wariness but is to some extent curious, and has a kind of teen-age lack of seriousness. These young bucks in rut are preposterously wacky, easy to outwit.

Past this stage, however, each season puts more knowledge and wariness into a buck. Deer of three years or so still have much to learn, but they already are plenty shy. And bucks that live to five, six, or seven are mature gentlemen with much wilderness wisdom. From this point on, if a deer survives, it is beginning to get old. Nine or ten years is a ripe age. Antler development may be poor now. But in good range and with deer in good health, you can bet the seven-year class or thereabouts are going to be tough to collect. They don't come to that age by being careless!

Hunters do not go after does as trophies, of course. But some imagine they can tell which doe they want. They shoot, as they say, "a barren doe." They might, by chance. Not one hunter in a thousand can tell a barren doe in the field, and has really no way to prove if the deer was barren even if he thinks it is. This old wives' tale always reminds me of the experts who pick out buck tracks. Once I followed such a track, a big one indeed, with a rather vociferous hunter who was going to show me the way to a monster buck. He led me straight to an old splay-footed mule deer doe.

The fact is, there are surprisingly few barren does. And when one does occur, it is seldom likely to be a healthy deer or in prime shape. Dozens of studies have been made—some are in fact made every year in numerous states—to check on fawn crops, and on doe pregnancies. Road-killed deer, which are all too numerous nowadays, are checked for fetuses. On good ranges and under optimum conditions, very nearly 100 percent of the does may bear fawns. On an average around 85 percent do. Range conditions make a big difference, but if conditions are normal almost all of the does in good health will be bred and will have fawns. There is no sure way whatever to spot a so-called barren doe. One of my most amusing experiences in this regard was with a hunter who bragged of his prowess for picking out barren does—the best venison, he said. He shot one at some distance as it stood in a thicket. Only it turned out to be a little antlerless buck!

There are several slants on collecting trophy bucks that many hunters overlook. It is well known that the health and vigor of all life stems at the beginning from the soil. Certain soils grow certain foods that nurture wildlife in better or poorer ways. Certain soil types, it has been shown, have a definite correlation with the size and heaviness and symmetry of deer antlers. There are, for example, some counties in the state where I live that seldom produce desirable deer antlers. Many are deformed, most are small. Some of the reasons have been traced to a lack of certain chemicals in the soil.

It thus follows that some places produce better antlers than others. A study of areas where record deer have been taken is interesting. Patterns show up. Further, an area which has produced numerous bucks with especially handsome antlers usually does so consistently, unless so hard pressured that mature bucks are collected too swiftly. If I were after an exceptional deer, mule or whitetail, I'd make a thorough check on places from which a substantial number of trophy-size animals have been taken *over recent seasons*. Range quality, deer populations, and other influences may change the pattern over a period of as little as a decade.

Some of my most interesting experiences with large bucks have come about through visits I've had with ranchers in the large-ranch states such as Texas, New Mexico, Colorado, and Montana. These men, who have had long experience with cattle, know that a certain range produces better cattle than another one, and even that a particular small area may be especially productive. They know, too, that a *good bull* begets superior progeny. On their lands, where many deer roam, they long ago concluded that the "good bull" mule deer or whitetail does likewise.

One time Gage Holland, a West Texas rancher friend who is an astute observer and extremely knowledgeable about both stock and wildlife, told me, "The biggest buck I've seen this year is hanging out near a little hummock of a mountain . . . " and he explained to me exactly where it was on his huge ranch.

We drove to the spot, and fortunately jumped the deer. It was a beautiful, vigorous ten-pointer. I know exactly what it weighed because later I killed it—185 pounds field-dressed.

One of the finest Desert mule deer I have ever taken—a ten-pointer, dressed weight 185 pounds.

After I had taken this deer and we had it hung up at headquarters, Gage told me, "The reason I found that deer is that there is always an unusual specimen in that general region. Take one and another will be along."

Does some other buck simply fill the vacuum? Not exactly. Gage knew why the place produced big bucks. These deer, as all healthy deer, did not wander far, and their *blood line* in this place was superior. Undoubtedly the area had everything necessary to produce trophy deer. But some old monster long ago had passed his unusual vigor and physical characteristics down to his progeny.

There is a pleasant little sequel to this anecdote. About five or six years after Gage and I had hung up that fine buck, I was on his ranch and rode in a Jeep with a mutual friend who was looking for a real buster. He had not found what he wanted. As we happened to take a trail that led near that hummock of rock I told him I'd show him one.

"Stop right here," I finally said.

We got down, and he loaded his rifle. It was midday and the deer were bedded. "If you'll climb to that rimrock and get over on the shady side and just pussyfoot along, you'll find what you want."

Now of course I was just gambling. But he jumped a deer up there that was a twin if I ever saw one to the deer I had taken some years earlier at the identical spot. He shot it, too, and ever since has believed I am some sort of expert. I never intend to tell him the difference! But mark my word, when you hear of a place where an unusual buck has been killed, make note of it. Not only are conditions proper there, but the blood line of that old bull has without question passed along to many a fawn.

If you are selective and don't intend to take just any deer that comes along, always, whether glassing does or bucks, check carefully on their condition. Mule deer look fatter than whitetails because of their build. But the coat of any deer will give you one clue to its true physical condition. If the coat is rough or off-color for the season, the deer is probably neither fat nor in vigorous health. Fat deer sometimes lick their sides, just as fat cattle do, and you can occasionally see that they have done this. It's another tip.

A deer with innumerable spots on its coat where the hair is raised, parted into small bumps that show plainly, is carrying a load of big ticks. Ticks suck the blood. Ticks seldom stay long on an exceptionally fat animal for they cannot get to the blood because of the fat under the hide. The coat of a prime deer should be smooth, glossy, and of rich hue and proper fall color. Such an animal will look rounded, never angular, even when you glass it out past rifle range.

I want to offer a brief aside here about selecting venison—a rule that unfortunately cannot be checked until after the deer is dressed. As I've said, mule deer will usually be fatter than whitetails. Mule deer venison rather often is also tastier and more tender. But in all deer, once you have a chance to look at the dressed animal, check the color before you decide how to cut up or use the meat. A skinny buck with meat looking almost bluish has probably been totally frazzled by the rut and is hardly fit to eat. A deer in good condition may have fat that is almost white, or it may be yellowish. This yellowish tallow color on a deer is a certain indication that the meat will be tough, precisely as in beef. It may taste fine but you will hardly be able to shoot a hole in the gravy. Make sausage or deer burgers out of this one. If the fat is white, however, particularly over the rump, and also thick, you have a much better piece of meat.

I realize that a great many hunters do not truly "select" the deer they shoot. The majority, I'm sure, grab the first opportunity and are happy. But we would have far better sport, better trophies, and better eating, if everyone actually *picked out a particular deer.* Long ago we developed too much of a competitive hunting spirit. Status was bringing home the venison. First it was bringing in a big deer and finally it deteriorated to bringing in any deer just so the license was filled. This is a patently ridiculous approach, robs one of much true sport and greater thrills, and puts a lot of low-class venison on the table.

There are many incorrect theories about which is the best deer so far as meat is concerned. All you have to do is listen to the hunter who insists that if you want a delicious piece of meat, forget the antlers and, in an any-deer season, collect a fawn. Nothing could be less factual. A fawn that has just been driven off and weaned by its mother, or has lost its mother, is one of the toughest deer on hooves. A fawn that has been weaned early and is fattening is excellent.

More hunters should take a course in meat cutting or a class in stock judging. I realize we cannot all be wildlife stock judges in the field. But we should know the basics. They are fairly simple. Any deer, at any age, that is as ranchers say "on the mend"—that is, fattening, going *up* in flesh and physical condition instead of down—will be good eating. I remember one year when I insisted that a friend shoot a gray-faced old deer that was obviously ancient by deer standards. But that old buck was one of the fattest I had seen. He insisted the deer would be tough enough to club back into the pan. It turned out to be a juicy, tender piece of venison. It was gaining, not losing. Age had no effect whatever.

Of course this is a difficult judgment to make in the field. A basic rule, however, is to forget the apparent age of the deer. Check as far as possible its condition. And again, I urge hunters not to be quite so eager. It really doesn't make any difference whether or not you fill your license. The sport is all that counts. Unless, of course, you truly want a deer to eat and the heck with the sport. Either way, you should make a selection.

The condition of buck antlers is varied, and always is an indication of the quality of the deer. Facts about this are more important to hunters

An exceptionally fine whitetail. Look for a smooth coat and dark-colored, heavy antlers. These indicate vigor and health.

This trophy whitetail has light-colored antlers. When they are this large and light, it is generally an indication that the buck is old.

than most believe. Most seldom think about it, or know much about it. A very old buck may show up some season as a long spike. I watched a big whitetail a friend had in a pen, under permit, for a number of years. At eight he was stunning, with a great trophy ten-point rack. The next year he hit the skids. He was poor, and grew long, rough spike antlers.

The condition of the antlers is directly attributable to the range and weather conditions during the time they are forming. Slender, white, or pale antlers usually mean there was a drought, or a severe winter, or poor forage. Deer may become fat by recouping before season. But a pale-antlered deer isn't a very good trophy. In a normally proper year pale antlers bespeak poor general quality of the animal. Or, it may be an indication of age. Old deer often in the last season of a full antler growth

A very old Desert mule deer buck. Old bucks "on the mend" are as good eating as younger ones.

have bone-white antlers that may have palmations, and splits in the tines. These may still be good trophies. But always look, when you are being selective, for a buck with dark-brown or mahogany-colored antlers. These are the vigorous bulls. Usually the bases are heavy, the tines long, and the deer carrying them is in prime condition.

I would like to interject here also that in my opinion the agony over antler point counting is ridiculous. Everyone has heard the old wheeze about "if you can hang a ring on it, it's a point." Any hunter who is so status-conscious he counts points in this manner is at the very least hungry for approbation. How often we have to hear about the twenty-point—or is it forty-point?—whitetails, the sixty-point muleys, and all such rot. A typical whitetail rack seldom has more than ten points—the main beam with three points off it, plus the brow tines. There are occasional honest twelve-pointers, but they are rare. I have won a few bets on the legit fourteens and sixteens and eighteens. The conformation of whitetail antlers just does not stretch this far except on rare occasions.

Granted, mule deer are different. For one thing, they evidence a trend in many areas toward nontypical heads. Commonly younger but big-antlered mule deer have no brow tines. Some of the nontypicals have a myriad points sticking every which way. But still, I get ready to explode over the "sixty-nine-point rack" that in reality is just an ordinary big eight or ten with a flurry of little knobs and stick-outs around the antler bases and on up the tines.

If you truly desire a trophy deer, how can you tell one when you see it? This depends on how fine you wish to cut it for trophies. If you simply want a good head to mount, the process of selection is not really very difficult. We're not talking now of attempting to break existing records or get "into the book." If you see a deer, mule deer or whitetail, running straight away from you, and the antlers are definitely wider than its rear end—shoot it! From the straight rear perspective decision you will have bagged a very respectable trophy. It may not be a record-book deer. Measurements for those come a lot finer.

If you are glassing a deer, looking for a good one, make up your mind the *type* of head you want. Mule deer, for example, exhibit many bucks with high, narrow racks. I passed up one several years ago that was stunning. I doubt if it would span twelve inches. Most hunters look for a broad rack that is heavy, and dark-colored, and in either species reasonably symmetrical and with at least ten honest points. Viewed broadside, or from three-quarters rear or front, antlers are difficult to judge. A friend of mine shot a monster last year and picked up a heavy rack with a 14-inch spread.

The surest judgment can be made if you have opportunity to glass or scope the deer straight head on and with ears cocked. Now bear in mind that a deer does not hold its ears straight out at exact horizontal. It cocks them up, and at varying degrees depending on age of the deer, species, how disturbed it is, and how much antlers may or may not get in the way. As we've noted, the mule deer ear, which is from 11 to 12 inches long, averages about 25 percent longer than the whitetail ear. Skull width varies among species and subspecies, but we have to use shotgun measurements because you don't have long to study the deer as a rule.

So, a whitetail with ears cocked fully, looking and listening, will measure from roughly 12 to 14 inches tip to tip of ears. This depends obviously on how upslanted the ears are held. If, looked at head on, the curve of the antlers appears to be well outside the ear tips—say 4 inches on a side—you're looking at a deer with a spread of 20 inches or more. One on my wall, a heavy ten-pointer, has a 24-inch spread, and the mount —which does not, of course, precisely imitate the angle of the ears on a live deer—measures 12 inches tip to tip of ears. Add on the 25 percent or a little more for mule deer and you can tell quite quickly and with fair accuracy what you are shooting at.

But remember, you have to be calm and look carefully. There is something about antlers that excites every sportsman. At varying angles a so-so rack can look deceivingly provocative. If you are truly trophy hunting, study a head meticulously before you shoot—or pass it up.

CHAPTER SIX

The Senses of Deer

For years, book after book, magazine article after magazine article, has rehashed "how to hunt deer" material by the traditional approach—that there are three methods, the drive, the stalk, the stand. This material is necessary and useful. But I have been fortunate enough to have hunted deer over a broad portion of the continent and to have spent days on end observing and photographing deer when not hunting. This experience has taught me what is really important: if you gather knowledge constantly about the *animals themselves,* stockpile it high, and interpret it properly, hunting methods will take care of themselves.

For example, it doesn't do much good to try to teach a tyro hunter by rote how to hide from deer so that they won't see him, if he doesn't know how the eye of a deer is fashioned, what the animal sees, what it sees best, and what it sees poorly. This is one facet of the type of knowledge about deer I refer to, and a good place to begin a discussion of the senses of deer.

Deer do make mistakes—like these skylighted mule deer staring curiously at the camera.

A great deal has been written about the fantastic ability of deer to sight danger at great distance. I have read about the "telescopic" eyes of a deer, which is pure malarky. All of us have heard the arguments about how that red or yellow coat is a blob of color that is certain to catch the gaze of a deer. This, too, is wrong, and in fact impossible from the deer's point of view. I have had hunters argue heatedly about color and deer vision. The deer may see the coat. But it doesn't do so because it is conscious of the *color,* and to believe so is to misinterpret fundamental knowledge, a bad habit to get into.

Deer see very well indeed. Their sense of smell is superbly developed, their hearing extremely keen. But hunters get into the habit of blaming their own failures on what they describe in flights of fancy as all but magical capabilities of deer senses. If the senses of deer—and the *judgment* the animals render from the information gathered by them—were as perfect as many claim, no hunter would ever kill a deer. Yet hundreds of thousands of deer are bagged annually. Thus deer do make errors. Many of them. Most errors are made because the deer brain is a kind of computer that lacks reasoning power. It is fed the information gathered by the various senses, and the decision of the computer is an instinctive one. That is why a hunter can outwit a deer, because the hunter is capable of reasoning, and thus can nullify the keen senses of the deer.

The eyes of man and of some other higher animals, most birds, and even most fish are fashioned similarly. The eye contains the cornea, lens, iris, and retina. There are groups of nerve ends, thousands of them, called rods. These nerve ends chiefly are a device for translating brightness, intensity of light fed into the eye. There is also another group of nerve ends, also counted in thousands, that deal with color. These are called cones. The cones must have enough light—brightness—so that color can be translated as such. When you look at a flower garden in bright sunlight there is a riot of sparkling color. Under heavy cloud cover the color is there but there is no "snap" and less contrast between colors. As dusk falls, color is washed out. The cones are unable to function properly and the rods must do all the translation.

Actually the eye doesn't operate quite that simply, but this will serve to illustrate. The eye of a deer is much like what I have described, except for one extremely important lack—at least to humans it would seem important. There are no cones in the eye of a deer. Thus, deer cannot see color. What they see is black and white, and all intermediate shades in between, which is to say varying shades of gray from light to dark.

Now this may not be any real handicap. In fact, since a deer does not have to recognize color of stop and go signals on a city street, its world may be simplified by its inability to see color. For its needs and purposes, it just may be easier to make quick judgments in a black, white, and gray world than to have to sort out the meaning of colors.

Hunters have long misinterpreted what a deer sees because many have believed firmly that deer see colors. And many have experienced the spooking of a deer by, let's say, a man in a yellow coat. Think a moment. Imagine you are colorblind to all the primaries. You are in the woods. There are gray-green trunks of poplars, dark green of balsam and spruce, and a mixture of lesser features in woodsy hues. But you, as a colorblind creature, see only the pale grays of the upright poplar trunks, the near-black of the conifers, and several other shades of brush and forest floor in between. The conifers (blacks) have their natural shapes, wide-based triangles; the poplars are vertical cylinders. Into this simple landscape now enters a hunter wearing a yellow coat.

The hunter moves—not with a gentle sway as limbs or small trees move in a wind. His movements are faster, and not very rhythmic. He wears dark trousers so they are not especially visible. But the yellow coat is a most unnatural vertical rectangle—and it is seen by a deer as a vivid, intense light gray, very nearly white. So, obviously, what does the deer do? Let's imagine it has neither heard nor scented the hunter. This pale unnatural rectangle moves through the woods. The deer tries first to bring other senses to bear, to gather more information. But it cannot. So, without knowing this is a hunter, the deer runs. The pale rectangle does not belong.

An interesting commentary is that another hunter, living in his world of color, might glimpse this yellow coat moving slowly among fall-painted aspens and not even recognize his own kind. The color blends. Thus his more *complicated* vision does not necessarily bring his brain more complete information for a snap judgment. Also, the deer, which knows this bailiwick in meticulous detail, instinctively realizes that a movable light-gray rectangle of high intensity or brightness does not belong here.

This should give you a pretty fair idea of how things look from the view of the deer. Now let's put a red soft wool coat on the hunter, a fairly dark red shade. This too will be a rectangle of unnatural shape. But it is not very bright. It looks to the deer like a much darker and less intense shade of gray. It is more difficult for the deer to distinguish. Now place our two hunters fifty yards apart and have each sit with back to a stump or a dark balsam. They sit absolutely still. If the deer neither scents nor hears them, it may or may not pick up the rectangles of gray. Chances are, however, that it will direct attention to the yellow (light, intense gray) blob. But it may pass over the other without ever seeing it. The dark-red one is just a stump.

If either rectangle *moves,* however, even slightly, the deer probably will catch the movement. It is attuned always to be watching for motion. Motion of any kind may mean danger. The light coat will be noticed moving much more quickly and easily than will the red one. But now it makes little difference, for if the deer sees the movement, one is as bad as the other, except that the light one is more distinct. So what we are really talking about when we speak of how well a deer sees a hunter regardless of color, is *how well a deer sees a hunter in motion.*

I have, for example, stood spang in the open in northern woodlands, dressed in one of the all-red wool hunting suits that at least at one time were popular there, and a buck, looking a hole right through me, could not tell what I was. Make no mistake, the deer was highly disturbed. This had nothing to do with color set off against the snow. This unnatural object—me—standing where it didn't belong and of a shape that did not belong here was bound to raise questions. I have also stood scores of times against a dark evergreen, dressed in red, and had deer pass within mere feet without sensing me.

In all this I have not mentioned the human face and hands. Nothing is more terrifying to any wildlife species than the human face. Hands are easily seen at close range because they are likely to be moving and light in hue. A face staring out at a deer is easily seen. But faces in shadow are not a giveaway at any distance. The camouflage headnet is a surefire way to keep deer from centering attention upon your face even when very close.

However, dealing only with deer vision and not with the other senses, we can now understand that color is meaningless except via intensity that contrasts with surroundings and to some extent by shape of the area covered by a given color. Movement is the giveaway, and the lighter the color of the mover, the more quickly the movement calls attention. It is true that a deer can see movement at great distance. But I have never been convinced that they see it any farther than a sharp-eyed man can. The difference, if there is one, is actually a difference in *alertness*. A deer is a keen observer of what goes on in its own living area. And movement means so much more to it than to most hunters that it is ever on the lookout.

The moral to be read here is that hunters should take a cue from their quarry, stay ever alert for movement. I personally have seen many a deer move at long range before the deer had any idea I was there. A hunter who will constantly train himself in visual alertness to *motion*—and to what a deer or any part of one looks like half-hidden—can match visual ability with deer under almost any set of terrain conditions. We will dig deeper into the matter of how to look for deer or parts of deer in a later chapter, but I want to note here as an example that you as a hunter can train yourself to see and properly identify just the lower legs of a deer a whole lot more efficiently than a deer can ever learn to spot your legs, when you are immobile.

The main reason for thoroughly understanding what deer can do with their eyes, and what they can't, is that many a hunter simply assumes the deer is so much better than he is that he can't compete. Nonsense! Regardless of how sharp-eyed a deer is, any keenly observant hunter who knows how to translate what he sees can readily compete. I know this theory flies in the face of what many others believe. But I'll stay with it. Note, too, that a deer is never *hunting you.* It certainly is on the lookout for any danger. But you are with utmost concentration hunting it. If you know enough about the abilities of your quarry and rate them honestly and intelligently, you can win.

While you are hunting the deer, how do you keep it from seeing you? There are a number of basic rules. One difficulty nowadays, what with the deluge of hunters making laws necessary for certain colors to be worn, is that mode of dress usually cannot be just what would be best. Blaze orange has been found to be the most readily seen color. It is an abominable shade to have to wear so far as outwitting a deer is concerned. Again, though not seen as a color, the "shine" or glare from it, plus the light intensity and hue, are certain to call attention.

Probably many readers are familiar with the newer red camouflage. Where that is legal, I have no doubt it is as effective as standard "camo"— camouflage—as seen through the eyes of a deer. I have a suit or two of wild yellow and orange camo. This is a step in the right direction for specialized wear. In fall colors with, say, birch and maple and oak leaves the surroundings, this otherwise highly visible camo is not bad. But in some instances it blends so well it may not be highly visible to another hunter. In most—but not all—settings, standard camouflage cloth, jacket and pants, gloves and headnet, is the surest way to obliterate yourself. If a headnet bothers your vision, pull one over your cap and let it hang down so you can see out from under but still have your forehead and eyes partly covered. Some nets have eyeholes, or you can make them yourself.

I have experimented with reversible camo suits, which I consider excellent. One has standard dark colors on one side, and sand and brown on the other. It should be obvious that a hunter fully dressed in dark camo and sitting out in sand-colored grass and brush is a dark blob that is unnatural. A deer may not be able to identify it. But the animal may be highly disturbed by it. Thus, the light-colored camo has its specialized uses.

If you know how to sit properly and walk properly, you really don't have to wear camouflage. A man sitting or standing atop an open ridge can be seen a mile away. One sitting just below the ridgeline is swallowed by his surroundings. One must sit still, of course. But even some movements are hard for deer to detect. For example, often I have raised a rifle, or a hand, or turned my head, when a deer was fairly close and even looking at me. By using extremely slow motion, the movement is accomplished so that the deer hardly detects it. A quick movement of a hand or turn of the head will alert a deer at some distance, even with its head down. It catches a flurry and instantly becomes alert, puzzling.

In country where trees and brush are scarce, I often sit behind a small bush, but in such a position that while my face is erased by a leafy branch I can see between branches or leaves. If on the other hand a good-sized bush such as a low juniper is available, even though it is the only one in the area, you can squeeze in among its low branches, and with your back to it. Bring a branch or two around you as a bit of a face screen, and deer will seldom see you.

In timber, never sit atop a bank. Sit below it. Never sit on or against a light-colored rock or bank if you are dressed darkly, and vice versa. Learn to select places where you will blend. If you must sit where there are large tree trunks, don't sit beside one, sit back against it. Small movements are blurred when you have a matching background. Never sit behind such a tree and keep peeking around. I have watched hunters standing behind a large tree and now and then sneaking a peek. This is laughable. A peeker is a prime spooker. If for some reason you must stay behind any object, don't sit or stand and then peek around. Lie flat. You will not be as easily detected because you are not so close to the plane of the deer's vision.

It is always best when selecting a stand to try to have some crisscross such as tall grasses, low bushes, down timber, a branch or two, or some sticks helter-skelter, to break up your blocky outline. Nothing in a forest or woodlot looks like the bulky shape of a man. But a man sprawled with legs apart and crooked, behind or beside a log, can become another log, to a deer. Always try in some manner to distribute your own human "shape" so it won't look that way. But always plan how you are going to shoot. Have the gun ready without any wild scramble.

One time out of curiosity I dressed in ordinary drab clothing while hunting on our ranch, and stood behind an old dead stub that had branches thrusting out at grotesque angles. I wanted to be able to get comfortable so I wouldn't have to move much. So, I spread my feet in such a way that my legs could pass for broken branches. I leaned one arm and let it dangle across another weathered limb. My rifle, held propped against my side, became another slender stub, and my face was behind a grill of small dead twigs. I so arranged myself that in one motion I could swing the gun over a branch for a rest and fire quickly. An even half dozen does passed me during the next hour. Not one saw me. But when they passed and picked up my scent on a small breeze they of course panicked.

In this same place I tried another tack, to see what would happen. I hung a length of camo netting over the old branches, wore a headnet, and hid behind the netting. In a period of two hours five different deer got close enough to have a look. They didn't like it. The camo wasn't in itself disturbing. There is a bare possibility some scent of mine got to them, but the day was very still. I am sure the problem was that the netting was a swatch of innocuous "nothing" that hadn't been here before. I took a walk around later and came back when a breeze was up. One end of the netting flapped. One deer looked at the spot from at least 75 yards, looked long and stamped a foot—and snorted and ran. Another closer one wheeled with tail up the moment the net flapped. It just was not a "right" thing, nor in a right place.

I presume any hunter would know that he should always try to walk or move in shadows. And in cover. Follow the same procedure a careful whitetail does and you will be on the right track. This doesn't mean to walk in shadow of trees atop a ridge. Anything below can see you against the sky. I've even spotted deer this way, which shows that they make errors because they use instinct, not reason. If you want to go from Point A to Point B, and a line of cover curves around so it is twice as long as a straight line, stay in the cover. Take a short cut in the open and you'll never know how many deer saw you because they'll drift away or sneak away quietly.

When the sun is low, watch your shadow. Under some circumstances a deer standing or feeding in cover at the edge of an opening can look into the opening and see a man's shadow 40 feet long moving in sunshine. The deer doesn't know what makes the shadow but it sure knows enough to vacate the area. An opposite slant can show you a deer. I have a vivid recollection of a photograph in the making I once saw that I have long anguished over, because I didn't get it. Two big buck mule deer were moving along a ridge where I could not see them from where I stood hidden in brush. But the sun projected their shadows in exaggerated fashion against a pale rock bluff. They looked like some huge Indian drawings. I grabbed for my camera. It was a once in a lifetime opportunity. But I was too late. I have even seen deer shadows across a woodland meadow as sun streamed through timber to throw a perfect silhouette upon the grass. These of course are uncommon opportunities. But as I have said, overlook nothing. Learn every last fact you can about deer and their homes and how they live.

It may seem that I am giving two kinds of conflicting advice when I say to stalk a deer with the sun in its eyes. This certainly throws your shadow toward the deer. But it all depends on the angle you use. In many years of photography I have learned that one can move right or left to keep sun full on a subject and throw the photographer's shadow away from the subject. In other words, three-quarter lighting, or quarter-lighting, or side-lighting.

One fall I was trying to stalk a big mule deer in open country. I was on a steep ridge. By walking toward the deer not quite directly out of the sun, but very nearly so, my shadow lay atop the ridge, or in its shadow, where the deer could not see it. A deer cannot see looking into the sun one bit better than you can. It may see some movement, but it cannot tell what is making the movement. Remember that backlighting, when a human looks at a backlighted scene, wipes out color. Everything becomes black and white and shades of gray (or yellow sunset hues). But if the sun is directly in your eyes, there is no color. It is blinding. A deer has the same difficulty. Don't let anybody convince you of the opposite. In fact, at close ranges it is so blinding that your shadow makes no difference. A deer can't see it.

But there is one little problem, a whim of nature that seems almost like some cruel joke. In many places and seasons and conditions of weather, particularly in fall during deer seasons, about the time the sun begins to sink in the west and the deer move out and you can put the sun to your advantage, the wind "blows out of the sun." Every experienced deer hunter has had this happen scores of times. He cannot shoot toward the sun because he cannot see. He cannot stalk downsun because the breeze carries his scent straight to the deer. Be thankful that it does not always happen. And never write off the advantage of the sun to you on crosswind or toward-sun breezes or still afternoons.

I am sure an entire book could be written about how to keep a deer from seeing you and how a hunter may better utilize his power of sight to see a deer. We cannot cover every detail here. But this should at least give you a sound idea of what a deer sees, how it sees it, and what you can do, using these suggestions as guides, to outwit the keen sight of deer. One suggestion I would make to all serious deer hunters who would rather beat a deer at its own game just for the joy of it than take a jillion trophies, is to get a long lens (300mm automatic will do fine) and a good 35mm camera and fast color film (160 ASA rating) and have a go at photography of living deer. I'll tell you something. My gun-hunting enjoyment has not been diminished one whit by pursuing this other hobby. But I have learned more about deer in twenty years of photographing them than in all my years of rifle hunting for them. The reason is that the photographer who is going to hand-hold his equipment, the only way for fast action and maneuverability, must get within no more than 75 yards for a fair picture and from 25 to 50 for a good shot. When you learn how to get these, believe me you won't have much trouble getting your rifle opportunities, and you will know a lot about deer you never previously imagined! The camera is one of the greatest schooling devices for the hunter.

Part of the exquisite anguish of deer hunting is that the deer's brain—his computer—is endlessly bringing all its information gathering agencies to bear upon the poor nimrod. Thus, though we have been discussing sight, and purposely shying from the other senses, the fact is that a deer is listening all the time it is looking. And it is using its nose every instant also. The other senses—taste and touch—do not concern the hunter. So now let us add hearing to sight. What a deer sees may or may not disturb it. But what it hears *as* it views a specific possible danger situation well may make the decision for flight.

I believe we can say that in the realm of deer vision it is *movement* in almost all cases that gives the hunter away. If you now add what a deer hears, the impetus to flee is at least doubled. Just how keen is the hearing of a deer? I will say this: writers and hunting observers constantly exaggerate it, because they really never know whether the deer was alerted to flight because of sight, hearing, smell, or a combination of any two of the three, or a combination of all three. It is in most instances impossible to tell precisely.

A few days ago as I write this, I read in a deer treatise of the nature-faker school that a deer can hear the clink of a rock a mile away. Utterly ridiculous. Or should we say, it depends on the decible measure of the clink and the size of the rock! I'm quite sure a deer has a sense of hearing more highly developed than that of humans. But I also am convinced it is not a great deal better—given the deer's advantage of much larger cupped ears as pick-uppers of sound waves. In other words, I do not intend to give the deer credit for supernormal hearing. I have heard deer, and hung 'em up to the meat pole, on numerous occasions when they didn't hear me, or with all their senses together make me out even at close range. So have thousands of hunters.

When I stand still, hidden, and in a place where sound carries well, and a deer happens to be moving so that the air movement carries any sound it makes to me, I will say that I can hear and interpret its sounds up to fifty yards or on occasion even a hundred yards. A hunter has only to *practice hearing.* Holding the breath while doing so helps immensely. I know one hunter, an ornery Irishman, who never can hear what his wife says at five paces but can hear a deer pussyfooting at fifty!

But now that we have a place from which to start, let me tell you the real problem. Hunters have long told wild tales about what a deer can hear, mostly to cover their own errors. Deer surely can hear the majority of inexpert hunters bumbling around the woods today. But what really matters is that there is a tremendous difference between *what a deer hears,* and *what a deer hears that frightens it.*

We've been over some of this ground. I have told how in a blind I mumbled at nearby deer and they paid scant attention. I stated also that deer seem quite accurate in their appraisal of sounds, but not infallible. The armadillo rustling, or another deer walking and clinking rocks are examples previously mentioned. I also stated that shots, at a distance and sometimes fairly close, aren't especially disturbing. On several occasions I have shot a buck and other deer a short distance away haven't even run.

An incredible trait now and then displayed by mule deer is that when one buck out of a group is shot and falls, the others—if they do not see the hunter—gather around totally puzzled, wondering what has happened. Apparently they do not associate the sound and the fallen deer. There may be other more complicated reasons for this. A somewhat similar habit of wild turkeys is well known. You shoot a gobbler from a group, and the others scatter wildly at the shot, then race back to peck at the downed gobbler.

Many modern-day sounds—a vehicle motor, for example—disturb deer little, especially in civilized areas. A most interesting phenomenon can be noted with deer and vehicles. This applies to whitetails as well as to mule deer. An animal, or group, will often stand to watch a closed vehicle pass, and will even allow it to stop. An open Jeep won't usually be tolerated, because the movements of hunters can easily be seen. If you intend to glass a deer and are driving in a closed vehicle, stop and have a look without getting out if possible. Usually the deer will bolt if you get out. Also, leave the motor running. Ordinarily as long as the motor sound continues the deer will stand. But nine times out of ten the moment the motor sound ceases, the deer becomes nervous and flees.

An aside here about deer and how they see vehicles. A few years ago, hunting in the brush country of Texas where vistas are long but deer hard to spot, several of us noted that in driving to a certain back pasture on a 9000-acre lease of a friend we were spooking deer some distance ahead. In watching other vehicles moving distantly over the ridges here we were struck by how brightly chrome and paint shone in the sun. In discussing this at the old camphouse one evening, someone remarked that the attention of a deer is always grabbed by any shiny article, and that deer are afraid of such reflections.

The late Paul Young, Sr., of Laredo, who owned this lease, and with whom I hunted a number of years, was owner of Gateway Chevrolet in that city. He decided to try an experiment. They had an old 1955 Chevvy four-door on the lot. He had his shop people repaint it with a dull, drab undercoat. Thus it did not reflect any light at all. Then they taped every bit of chrome on it with dark, dull tape. We used that vehicle as a "hunting car" and I rode hundreds of miles of rough *senderos* in it over the next few seasons. It was astonishing the effect this lack of shine had on deer. Many a whitetail simply stood to watch us pass by!

Loud and unusual noises definitely frighten deer. Everyone has heard of chousing deer out of canyons by rolling rocks down from above. This is not infallible. In canyon country deer often hear rocks roll. Some will just pay no attention and some may simply move out of the way, if the rolling rock is close. What will spook them out is a rock that falls directly into a canyon.

John Finegan, a friend of mine who owns a ranch along Devil's River in Texas—an exceedingly rugged ranch and loaded with very handsome whitetails—practices as unusual a method as I have ever seen to get the deer out of the canyons. Point is, if you walk up a steep draw the deer run out ahead unseen. Deer will almost always go up rather than down when disturbed in any coulee, gully, canyon, or draw. John gets up on top and places a hunter or two near the canyon head. He carries a big leather slingshot. Not the sort on a forked stick, but a true sling, with a pouch and two thongs, to be whirled around and the one end released. He loads with a fist-sized rock and is so adept that he can hurl it far out over the canyon. When the rock crashes down into the brush cover, any deer in that canyon is alerted. After three or four throws, out they go. From above the hunter also puts his ears to use. He can hear the clatter of deer hooves on rock. The shooting is tricky, because since these deer are whitetails they really barrel out of there.

The sudden crack of a stick is frightening to deer. So is any unnatural noise like the clang of metal, or a whistle. Sometimes, however, a sharp whistle will stop a fleeing deer. This depends on whether or not the deer has also been disturbed by human scent, and also upon what it has seen. A friend of mine always whistles at a buck if it has flushed without seeing him. On occasion one will stop and look back.

A sneaking approach, as has been discussed earlier, will send a deer from its bed, either sneaking away or else on the run. The reason is obvious. All predators prowl and attempt to keep from making a noisy

Hunting whitetails in rough canyon country, John Finegan spooks them out with rocks hurled from a big sling.

approach. The stalking deer hunter must be absolutely still, selecting each step with utmost care.

All deer are nervous when their hearing is impaired in any way. On windy days there are noises from leaves and branches. Especially on gusty days, the sense of scent is also to some extent impaired. Thus a deer cannot go about its routine calmly because it cannot hear properly except from a single direction and in whimsical, changing gusts no direction is secure. Wind that is steady certainly favors a hunter. His sounds are covered. But his best hunting at such times will be when his quarry is bedded. When feeding or moving the deer will be uneasy.

Years ago I used to believe that hunting along a noisy stream was a great idea. But it finally dawned on me that I seldom saw deer, and never killed one, near a loud-rushing river. Deer shy from such places because the water noise impairs their ability to hear. You have to temper this fact with some judgment. A creek that babbles quietly doesn't inhibit deer. They can hear other sounds easily above its small rilling.

Natural sounds that belong in any given deer habitat are, of course, not frightening to the animals. But it takes only slight deviation from the norm at least to alert them. I've used an owl hoot to signal back and forth with a partner and watched deer raise their heads to listen, even when I had to use a binocular to see them well. But this did not mean they were uneasy. They were simply aware. The human voice making normal, high-decibel human sounds, such as shouting or talking, is one noise no deer will tolerate. It is amazing to me each season to listen to hunters.

"Hey, Bill," one calls, "where are you? I just saw a deer."

"I'm over here. Which way is he headed?"

After such an exchange every deer in a half-section or more of land is not only aware of the hunters' presence but undoubtedly moving off.

There are times when hunters purposely make noise to frighten deer. This is when making drives, which we will discuss in a later chapter. But there is one odd use for noise that I doubt many hunters know about, and I want to mention it here. This is the use of an ordinary coyote or fox call for the express purpose of scaring deer out of thickets. It is not an attempt to call the deer to you, but to move them. It works better with whitetails than with mule deer, although muleys will bolt sometimes.

One recent season, for example, I was trying to help a friend from the north find a real trophy brush-country whitetail in South Texas. This is rolling, generally treeless terrain, with thornbrush and cactus. Deer are exceedingly difficult to see in it. When they are bedded there isn't a chance. And when they are up and moving, they are so infernally wild that getting a shot at a good buck is a major project.

We had been slowly cruising the *senderos,* or trails, for several hours, from dawn on. This is a traditional hunting method here. You spot a deer on a distant ridge, get out and get a rest across the hood perhaps, and have at it. But not a deer had we seen. They were not moving at all.

Finally I said, "When you come to the next high hill, park on it. The pickup will be in plain sight, I know. But I want to try something."

When we were on the hill I instructed my hunter to get out and load up and get into the bed of the pickup and get a rest across the top.

We were on a fenceline and any shooting would be done to the left. There was a large, low basin of dense brush and cactus on that side, just the sort of place a big deer might stake out. On the far side of it was a high ridge running at right angles to the one we were on.

I hauled out my coyote call, kept my binocular ready, and began to squall as loud as I could. In less than a minute three deer simply hurtled out of a thicket in the basin. I grabbed for my glass and was looking at one of the biggest whitetail bucks I have ever seen.

"The third deer!" I yelled. "Shoot!"

He had a bit of trouble picking up the deer. The range was possibly 150 yards to where they'd jumped. But they were a good 250, going up the far ridge, when he touched off. It was a close miss. The next shot was closer still. But at that one the buck sailed over the ridge and was out of sight. Nonetheless, the action was thrilling. I have run whitetails out numerous times by this method. It is useless to do it unless you have a wide area to watch. And you don't blow as if trying to call a coyote, you simply pour the steam to it, making a hair-raising racket.

As I have said, I'm convinced that any hunter who will practice can learn to see well enough, given normal eyesight, so that he can readily compete with deer eyesight. And, if he will practice listening, though he certainly can't hear everything as well and as far away as a deer can, he can do pretty well. But when it comes to the sense of smell—well—no human nose can even remotely compare in ability with that of a deer. I'm sure that if deer did not have this amazing scenting ability they would be easy to bag. This is the sense a hunter must understand the best—that is, the all but unbelievable keenness of it—because this is the deer sense that gives every hunter the most trouble.

Any time a deer is looking and listening, which is virtually all the time, it is incessantly testing for smells. If an air current carries an undesirable scent to the deer, it doesn't need to hear or see where the scent came from. It is long gone. If it sees, or hears, or sees and hears something it is undecided about, it will depend on its nose to identify the object or sound or the two together. Thus, with eyes, ears, and nose all operating, it might sometimes seem that deer are invulnerable. Nonetheless, this acute sense can be outwitted. But the single most important lesson any deer hunter can learn is never to underestimate the uncanny ability of a deer to use its nose for protection. If you are careless regarding scent, you will never be a very successful deer hunter.

Even though many hunters know that the sense of smell is acute, still they refuse to believe or fail to realize just how astoundingly acute it is. Several years ago I went with a friend to a cleverly designed photography blind he had built on his property expressly for taking telephoto deer photos. It was like a small cottage, with photo ports on three sides. All had sliding closures so that movement inside could be blotted out by closing one on the left if you were using the one on the right. Behind the blind there was a small shed into which the vehicle could be driven and parked. (A vehicle parked out in the open will usually make deer shy.) The interior of the blind had a dirt floor, to avoid noise, and it was padded on the sides with burlap to dampen any sound. Once you were inside, with the vehicle shed door closed and the inner blind door closed, I would have sworn no deer could scent us even if it was within six feet.

He had put out corn some distance from the blind, and had in fact been feeding deer there to toll them in. We sat quietly for some time. Then from our right we saw two deer coming. They walked along unconcerned. When they were almost to the spot where the bait was placed, both whirled and looked toward the blind, snorted, and ran with flags flying. We couldn't imagine what had happened. But within the next half hour, after two other small groups had done likewise, we realized what was wrong. Watching grass and small branches out front, we deduced that while we'd been waiting inside the wind had shifted. It was not a severe wind. But it was blowing from straight behind the blind and shed. Somehow enough of our scent was wafted out so that the deer could pick it up yards away, even though we could not feel the slightest draft. This will give you a good idea how important it is to watch where your scent goes, and how amazingly keen the nose of a deer is.

In some regions—where it is legal—hunters use tree seats for blinds. Deer do not look up much, and thus are rather easily outwitted by a hunter from above. Some writers have even claimed this is a neat way of keeping your scent from alerting deer. The statement needs qualification. In very flat country a hunter up in a tree keeps his scent well above ground in dry weather, within a circle probably of short gunshot range. But at longer ranges the scent may settle enough to get to deer. And on humid days it settles without much predictability. In rolling to steep terrains, where breezes may be whimsical, although the tree stand is an assist, it is by no means infallible.

I'm not much good at sitting for long periods. But some years back when I first came to Texas to live I was invited each fall to hunt on a

This hunter in his Texas hill-country blind is about to bag a buck.

ranch whose owner had blinds, both enclosed blinds on stilts and a number
of tree seats, all of them scattered widely and wisely so that hunters in
one could not possibly endanger hunters in another. He did not allow any
guest to get down and walk around. Thus, I had many hours of sitting
and observing deer, which were plentiful. He did not allow shooting of
anything less than eight points, which made the endeavor at least somewhat
sporty because you had to look sharp—and you paid a husky fine, which
was given to a charity, if you broke any rules.

At any rate, in various tree seats I observed that deer as much as
300 yards from me on a fairly flat mesalike area moving and feeding
suddenly become alert. This was because even the gentlest air movement
in that direction took scent from my tree stand with it. When the deer

got in the right position they'd pick it up and leave. Had I been on the ground in that instance, I doubt the scent would have carried so far. When the afternoon was utterly still and the air dry, scent apparently rose and moved away at a level no lower than where I sat. But on "heavy," humid, still days I often watched deer become very disturbed when they got within sixty to seventy-five yards.

I noted earlier that scent has an "oozing" effect. On a still day a hunter on a stand has a ring of scent around him and it expands the longer he stays on the stand. I presume it is diluted enough after a certain unpredictable number of yards so it does no harm. But if shots are going to be short—that is, in dense cover—it is a good idea to move from time to time to other stands to thwart the expansion of the scent circle. In the following chapter we will discuss what a hunter can do to blot out his own scent, or what he can use that is presumably attractive enough to deer to overpower it.

The basics of minimizing the scent problem are fairly simple: scrupulously avoid letting air movement carry your scent to the deer. This is not always easy in practice. You just have to do the best you can. Establish very carefully the wind direction. Hunt with it in your face. This means to take a stand, if you are going to hunt that way, with the breeze moving straight toward you. Obviously the *selection* of a stand in this case is extremely important. It must be a place where deer are likely to be moving, a place where you can see them if they move, and a place where the breeze is moving toward you. If you are going to stalk instead of stand, then you must plan your prowling by roughly the same rules. Select a movement line that is first of all in country where deer are most likely to be—moving or bedded—and where you can see them distantly or have a chance of jumping them, and during your entire walk the wind is never anywhere but directly toward you.

I use the word "directly" because air movements in any location and especially in mountain country or any hilly country can be tricky. Get into a habit of hunting with the wind quartering across you or from a right angle, and sudden gusts will whip the back of your neck and move out deer you were after. Further, while it is certainly feasible in special situations to hunt into a quartering or cross wind, you cut down on the *area* where your scent is blotted out by anything other than a head on breeze.

For example, there is a ridge we hunt annually on our own place that is a real deer hangout. Moving along it from north to south, the cover where deer hide is on the right. Moving vice versa it is on the left. We don't like to disturb the deer in cover, on that slope, if we can help it. But if we walk the ridge with a breeze from the east, though deer atop the ridge in front of us can be tricked, we move every deer out of the cover on the right slopes, and they leave and head down a canyon onto another property.

So, we wait for a breeze straight north or straight south. This way if we are very careful we can hunt the ridge along its length, drop off the east slope, and come carefully back and after half an hour do it again. Meanwhile, as often happens, a deer or two will have moved out of the cover to feed in the scattered oaks on the ridge.

If you sit on a stand with the breeze directly in your face, you have a chance over the entire 180-degree arc in front and to left and right. A quartering breeze cuts down slightly on one side or the other. There are places where it doesn't matter. I think of a lakeshore that is a top piece of deer country. Here one can sit, or prowl, with the wind anywhere from straight on one shoulder or the other to straight in the face. No deer is going to be on the water side anyway. However, any time a hard breeze blows there is always a chance of sudden shifts of gusts. The broader the angle, from quartering to side-on, the greater the chance of a quick gust from behind quartering or full.

Many hunters are not careful enough to make certain there is no air movement. A hard wind whips scent far, but also to some extent dissipates and dilutes it. A gentle, steady breeze is bad, because it keeps scent more concentrated. But the most evil air movement so far as the hunter is concerned is the barely detectable one that "lies" to him.

"There's no breeze at all today," a hunter says, "so we can hunt in any direction."

Too often he hasn't checked thoroughly. Look at tall grass stems or the smallest branches of trees. Try sifting bits of grass, or dandelion seeds or any light dust, held high above the ground and released. If there is any drift at all, you can be absolutely sure a deer will pick up your scent if you move with it. Remember that there is seldom a day or time of day when the air is absolutely still. Remember also that in mountains air movement is usually uphill from daylight until late afternoon, when it reverses.

The only time when a deer hunter goes with the breeze is during a drive. I personally am not keen on the standard deer drives—more about that later. But the drive is used in many parts of the country. The drivers move downwind so that their scent, along with their racket, carries to the deer and pushes them to the hunters, who face the breeze, or are above, out of it.

There is really little more to be said about how to outwit the sense of smell of deer. The only way it is possible is to so arrange yourself in the picture that your scent cannot carry to the deer, or at least so that the odds are as high as you can make them that it won't. The all-important consideration is to convince yourself of just how magically keen this sense is in deer. Never underestimate it!

CHAPTER SEVEN

Attracting Deer

Undoubtedly if we knew how to do so we could call any animal or bird by using a sound, or a sight, or a scent that has some special appeal. I have tolled pronghorn antelope on several occasions exactly as Indians and pioneers did, by hiding and waving my hat, or a white handkerchief. This *sight* appeal works because antelope depend mainly on their eyes, and because they have much curiosity. Ducks and geese come to decoys because they imagine these are their own kind, feeding. But usually the sound of a call is used in conjunction to enhance the illusion. Moose, during the rut, are called by imitating their own sounds. Bull elk are "whistled up" during the rutting season by challenging them with an imitation of their bugling. Squirrel chatter will attract squirrels at any time, and of course nowadays predator calling—the "food" call—is well known.

As stated earlier, deer are not very vocal creatures. Thus there are difficulties with making vocal sounds to attract them, although there are possibilities, which we will discuss. Indians used scents, some to attract, some simply to mask their own scent. This we will also talk about later in this chapter. However, the one most successful method for attracting buck deer, a technique seldom used to any extent except in parts of the Southwest, is "rattling." This is the use of deer antlers, rattled together, to give the impression of two bucks fighting during the rut. It is a tremendously dramatic affair. I want to cover it in detail here because many hunters who scoff at the idea and many others who don't even know about it can bring deer to them with amazing regularity and great sport, if they will learn the details and practice this method.

Rattling will not be successful except during the rut, and for bucks only. But almost all deer seasons fall within at least a portion of that period, and many are set right at the peak of it. Doe deer will pay little attention to the sound, although very occasionally one or more will show up, presumably curious or else ready to be bred.

Although I had heard of this phenomenon for some years, I never witnessed it until I came to Texas to live. It is believed that certain Indian tribes used the method long ago, even rattling sticks together to simulate sounds of antlers rammed together during a buck fight. Oldtime hunters rattled a stick on a gunstock. The modern method, so far as it can be pinned down, seems to have evolved for the whitetails of the brush country of South Texas and the Mexican border some time back in the 1800s. No doubt it had been passed down even then by more primitive peoples.

Because the thornbrush and cactus are dense, it is difficult for a hunter to see a deer, and it is also easy for a hunter to hide. I have been told that in its early use rattling was a South Texas method because, although you might at times get extremely long shots at deer on ridges, usually shots had to be short because of the poor close-in visibility. By rattling up a buck it was practically in your lap before it realized the mistake.

I was also told, some years before we lived in Texas, that for some odd reason the method was successful *only* in the border brush country. This of course is nonsense. It simply was not practiced elsewhere, or if it was the incidents were obscure. Within the past fifteen or twenty years Texas hunters began using the technique outside the brush of the south. Charlie Schreiner, owner of the hunt-famed YO Ranch, taught me the tricks of rattling, demonstrated the amazing success of it, and made me a convert. Charlie was one of the pioneers in using the method outside the brush country. The YO Ranch is located out of Mountain Home on the edge of the Texas hill country, a couple hundred miles north and in totally different terrain from where rattling deer originated.

I will never forget the first time I went with Charlie to see how it was done. The dawn was frosty-crisp and utterly still. This is a perfect combination for the method. We drove out from ranch headquarters a couple of miles and parked the vehicle. Taking his set of "rattling horns" and beckoning me, Charlie walked quietly some fifty yards off the ranch trail. Scrub live oak and cedar make up a large part of the timber on the YO. There was a small cedar thicket from which we could see out into openings surrounding it. Charlie motioned for me to crawl in.

When we were settled, he began the rattling. He didn't have time to work up to his varied additional sounds. The antlers had barely clashed and rattled when we saw the buck coming. He was running, about seventy yards away, coming straight to us. Charlie tickled the antler tips lightly and we hunched low. The buck was an eight-pointer. He stopped possibly ten paces from us. His eyes were wild, his neck hair slightly raised. Here was a buck ready to fight.

There is no question about whether or not he could see us. We could not possibly hide well enough to go undiscovered. Yet so convinced was the buck, and so aroused, that caution was tossed away. He stared at us. He held his tail out straight and minced closer. For a moment or two I actually thought that gentleman was going to come right into the thicket with us—or after us. We had no intention of shooting. The deer finally trotted away. But when Charlie rattled again he turned back and stood staring. I had been initiated—and fully convinced.

Later, when I had learned more and had some confidence in my own ability, I proposed one year to Marlin Firearms a film for national TV distribution about rattling deer. A partner, Ebb Warren, and I put together War-Dal Productions some years back, a firm that produces films for various firms, to be shown chiefly on TV. I thought this rattling phenomenon would make a stunning film, but frankly I was nervous about being able to bring the deer close for Ebb's movie camera. He was also worried, for the fact was he had never seen this done and was somewhat dubious that we knew what we were talking about.

The launching of this production was an astonishing and somewhat comic affair. Ebb flew to Texas, and we went out a few days before deer season opened—not to do any rifle shooting but hopeful of getting footage of bucks "coming to horns" before any hunter disturbance. With Ebb toting the movie camera and me with rattling antlers slung on a thong over my shoulder, we went into semi-open woods, again on the YO Ranch, where whitetails are extremely abundant and many good heads show every season.

I motioned Ebb in under some live oaks with low limbs and I followed. We hunkered low. There was a rather large opening here dotted with scattered cedars. I let fly with the rattling. Instantly we heard stones klink and could actually hear the hoofbeats of a buck pounding toward us. I will always remember Ebb's expression. The buck was a big fellow and was really barreling down on us. Ebb was so astonished he just hunkered there, camera on its gunstock under his arm.

"Shoot, dammit!" I hissed. This was a chance of a lifetime—or so I thought that instant.

That brought Ebb around. It also startled the deer. The buck slid with forelegs braced, looked us straight in the eye from almost close enough to touch. He let out a snort as the camera whirred, wheeled and ran. But when I rattled again he turned, plunged clear around the edge of the opening, and came back. We got the whole bit on film.

This was only the beginning. It happened that the rut that fall was quite concentrated and the weather perfect for this technique. During ten filming days I rattled exactly *fifty-two bucks* into camera range! On two occasions I had four around us at once. Wally Chamness, a Marlin representative who was in the film with me, and I each took a good buck and we had all of this on film, too. That film has been shown to many millions of viewers throughout the nation. Whether they all believe it or not, I can't say. But this should give you an idea how successful and how awesomely dramatic rattling deer can be.

Bucks come to the sound of antlers for several reasons. Each buck has his own territory, his living area. During the rut this is staked out in stricter fashion than at other times. Of course there may be overlap between territories. But in general a buck runs his own area, fights off interlopers. However, he may become an interloper himself, crossing into other nearby buck territories and attempting to run off does from these. A buck may thus be defending his own area when a fight starts, or it may be that a buck from outside the area is trying to put the established one to flight. In some instances undoubtedly two interloper bucks get in a battle over a doe, or imagine they are fighting with the territorial baron.

Therefore, a buck coming to the sound of rattled antlers may come ready to fight because this is his territory and he imagines two other bucks are in it and fighting. Or, the buck may come because he had heard the sound of two others fighting and hopes to take on the winner. Again, he may come sneaking, not spoiling for a battle at all. They commonly do this, obviously hoping to sneak off with the doe over which the fight started, while the other bucks are busy at battle. You have to be alert for either

This illustrates how intrigued bucks are by rattling. This young buck is coming almost to me, and I'm not even well hidden.

a rush-in approach or a sneaking approach. I've had a buck come in so quietly on a breezy day, and from behind me, that it was within mere steps when it decided this was no place to be. When one practically turns wrong side out at arm's length at your back, I can assure you it's a thrill you don't need too often!

Bucks also come at times most warily. They are not sure what's happening, are suspicious, yet drawn to the sound. Also, when a buck is worn out from doe chasing and has bedded down it may not be eager but nonetheless finds the urge to have a look irrepressible. I recall one particularly interesting session with a hunter and a cameraman when I rattled for fifteen minutes with no result. It was time to move. But then we saw

This buck is cautiously moving in to the sound of rattled antlers.

a movement on a ridge at least 150 yards distant. Glassing proved a buck was there, standing in brush, watching the spot from which the sound emanated.

The buck came a step or two at a time during the next half hour. We could see it every now and then, just a glimpse. At the end it made a most foolish move. In order to get near us, it had to move out of cover and cross an open swatch about sixty yards wide. By the time the deer got to the edge of the cover presumably it had made up its mind. Why it would imagine two bucks could fight so long, I'm not sure. But at last the buck stepped into the open and came walking right across, ears alert. The hunter reared and took aim. The deer hauled up abruptly and just stood staring in disbelief. It was a handsome ten-point, well worth the trouble. But from the first rattle to the conclusion of the hunt the time span had been almost a full hour.

Age groups react to rattling about as one would expect. The condition of the buck influences this too, of course. That is, a buck in full rut loses caution. One just starting is more wary. Spike bucks coming in are plain silly. I have let one come right to me, then stood up and rattled the antlers gently practically in its face. It throws up its tail, runs a few steps, then likely as not comes back. A forkhorn is almost as giddy and determined. Mature bucks may come really charging. Or one may rush up to within fifty yards and stop, looking things over. Or it may sneak in or sneak way around. Weather and wind are important influences.

On still, crisp mornings results are usually best. Windy days are difficult regardless of how excited the bucks are. They will invariably circle and come upwind to the sound. Now and then one is so intent it pays little heed to man smell, but not often. You can trick one on a breezy morning, however, by making a setup near a piece of likely cover—a draw or a large thicket—in such a way that in order to get the wind on you the buck will have to show himself. Very occasionally one will come downwind, if wildeyed with the breeding urge. Ordinarily this is not to be expected.

Two good whitetail bucks that came to rattled antlers. A moment later the larger one drove the other away.

I have experienced overcast, chill days when bucks would come in almost all day long. It is a fact, however, that much actual breeding among deer takes place at night. Dawn is therefore the best time for rattling. By nine a.m. as a rule the action is pretty well finished. Frazzled bucks are bedded and resting up. Toward dusk the activity will begin again. Even so, many a buck has been rattled up in the middle of day. You never know. Perhaps one has had difficulty finding does, and is therefore eager to investigate any battle scene.

Whenever a young buck comes to the sound, and you don't wish to take him, be sure to watch his every gesture and movement. A spike or forkhorn does not wish to tangle with an old buster of a buck. I remember one morning having a spike rush in and stand around flicking his tail. Then suddenly he flicked an ear backward and turned that way. He stared a moment and then started to sneak off. I looked where he had been looking and there was a heavy-antlered eight-pointer. This is a fairly common experience.

To take advantage of the rut for rattling, or other methods, you must be informed about it. The season differs to some extent from north to south. Cool weather activates it, scientists believe, by assisting certain hormone changes. What is cool weather, however, depends on where the deer live. A gently cool zephyr blowing in from the north after a hot spell of deer season on the Mexican border may set off a session of bucks chasing does. In northern Wisconsin it might require a zippy cold spell to do the same.

Most hunters believe the rut is a short period—possibly two weeks. It may be. But usually it is much longer, at least forty days, although maybe not concentrated all the time. Hot and cold spells shut it off and turn it on, or at least we can say they decrease or increase the breeding urge. All does do not come in heat at the same time. This further complicates matters. In the region where I now live I have seen a buck rattled up in September, long before the season, and have seen one the same year avidly chasing a doe in late January, after the season had been closed a month. Nonetheless, most years the period of greatest activity, given normal weather, falls in November in my area, but comes in late December down near the border. By and large it can be said that the best time to get trophy bucks in rut is during the latter part of the peak.

Every deer state has done studies on timing of the fawn drop in its latitude. Biologists realize, of course, that fawns may be born over a period of some weeks. But they know, for their state or certain portions of it, when the *most* fawns are born. By figuring back the gestation period one can arrive at the several fall or winter weeks when the majority of does were bred. That will be the peak of the rut and the best period for successful rattling. A check with deer management people in your state or where you intend to hunt will turn up this important information. If you know the peak weeks, and if you watch the ups and downs of the weather, your odds are better.

As I mentioned, rattling for fifteen minutes or so at one spot will in most instances be enough. Then move a half-mile away and try again. Conversely, it is sometimes a good idea to stay put, rattling a few minutes and then quitting, and starting again fifteen minutes later. The theory here is that bucks out running, looking for does, may cross the sound in due time. Much depends on the size of your hunting country, and how abundant the deer are. In places of low deer population it may be best to keep moving. Always be alert for the big trophy buck that neither sneaks in nor races in, but comes slowly until it is possibly seventy-five yards distant, then stands immobile in a thicket. Sometimes such a deer will stand for fifteen minutes, listening, watching. It may then come on into full sight, or it may leave just as quietly.

I would like to convince those who have not tried this sport that it is one of the truly classic methods of deer hunting, and that it will work *anywhere,* if bucks are in rut and within hearing, and you do your part properly. It is not difficult. Anyone can do it the first time out, although practice and experience increase your chances. I do not mean to imply that rattling is infallible. There may be many reasons why no deer comes to your racket. But the method is definitely not regional. Deer have been rattled up from Texas to Kansas to Minnesota, and Canada to Maine and Pennsylvania. The reason more are not is that so few hunters ever try it.

In a region where deer are extremely abundant it makes little difference where you take your rattling stand. But even here, and especially in areas of fewer deer, it is a good idea to do some pre-scouting, just as you would for any other hunting. Thus, this will apply to stand or stalk hunting and even to driving, too. During late summer and on into the fall, bucks rub the velvet from their hardened antlers and then are constantly polishing them by mock fights or rubbing on bushes or shrubs. Find a place where there are a number of rubs, and you know at least that a buck or several are present in the general area.

A facet of information regarding buck rubs that has had little attention concerns the type of vegetation in a given region most likely to be selected. In fact, I have never hunted with anyone who checked for rubs with this

A buck rub on a retama shrub.

in mind. I will cite some examples here. In any latitude or longitude most trees or shrubs are not suitable. A large tree—of four inches or more in diameter—is not selected by the buck for the simple reason that it has no "give" and it is too big to polish single or several tines.

Some shrubs are too thick. In my part of Texas most young cedars have the branches rounded out at the bottom. A buck can't get to a semi-solid stem properly. But among the thousands of cedars that grow in the hill country, a few have a single trunk, and young ones may have branches up at a height beginning perhaps at two to three feet above ground. Such a cedar is an ideal "rubbing tree" when the trunk is about an inch in diameter. The rough bark polishes or cleans away velvet. A few small branches assist.

Farther south in the cactus and thornbrush there is a viciously thorned small tree with fairly smooth green bark called a retama. For some reason stands of retamas quite commonly spring up below the earthen dams where ranch tanks have been built. Probably because of the fairly soft bark that can be scrubbed off, and a few thorns at small branch crotches, whitetails here very commonly select retamas on which to make rubs. When I am checking an expanse of deer country here, I keep an eye out for retamas and check them for rubs. They'll often give a buck away. In northern Michigan I discovered that small balsams are a favorite rubbing tree for deer. Some young Juneberry shrubs down in river bottoms also were invariably attacked. A birch an inch or two in diameter might be also. The bark peels off and makes a rough place for antler scrubbing.

As I have said before, you can never learn too much about the quarry, and this is one of those small items that shortcuts the puzzle of where the bucks are. I cannot tell you in every state or county which shrubs or small bushes and trees the deer will select. But if you are observant you will discover that they have localized favorites. Constantly keep checking these for rubs as you pass.

A deer rub does not necessarily mean the deer will be back there. It just means a deer lives within a section or less of land in the vicinity. A very fresh rub with juice still wet is a hotter sign. Now comes the search for a much more important and pinpoint buck sign made during the breeding season, a *scrape*. This is without any question the most useful buck sign you can discover.

Ordinarily a scrape is made in dry soil. It is pawed out by the front hoofs. It is not a deep hole, but the scraping may cover a couple of square feet or more. A very special location is selected for a scrape. Almost without fail there will be a branch or branches reachable by the buck's antlers and his mouth directly above the scrape, or at least within reach if the scrape is anywhere beneath the animal.

The buck makes the scrape, then urinates in it. He reaches up to jostle a branch with his antlers and he will also reach up to pick at twigs or leaves with his mouth. Why the buck does this last is not clear, but I have seen it on several occasions.

Scrapes are made only during the rut. They are signs saying the buck is in breeding condition. Within his staked-out domain there will be several scrapes. The buck will patrol from one to another without much system, renewing the urine, wetting on his hocks in the process so he leaves a well-marked trail, nuzzling or chewing at the overhead twigs meanwhile.

Does go to these scrapes, too, and often urinate in them and leave a trail for the buck. Other bucks find them and brace the one that made them. Thus a patrolling buck in his territory is always checking to run off other bucks and to find does that have recognized his marks and his signals. At times a doe may even pursue the buck.

Because a buck comes back time and again to scrapes, there is no better stand. As for rattling, nothing is more infuriating to a buck than to hear a "fight" in progress right near one of his scrapes. It may be tricky to pick out a hiding place, with the breeze right, where you can see the vicinity of the scrape and still have the deer in the open somewhere along. It is a good plan, incidentally, when rattling, to use two hunters. One does the shooting and one the rattling. If you are alone, keep your rifle where it can be seized swiftly as you drop the rattling antlers.

Old hands at this game are a bit choosy about what they pick for antlers. The best-balanced sets are made from eight- or ten-point typical whitetail racks, or else mule deer antlers about comparable. They should be reasonably heavy, if they are whitetail antlers. Extra-heavy mule deer antlers are simply too large and unwieldy to use with adeptness. Smaller mule deer antlers comparable to a fairly heavy whitetail set are okay. An amusing aside here is that I have a set of rattling antlers made from a mule deer rack of modest size. One time I was rattling for another hunter who was solemnly telling me he had heard that a whitetail wouldn't come to mule deer antlers. Obviously this is ridiculous—the deer doesn't stand out there listening and thinking, "Nope, that's a mule deer." At any rate, up came a fine buck and the man killed it. I was using mule deer antlers.

Pale-colored antlers are not as good as dark ones. They are invariably lighter and less resonant. Many expert rattlers saw the individual antlers from the skull just above the burr. I do it just the opposite way, leaving the burr on. The brow tines are sawed off. They get in the way and hurt your fingers. If there are any crooked points or small extra points, these should be sawed off, too. A heavy file or rasp serves to smooth down the sawed places. If you have left the burrs on, you may want to touch up rough spots on them. A thong tied between the antlers above the burr on each serves as a carrying string or to loop over your shoulder. If you have sawed above the burr, then drill a hole through each antler butt and run the thong there. If the antler points are very sharp, it's a good idea to saw those off, too, and smooth them down.

The finished pair should mesh well. Some rattlers like to use the left antler in the right hand and vice versa. Some others hold them just as they came from the skull. Either way is all right, just so they feel comfortable and fit together well. There are several theories about rattling routines. The sound does carry far. Some believe in very light rattling. Others really smack 'em.

My own routine is as follows. I try to select a sitting place with good view where I can be obscured. There should be a rough bush within easy reach, a larger tree with rough bark, and a patch of gravel. I begin by whacking the cup of one antler across the curved back of the other. Just a loud crack as an attention-getter. This is followed immediately by meshing the two antlers with a crack and a simultaneous rattling of tines on tines. Generally I follow this, keeping tines meshed, with a lighter cracking and rattling.

This is followed by whacking the bush with one antler, or clawing at it. This sound is much like deer slipping and mauling brush. Next I

Scraping and rattling antlers on tree to simulate a buck fight.

rake the bark of the tree hard with one set of tines, and then rake the gravel patch with tines turned down, to simulate deer hoofs on stones. The exact sequence is of course not necessary, but that is a general run-down on my own approach. These sounds are followed by more rattling. After this entire sequence all sound is stopped. After a few seconds more rattling is done, with portions of the other sounds intermingled.

If a deer shows, cut down the noise. Most rattlers just tickle the antler tips together lightly when a buck comes partway and stops, fully alert and puzzled. I've often raked gravel and brought one on in, never touching the antlers together again. Another little trick is to grip the antlers firmly, with the curved backs to the ground, and pound them two or three times on the ground. This sounds like the foot of a buck stamped hard. It will carry for some distance and at times this alone will bring a buck to investigate, after a series of rattles.

Only observation of rattled-up individual deer will teach you what is needed and what may make a buck shy off. You have to learn, as in calling geese, for example, when to make a sound and when to keep quiet. Never get into a tree to rattle antlers. This is unnatural. The sound must come from near the ground. It will carry, don't worry about that. If you have confidence in this unusual method and keep at it, you will finally succeed. When you do, you'll agree this is the ultimate.

I have been explaining this technique with whitetails in mind. Because they are so much more aggressive during rut than mule deer, they come to antler rattling more readily. In fact, not a great deal is known about the effect of this method on mule deer. A few have tried it. I have. But in my own experience I was never certain my timing, in relation to the rut, was proper. A few rattlers claim to have brought mulies in. I haven't with any certainty. I feel this is an area of deer hunting lore that needs more exploration. I have a hunch the coastal blacktails should be easy to rattle up but have never tried.

Some hunters are enthusiastic about mouth-blown deer calls. Certainly a good many are sold. In an earlier chapter I told how the loud squalling of a predator call can be used to spook deer out of thickets. The so-called "deer call" is designed just like a coyote or fox call, but the reed gives a much lower tone and the resonating chamber is larger. Supposedly the sound simulates that made by a young deer in difficulty, or possibly the low bleat of a doe.

Probably no one has done more experimentation with deer calls than the Burnham brothers, Murry and Winston, long known for the predator,

Occasionally deer calling with a mouth-blown call does work.

and other, calls they manufacture. For some seasons I was fortunate in being able to work with them. At one time I began to be convinced the deer call would eventually be a really lethal approach. In fact, as far back as 1960 in one of the first magazine articles about deer calling, I suggested this. But I do not believe it has developed that well.

We discovered that in summer whitetail does would come running to the low bleat of a call. During a summer session in the western mountains mule deer did the same. These reactions seemed patently to be doe concern for possible harm to fawns. However, here and there throughout the nation hunters using calls have become excited when a buck came right in. Regardless, results with deer calls have been spotty and erratic everywhere. Last season for some reason known only to the deer, a number of whitetails came eagerly to Winston Burnham's call, used in South Texas brush. It had not happened to that extent previously.

Deer—mule and whitetail—have been known to come to a coyote call. But usually it was a low-pitched call, or one supposedly imitating a jackrabbit, which has a lower-pitched squall than a cottontail. And usually results have come when the call was blown very low in volume. There seems to be a fine line between appealing to a deer with a call, and frightening it. Many deer calls have been unsuccessful, undoubtedly, because the hunters using them were careless. The deer must be wholly unaware of the hunter's presence before it will respond.

My enthusiasm for deer calls is perhaps dampened a bit because over all my years of observing deer I have so seldom heard them make vocal sounds, and most of these have been made by fawns in distress or else trying to locate the doe. Once in Michigan I watched and listened to a fawn as it wandered through the woods bleating at every step. This was during deer season, incidentally. I have heard young mule deer make soft calls a few times, too. And I have heard a badly wounded adult deer bawl in anguish, although this is a rare happening. Once in the north I shot a big buck that was following a doe. He fell and let out a series of guttural blatts that would raise your hair. I've never heard such a sound again.

Most early deer calls were based—so the makers alleged—on practices of Alaskan Indians. Whether this was a sales pitch or the truth is impossible now to sort out. If it was based on truth, which is unlikely, then the deer in question had to be the Sitka deer, and of all our deer this one is possibly the most naive.

My conclusion reached over the years is that deer definitely will come to properly pitched calls. Does are more gullible about it than bucks. But at times, for obscure reasons, bucks can't seem to wait. When I was researching this subject a decade or more ago, I corresponded with a man in Pennsylvania who claimed to have called several hundred deer. It was a hobby with him and I had no reason to disbelieve his accounts, although I could not prove them either. I have corresponded with numerous hunters who have brought bucks in, of both varieties, and killed them.

To sum up, I suspect one may as often frighten deer with a call as interest them. On the other hand, I don't like to carry around black-and-white opinions. Both whitetail and mule deer certainly can be called. Possibly someday hunters will learn how to do this consistently. They haven't as yet.

Scents of various kinds are widely advertised as "deer calls" or "deer lures." Scents can certainly be useful. I am skeptical, however, that they actually *call* many deer. One scent manufacturer some years back told me in all seriousness that his scent smelled like apples, and deer, which like apples, were therefore attracted by it. I found this rather amusing. His operation was in the East where there were numerous apple orchards. I wondered about the whitetails in the northern Maine forest that had never seen or smelled an apple, or the ones in the Montana Rockies or down in South Texas. It is interesting to note that whitetails in some remote places where they have never seen grain of any kind cannot be baited with shelled corn! They won't touch it. They don't know what it is. Thus I doubt that these same deer would be greatly attracted by the smell of apples. For all we know it might scare them!

Most deer "lures" of the scent variety are *masks* for human scent. It may well be that the apple scent I mentioned neither appeals to a deer nor disturbs it, yet might meanwhile overpower human scent. A smell that is common almost everywhere deer range—skunk musk, for example— probably neither repels nor frightens deer, and it certainly wipes out human odor. Whether it is worth living with for the biggest trophy in the woods is to me at least questionable.

I am quite convinced that mask scents are an assistance. On numerous occasions while rattling deer I have used the wet musk glands from the legs of deer, carried in a jar and hung on nearby bushes. This seems especially effective on a day when there is a breeze. It helps to mask human scent and is confusing to a deer, which may get whiffs of both. In fact, some scent makers believe musk that smells to a deer like another deer, used in conjunction with the sound of a deer call, actually brings deer to the hunter. There is merit in this theory. Human odor is blotted out by the deer musk, and the low bleat sends out its appeal.

Some hunters who like to prowl the woods stalking deer swear by scents. Let us suppose the scent, worn perhaps on boots and clothing, does have a direct appeal to the deer and at the same time covers up human odor. The crack of a stick as the hunter walks may alert or frighten the listening buck, but the scent the buck picks up is reassuring.

Indians used deer musk as a scent supposedly appealing to deer. Some wore fresh deer hides, burned wild aster, which supposedly is attractive to deer, or took a gummy material exuded from between the toes of deer as a human scent mask that would appeal to deer. Some of these ideas may have been worthwhile, some may have been pure foolishness. Just because Indians used them doesn't mean the Indians were necessarily correct. Much hokum has come out of Indian lore. A fresh deer hide may have a smell to a deer that is horrifying, for all we know.

I suspect we all need to use the proverbial salt grain with lots of such deer-hunt theories. Should you avoid smoking? Or wearing clothing smelling of tobacco? Maybe. But how do you know this odor frightens deer? Maybe they like it. Tame deer love to eat tobacco. Should you avoid use of deodorants? Perhaps deer like the smell. Some of the recent modern musk scents women now wear will certainly mask human scent and just might make a deer dizzy enough to catch by hand! Some hunters don't bathe because they don't want that fresh soap smell. Some bathe to get the man smell off. The fact is, the nose of a deer is very keen and it makes not much difference *what* you smell like if it can be related somehow to something not supposed to be there. The deer smelling it will undoubtedly be frightened regardless. I've heard that new clothes must be washed to rid them of their "new" smell. And that new boots must be oiled to kill the "new" smell. How do we know that your old clothes and boots don't smell worse to a deer as well as to a fellow hunter?

To sum it up, I am sure mask-type scents inoffensive and undisturbing to deer can be helpful tools. But the best of success will always fall to those hunters who so arrange matters that the deer does not smell them at all!

I have a good friend who is avid for scents. On the left breast of his hunting coat he pins a square of sheepskin. Before each hunt he soaks it in some musk scent that is utterly vile. He is certain this helps him bring in his buck every year. It may. But I'll tell you one thing for sure: he hunts alone and he brings it in alone. Nobody will even get near him for a month after the season closes. The moral here is that there just have to be more pleasant ways of hunting deer.

CHAPTER EIGHT

The
Movements
of Deer

In some ways the life of a deer may seem to be idyllic. It has nothing to do but eat, drink, and seek comfortable and secluded resting places. Food, water, comfort, safety—these are the prime motivations or *movers* of all wildlife. Although the needs of deer may seem extremely simple, the myriad influences bearing upon each of their needs form extremely complicated combinations.

Basically the terrain and its soil will lay down the rules for the deer to follow. Upon terrain and soil depend what the deer will eat and where the food will grow. Upon terrain, too, will depend the water sources— whether desert or a country of abundant lakes and streams. Where the deer will find comfort and where they will feel safe are also related to terrain. But to complicate the matter further we must now add weather. And by weather I mean to include day-to-day weather, plus the whimsical annual patterns, plus the general climate in which any given terrain is situated.

For example, in one type of habitat a deer will invariably move up to find a cool bedding place. In another, as we will see, it will probably move down. Temperature—weather—dictates these movements, but the terrain is the factor which forces the deer to go in one direction or the other. A severe drought in early summer will directly affect the food equation—where the deer will be and on what it will feed and perhaps even how concentrated the deer will be in fall hunting season. Conversely, a lush summer, actually a weather effect, will change deer habits.

When we begin to put the combinations together it may appear discouraging. Scarce food, for instance, plus unseasonably hot weather, plus a dearth of leafy cover that makes comfortable, safe hiding places few, plus scarce water. Let's suppose this combination occurs where you intend to hunt, and that under normal conditions this area would furnish ample food, water, and cover, and crisp weather. The habits of the deer will be vastly altered that season, by necessity.

Instead of discouragement, however, a hunter should have firmly in mind all of the influences upon his quarry and have stored up a knowledge that can help him solve the problem, regardless of intricate combination. Pared right down to the bare bones, *terrain, weather, cover, water,* and *food* are the five fundamental concerns of both the deer and the hunter. These five dictate completely the *movements of deer.* And it is upon these movements that the success or failure of deer hunting depends.

When a deer moves from Point A to Point B to feed, or to drink, or to locate a place of comfort and safety for resting, the hunter's chore is to intercept it, or pursue it. When it has found its resting place, a stalk will move it into sight. Knowing *why* a deer moves from Point A to Point B, and the ability to predict that it will make such a movement, is the highest art and craft of the deer hunter. If you know what deer eat *in your hunting area,* where they drink, where they rest, the general routes they travel normally to and from any of these points, and you also know how weather and terrain will affect both the deer and their basic requirements, restricting the animals or giving them utmost freedom of movement—if you know these fundamentals thoroughly, then you are indeed a schooled deer hunter and will invariably bring in the venison.

Let us deal first with food. I was in Maine one season when a friend shot a fine buck in an old abandoned apple orchard as it ate fallen, frosted fruit at dawn. This man, a Maine native, told me that apple orchards were his favorite stands. He had killed several deer in one or another. Amusingly, I later read in a national magazine article written by an Easterner

In the East and Great Lakes region particularly, abandoned apple orchards are a prime deer attraction, and can furnish a snack for the hunter as well.

that apple orchards were among the hottest spots for deer, during years of course when the trees bore. What, I wondered, would the hunter in northeastern Wyoming think of this? Or the hunter in an Alabama swamp, or the one in the southwestern cactus patches, all places where whitetails are numerous? He'd spend a longer time finding an abandoned apple orchard than he would need to kill a hundred deer!

So, first of all it is necessary to know what deer eat where you will do your hunting. Deer food is highly varied. Further, it does little good to bone up on what the deer are eating on your proposed hunting ground in summer. When deer season opens much of the lush summer forage will be long gone. One needs to know area foods likely to be most abundant and available during the fall season, and in a specified area or terrain. Additionally, once on the ground, the hunter should establish whether or not there were good "crops" this year of the food the deer would normally take.

The subject of deer forage and preferences is an extremely involved one. Many detailed studies have been made of it. We cannot possibly do more than skim the surface here, with portions of the subject of greatest help to hunters. Deer are attracted to succulent green feed and will graze when such foods are available. In most places the grasses are spring and early summer foods. But as soon as these get too high and tough, deer switch to forbs and other green foods. In fall in most areas deer will be browsing more than grazing, because it is now that the woody plants are available and the grasses are gone.

Suppose that you hunt an area where a crop such as winter oats is planted. Deer will swarm to a patch of this green grasslike grazing feed because it is nutritious and a change from browse plants. To illustrate, however, what a study you can make of deer foods, let us suppose that a cut-over field with stubble in it, and thus much dead material, is sprouting green shoots. Across the fence there is a patch of winter oats just nicely sprouting. The woods edge to watch is the one bordering the oat patch. While the green sprouts in the stubble field might be utilized if the oats were unavailable, deer dislike feeding in the dead-and-green stubble mixture and will take the all-green oat patch in preference.

Deer seem to recognize palatability of various foods, and to be in best condition on ranges where a variety of foods is available. It is obvious that deer living in sagebrush foothills with scattered junipers do not have as wide a selection of foods as, say, a deer in the New England woods. Where a habitat is sparse, a hunter can more quickly deduce what is making up the bulk of the diet. In the South Texas brush, huajilla, a shrub with feathery multiple leaf fronds and tiny but fairly inconsequential thorns along the stems, is a prime deer forage. It is never amiss to seek deer where there is a heavy growth of it.

In an eastern woods there may be red maple, greenbrier, dogwood, poplar, and blackberry scattered through a given range and all in fair abundance. There will also be patches of clover that stay green far into fall, and possibly wild strawberry patches also, plus low-growing wintergreen. All of these serve as deer foods in fall. And in a good year the animals may be feeding on the mixture and difficult to tie to a specific "food patch."

Bear in mind that forage must be within reach. Some hunters have an exaggerated idea of how high a deer can reach. If there is an abundance of a preferred forage, but too tall, it is useless, and trying to tie a deer to the spot would be silly. Also, weather has drastic effects both good and bad on foods. As noted, a drought may force deer to live on undesirable varieties some seasons. Conversely, there may be a real bonanza of a certain palatable food some falls. It is these happenstances that a hunter should be quick to grasp, and utilize to his advantage.

Certainly those old apple orchards, where found, are excellent deer attractors. Here is a food that is desirable, in limited seasonal supply, and not scattered all over the place. Acorns are another good example. In oak country—there are many species, of course—not all years furnish a good crop. Nor do all oak trees even in good production years bear acorns. Some may bear none. Some may be loaded but every acorn drilled and ruined by insect parasites. But there may be a single large tree that is heavy with acorns, all of them healthy nuts. Such a tree commonly draws deer like a magnet.

In my back yard, in fact barely outside our back door, there is a live oak that is especially vigorous. One recent fall it bore a fabulous acorn crop, the major portion untouched by parasites. For days two small bucks fed under that tree. They'd scatter as if ready to explode with fright when one of us went out the door. But soon they'd be back. Curiously, many of our live oaks had acorns that year. But that tree had a particularly huge, good crop and the deer—does as well as those two little bucks—selected it. Such a tree can serve you as a "deer call" if you are a sharp observer.

On numerous ranches near us, low shin oak grows profusely. The little scrub, when it bears, has amazingly large acorns, and deer are invariably in the patches to eat them. On our Bushwhack Creek Ranch we have five species of oaks. It is interesting to observe that the deer favor certain ones. This is vitally important to the hunter. In the stream bottom we have a few enormous oaks of the chestnut-oak group, with broad, nonlobed leaves. These bear acorns to match—huge. In years when they and all the other species produce a bumper crop you can just bet a deer or two can be bagged by taking a stand near one of these scarce trees.

Thus I emphasize that any unusual abundance of a fairly scarce and extremely desirable food can be a clue to a good deer hunting location. It is well known, for example, that deer like mushrooms, even though the nutritional value is very low. I recall a spot in the north where I was puzzled to see deer consistently feeding, during an unseasonably balmy fall. I could not see anything attractive enough to bait them, until I stumbled upon the fact that the entire area was littered with small puffballs hidden in low grass. These do not last long, nor come into such profusion often. The deer were making the most of it.

In Michigan one time I stumbled upon a real deer bonanza tied to a food source. Although some normal foods here would have been balsam, white cedar, oak and maple twigs, serviceberry shoots, and under duress jackpine, a starvation food when deer are forced to take it and nothing else, the deer were feeding where a heavy cutting of poplar had been made

An exceptionally fat Utah mule deer, bagged in country where piñon nuts and cedar berries were plentiful.

the previous year. A maze of young poplar shoots had sprung up here. This is prime browse and the deer were utilizing it. Aspen, of course, is a top deer food in the West, as its relatives the poplars and birches are eastward. But the problem there is the abundance of aspen in most areas, which hardly ties deer to one small feeding ground.

Where deer utilize different ranges in summer and winter—the classic example is the vertical migration of some Western mule deer—you must relate your knowledge of deer food to which range they are on. On winter range the forage may be entirely different from that on summer or pre-migration range. It will do little good to know that high-country mule deer love to eat mountain mahogany, if you are hunting a winter range where none exists. Here again it is an excellent idea to be ever alert for an unusual crop of some delicacy. Piñon nuts are the classic in some parts of the West. In good years deer gorge on them. In some areas, too, when an unusual crop of cedar berries (juniper) appears, deer stomachs will be stuffed with them.

On a general level it is a good idea to bone up on how deer foods change by latitudes as the vegetation patterns change. In parts of eastern

Oklahoma and across the Ozarks, where oaks are prominent, acorns are an important fall diet, and so is oak browse. Conifers such as pine, when present, are seldom touched. Yet deer in the Great Lakes region utilize the conifers heavily, and they also do in parts of the South. These are simply general patterns one should know. You should also be aware of the rather exasperating fact that a food taken avidly in one place may be shunned in another. Studies by biologists have shown, for example, that certain plants eagerly eaten by whitetails in one state are almost entirely shunned in another not far away. On specific ranges of the West, mule deer eat rabbitbrush as a preferred food. Only a couple of hours away as a hunter drives his vehicle, they pay no attention to it.

On the less discouraging side, although the list of vegetation species that deer eat is a long one, in *any* location the bulk of the diet will be made up of only a few. Part of this is because of availability, part because of palatability to the deer. Diet studies have been meticulously made for many years. Most have shown that on any given range, though the list of plants (grasses, forbs, shrubs, trees) eaten by deer may encompass well over a hundred species, some 75 percent or more of the diet is made up of less than ten. Further, among those ten, 75 percent or more is usually made up—given availability—of only three or four.

This makes it easier for the hunter. Further, *during hunting season* the choice of standard foods is whittled down drastically. That narrows it farther. My suggestion is to find out what deer eat in the fall in any area where you will hunt. That is not difficult. If you hunt on private lands owned by farmer or rancher, most of them are well aware of favored deer forage on their property. A query to the deer management people of any state can bring you printed information about forage studies in that state, and often right down to specific ranges. But don't deluge these people with a lot of silly questions. Be specific. Ask how you may obtain study results. They don't have time to write long letters. If you have to pay for these study results, you could not spend your money more wisely.

In addition to the standard favorites, ferret out what unusual bonanzas may appear in a good season and which traditional crops are best. These will be like dessert to a deer and tie the animals to specific places. If you are interested enough to pursue the food study with fervor, learn also what deer do *not* eat. As I write that I think of a gentleman who was having his first Desert mule deer hunt on the huge ranch of a friend of mine in West Texas. He wanted to hunt alone and to walk, so the rancher gave him a pasture to himself. We picked him up at noon, and again at evening,

Creosote brush. There is rarely much point in hunting creosote flats—there is nothing there to attract them.

and all the time he had been prowling a huge flat of creosote brush. Now creosote brush grows on the worst possible soil, where practically nothing else will grow. Further, it is wholly unpalatable to any living creature. Crush a few of the tiny leaves in your fingers and smell it and you'll know why. I have seen small mule deer bucks lie up in midday in creosote, cooled by a breeze across the flat. The odds of killing a big buck here are long indeed. There is absolutely nothing here he can use, unless he happens to chase a doe across one!

You should be aware that food has a great deal of influence on what sort of rack your buck will have. The size and condition of antlers are directly related to how well the deer ate and how nutritious the food during the period when antlers were forming. Any fair-to-middling hunter can predict what antlers should be like in any given season by checking on food conditions—obviously an aspect of weather influence—back in the spring and early summer. The effect will be emphasized in direct proportion to the quality of the range. A desert habitat, for example, sparse to begin with, will turn out small-antlered deer when there has been a super-dry spring, and chances are the antlers even on older bucks will be thin and pale.

Whenever possible, set your sights to hunt deer on a range where a fair *variety* of food is abundant. I do not mean necessarily during season, but where the year-round life of the animals is in proximity to a highly varied diet. It may be that the deer utilize heavily only a few plants. But it is well known that deer on ranges with varied forage possibilities are invariably in better condition than those on ranges where food selection is slim. And, don't misread this or interpret it in simple terms, such as "desert is sparse, northwoods is lush." Arid habitats are not necessarily lacking in variety, and non-arid ones may be. A big green woods doesn't automatically mean healthy deer—not unless there are desirable foods for them available.

Also, if you are going to delve into deer hunting in relation to foods rather thoroughly, you must learn that certain plants have many species, and among the group not all may be utilized by deer. A classic example is sage. There are numerous species of sage growing throughout the West. That "silver and purple" line may sound nice, but not necessarily to a deer. The variety of sage known as "silver" has in fact little appeal or value to feeding deer. But a few other species do have. Check out which ones, where you will hunt, are important, and which are not, and learn to recognize them. After all, this may sound terribly scientific—but what could add more to your hobby?

It is certainly true, particularly in our crowded conditions nowadays, that a great many deer hunters are plain "lucky." Somebody spooks a record buck into their lap. Is that very satisfying? I'd much prefer outwitting the big blighter with knowledge and craft! And so it is that deer moving to or from a feeding place can be intercepted, if you know what they prefer to eat, in your region.

The chief reason movements of deer to and from forage is of special importance to a hunter is that in the equation of daily life of deer the food digit is the most fragile. Water, and cover for comfort and safety, are seldom problems. Food often is. In fact in the science of deer management this is the most vital concern. On optimum range, deer thrive. But if this range spawns overabundance, the animals then begin to overbrowse their habitat. If this continues long enough without proper herd cropping, the range will be impaired even past possible rejuvenation.

The one phenomenon difficult for many a hunter to understand—and I've indicated some of this—is the difference between summer feeding conditions and winter feeding conditions. When I lived in northern Michigan, hunters from the cities scoffed often at the idea of deer starving to death in large numbers, in winter. These people had seen in summer the lush greenery of the northern woodlands. In fall while deer hunting they had seen animals in good condition and ample forage available. But most of them had no idea what happened as the winter dragged on. February and March and even April in a cold year are the crucial months. Deep snow inhibits deer movement. Deer yard up, eat what is available, and then starve. Or, weakened by severe malnutrition, they succumb to other diseases. At one time hunters urged feeding, of hay for example. Deer can starve on this diet, too.

One time some years ago during a hard winter I went with conservation officers on snowshoes in March, in northern Michigan, to check on deer condition. On one forty-acre tract laid out for careful check, we found fifteen dead deer. We also found several almost gone. I walked up and put my hand on one deer that was able to stand but too debilitated to walk or run.

This is why I describe forage as the most fragile part of the equation. Nor should hunters get the idea that difficult conditions arise only in snow country. Anywhere on the continent there is a growing season and a season of little vegetative growth. By the fall deer season everywhere the food available for deer has been drastically cut down from what it was in summer. Variety is less. Many former foods—grasses and forbs—are now dry and unpalatable. The deer flexibly change diet. If you know what forage they are utilizing, and where, the movements of the animals related to food can result in filling your license.

For some reason there has always been stigma attached to taking animals at their water sources. Some of this is justified. In some states hunters may not legally camp within a specified distance of a waterhole, or shoot a deer at a watering place. In others it is illegal to kill a deer in a stream, or from a stream while in any type of craft. Probably some such laws are nitpicking. Moose hunting is commonly done from boat or canoe and this is not frowned upon.

It is not easy in most deer ranges to tie deer to watering places. In New England or the Great Lakes region, for example, water is never any problem for a deer. Sources are so numerous that deer seldom have pinpoint drinking spots utilized daily. However, in certain steep country where stream crossings easily accessible are few, deer do use the same drinking spots habitually. In extremely arid situations, deer are forced to get water from only a few places. In such instances if not illegal it is probably all right to watch a waterhole. The only stigma is that you may keep numerous animals from drinking. A more sporting arrangement is to check out trails going to or from the water. Invariably when sources are few the trails will be distinct. Watching such a trail some distance away from the water can be a most effective method of hunting.

What hunters fail often to understand is that deer know many places to drink that a hunter never discovers. It does not take much of a seepage or rainwater puddle to satisfy a deer. Even in desert regions there may be scores of such small drinking holes hidden away. I think of a spring in Big Bend National Park. There is, of course, no hunting here. But as you drive through the burning desert you would not remotely imagine flowing water anywhere near. Yet this famous spring is only a short hike back into the foothills. It is secluded, and there are always deer nearby.

Mule deer in particular, because they have lived for centuries in several remote desert areas, have an uncanny way of getting along on what may seem to be very little water. There is a vast expanse on the Gage Holland Ranch in the Big Bend country of West Texas that shows on many maps as "Hell's Half Acre." It is an exceedingly rough expanse of desert mountains. I rode this country for some days a few years ago on horseback, with Gage. At that time there were no roads, and no windmills here. Thus it could not be utilized for cattle, except on one edge where San Francisco Creek flowed meagerly. At that time Gage was preparing to open up the region for cattle, by pushing in roads and putting down windmills. What struck me as unique during our long treks in the saddle was that there were Desert mule deer galore. Some of the biggest trophy bucks I've ever seen in West Texas we spotted and photographed. Where did they get water? Only the deer knew.

Some students of desert-habitat deer are convinced they can get along without free-flowing or standing water, that they take in their requirement from plant moisture. This is not true. But watery plants do provide part of the water needs. Prickly pear cactus, for example, is at least half water (juice) by weight. Until you have watched a big mule buck stand placidly munching on those spine-studded pear pads, you might not believe they can handle such fare. But I have watched this on numerous occasions. Whitetails also eat pear to some extent when necessary.

As we have seen earlier, ranges of individual deer groups are small. Most utilize no more than half a square mile, some as much as a mile. But if conditions are spare, the range has to be somewhat larger. However, if food and cover are abundantly present, but not water, the deer may travel some distance to get water. This is one instance where knowing their drinking habits may assist a hunter. Because deer are basically nocturnal creatures, both varieties have a habit of drinking just before bedding down in the morning.

This may not be so noticeable with whitetails, because almost always their water source is very near to good resting places. Mule deer, on the other hand, may be in the valleys and on the flats feeding at night, but their bedding areas may be up atop a ridge, under a rimrock or on a high point. Thus it is common to see mule deer at dawn or shortly after going for a drink. Then they start casually climbing from the watering place upward and on average days by nine o'clock or shortly after they will be lying down.

Last season, for example, I watched bands of mule deer come to a cement windmill tank to drink. The water was of course primarily for cattle. By eight a.m. I had counted more than forty deer idling along to the water, drinking, and then going on. The big bucks came earliest. They didn't want to hang around in daylight. But they were headed, I was sure, for the top of a mountain backdropping the water source. There were well-worn trails up the mountain easily visible with my binocular. A hunter up on the mountain, away from a main trail a short distance, would have been in a perfect spot to take an excellent buck. The updraft thermals were beginning and the deer would have walked right to him. This is one example of how water can help you in your hunt.

In the major share of whitetail habitats in the North and Southeast, as I've said, water is seldom a problem and you just cannot tie a deer to a specific watering place easily. In snow country, deer often utilize snow to give them their water quota even when lake and stream waters are available, and not frozen over. Conversely, in dry areas, knowing where deer go to water can be most helpful. In the brush country near the Mexican border, all cattle country, tanks are dug usually at about half-mile or mile intervals. The soil here holds water quite well. Vegetation grows up in dense thickets near the water, and hunting deer near a tank is one of the best ways to connect in this country which is difficult to hunt. There will always be deer hanging around near a tank, not just for the water but because cover is so excellent here. Taking a stand hidden along a tank dam or on a *sendero* leading to a tank is a productive method.

Deer may, or may not, drink more than once every twenty-four hours. If the trip to water is far, once may suffice. But again, it usually isn't.

Where water is not abundant, hunting the creek bottoms is apt to pay off.

During the night when deer are active they undoubtedly drink. But the morning habit, as I've illustrated, is quite common. And after deer have bedded much of the day they will soon go to water after moving out. If the weather is hot, contrive to hunt the "water trips" with some concentration. If it is cool to cold there will not be so much urgency to drink. A deer of 200 pounds live weight will drink in average temperature two or three quarts of water daily. In very hot weather the average will run as much as double that. On certain diets water consumption is high, but of course the hunter would be unable to judge how high or what those diets might be. Salt content raises water intake progressively. It is easy to understand that a deer in warm weather undoubtedly drinks at least twice daily and possibly more. Where a water source is close to bedding and feeding ground, the animals drink more than once daily even in normally cool weather.

We have dealt at some length in previous chapters with cover preferred by the several deer groups, and we have seen that cover is directly related to safety and comfort and also to food. Of course, safety and comfort depend upon weather, too, and in turn weather may be closely related to terrain. The most important point to be made about cover alone is to be certain you are able to interpret what is good cover in any situation. Deer must hide, be shaded, or be in sun as temperature dictates. They must be able to feel that they have secure places where they will be undisturbed.

I have seen deer in open areas of eastern Wyoming bed down on high shale ledges of buttes thrusting up from the treeless floor below. Thus in this case the ledge and the rock behind the deer is the cover. In the same region, deer get into deep coulees or eroded gullies, and select small lie-up spots where perhaps only a few small bushes grow. In northern woodlands obviously cover is all but limitless. In the Midwest there may be open, tilled fields but also brushy small creeks. Both whitetails and mule deer will use the vegetative edges of stream courses anywhere in their ranges. In the broad and horribly jagged lava beds of parts of the West, deer will hide in crevices or among upheavals. During deer seasons it is a law of nature that deer will seek out more dense cover in cold climes than in warm ones.

Thus as an all-round deer expert you must be able quickly and accurately to spot what deer will use as "cover" regardless of the topographical features. If you spot a deer in what you think is a wide-open spot, a long gunshot from any cover, you had better look again, for you can learn from this animal. Some kind of cover is not far away. Though whitetails and mule deer may have different ideas about how dense and expansive cover must be, each is found only rarely more than a quarter-mile from a hiding place. Usually the distance is much less. In hard-hunted Pennsylvania, whitetails may race across an open field, but only because some hunter has forced them. They will make more errors when heavily pressured because there are simply too many dangers harassing them. When you watch, as I have many times, a group of mule deer bucks moseying along unconcerned up the slope of what you'd be inclined to call a "barren mountain," glass carefully. Those "little" outcrops or ragged boulder slides or rims are big as houses once you are up there. Among them are crannies to bed a hundred deer.

So, size up the range. What are the deer eating here, where are their water sources, what serves as cover here? In all of this, beware of putting too much faith in deer trails. I know that many hunters dote on them. Trails to or from water or favorite bedding places may make useful stands. But deer do a lot of wandering. They also, remember, move around just as much in summer as in deer season and maybe more. That distinct deer trail you have selected for a stand may be a trail laid down in summer and not used at all now. This is not to say trails are valueless for watching movements of deer. Just make certain the trail is in use—up to a rimrock, up a brushy draw—and that it has a specific use by deer for the season in which you are hunting. If you want to have your faith in trails somewhat weakened, have a look when snow is on the ground. A trail you may have bet on before the snow fell may have no sign of a track in it, but other tracks will be wandering seemingly aimlessly all over the forest.

Weather, of course, cannot be left out of this. The reason those tracks wander now far more than they did in summer is that, as we've indicated,

Some hunters are inveterate trail watchers. That's all right—if the trail is being used. Some are only seasonal.

food is now becoming less varied and more scarce. Deer now have to *work harder* to survive, as this most fragile part of their habitat is cut down to size long after the growing season is ended. There are advantages to the hunter. As the forage gets thinned, deer must move more in order to fill up. In addition, as temperature drops they must *eat more.* No one can say at what temperature a deer anywhere is most comfortable. A Southern deer probably gets cold at medium temperatures because it is not conditioned to cold—just like people who live in the South. The same deer may be uncomfortable in hot weather but not as much so as the Northern whitetail that experiences little hot weather.

It is believed by scientists that by and large the temperature at which most deer feel the maximum comfort is probably a bit lower than for humans—somewhere around 60 degrees, a little less, a little more, as opposed to our 70 degrees. In temperatures anywhere from about 40 to 60 degrees, deer will be vigorous and active in a normal manner. But even though they must live out in the woods in bitter weather, they certainly do get cold. In fact, when the temperature goes down to a few degrees above freezing even a fat deer cannot maintain a constant weight, regardless of how abundant and fattening the food supply. From there on down, deer suffer. They must get into dense cover to ward off cold, they utilize conifers and deep snow beds to help them keep warm, and they must constantly travel—if snow does not prevent this—to fill their bellies.

If you understand these facts, your deer hunting is to some extent simplified. As an example, if you are hunting in severe weather on a deer range that has excellent cover, you will probably bring in a deer in good condition. And you will have to hunt the dense cover to move it out in the daytime. If cover is sparse, even though food may be ample enough, the deer probably will not be in good condition and they will be wilder because hiding and comfort are below par.

I am quite certain deer sense drastic weather changes. When wispy mares' tails ride the western sky and forecast a stiff blow from the north, deer will usually be out and active. When the bitter wind with its snow, or even just its biting chill and no snow, strikes the range, the deer will drop from sight. I have seen times when you would swear they were absolutely gone. At such times they will be in dense conifer thickets in the North, or in steep canyons in the lee in such country. In open mountain regions you should glass closely the sunny slopes, because now deer require warmth. In the mixed forest of the North, deep tamarack or cedar swamps or pine plantings will form protection for deer, and a quiet stalker, using the snow to advantage, may walk up on many a bedded buck.

In Eastern woodlands the calm morning after a big storm has ceased is a great time to be out. Hungry deer will move, and their tracks are fresh.

After the storm has passed, and the air quiets down and the sun shines, even though the day may be chill the deer will begin to move again. They must. I want to emphasize that during short periods of severe weather you can forget all about any "movements of deer." The comfort factor at times overshadows desire for food and water. I remember a hard storm in the Great Lakes region when every deer track disappeared for three days. A friend and I pussyfooted around a silent, deep cedar swamp, and he jumped a nice buck and killed it right there. On the fourth day with the sun out and the air crisp and still, every deer was moving. They had to make daytime movements because they had been penned up too long. There will be exceptions, which you have to dope out. If food and water and cover are all in the same place—I noted this phenomenon earlier on our own ranch—the deer don't have to move out to get along well.

In open country after a hard storm, mule deer will literally swarm. A couple of years ago during a severe norther three of us used a four-wheel-drive with chains to cruise steep snowy ranch trails in West Texas. Weather was simply awful. In three days we saw exactly two deer. We just could not believe they could drop from sight so totally. There was not a track. Then the weather switched. The skiff of snow melted, wind settled, sun blazed. In one morning we glassed by actual count over 200 deer! Year after year hunters in the Rockies swarm to high areas to find themselves suddenly deluged by an early storm. Seldom does such a storm put down lasting snow. Sit tight and bull it out. When weather clears, deer will be all over the slopes.

We have already covered mule deer migrations in the Rockies, an influence of weather. We do need to have a closer look at high temperatures and their effect on deer movements. If a deer is comfortable at from, say, 50 to 65 degrees, it's a cinch that from around 65 degrees upward deer will look for shady places. In much whitetail country these resting places will usually be up on a slope or at the head of a draw or under shady cover on a ridgetop, where a breeze will blow. Occasionally deer will seek coolness elsewhere. On our ranch there is one particular place along the creek where high soft-rock bluffs drip water constantly. Often deer will lie in ferns here, in the shade of the bluff. But I have yet to see a buck there. Always does.

In mountain country where there are rimrocks without trees, the deer will go up and without fail bed down on the shady side. In timbered

High rims like these in Utah are excellent places to find deer bedded, but they require patient glassing.

mountains they will seek shady ledges or thickets overlooking valleys. There is a most crafty little trick a deer hunter can play, once he knows this shady-side habit. A north-south ridge or one quartering north-south will have the shade on the west side of the rim part of the day, and on the east side the rest of the day. Deer will move to get out of the sun. I'm talking about when weather is warm—65 or above, which to a fat deer is not comfortable. By selecting a proper watching spot you can intercept these moving animals.

Nor does this apply just to rimrocks and open mountains. In whitetail country and in dense blacktail country, a hot sun will force deer to move. It will do the same in the Rockies, whenever the situation is such that hot sun can slant into a hideaway. Movement, to be sure, is seldom as far because the deer does not need to move far to find shade again. But always remember that a deer that is undisturbed except by temperature, and gets up to re-bed, may well wander around briefly. They may snatch a few bites, drink if water is close, urinate, then find a new, shady bed. Some excellent midday or early-afternoon opportunities are afforded by this habit. Remember, too, that as a general rule the hotter the weather, the earlier, and later, the deer are out feeding. In unseasonal weather in some areas it may be too late or too early to allow shooting light.

There are isolated instances when deer move directly opposite to what one might predict. The classic example I think of occurs in my state. In the open mountains of West Texas the mule deer move *up* to bed down because this is where they find the most shady, cool places. Place a stranger in the whitetail country of the South Texas brush and cactus, however, and he might be totally puzzled. I had a man from Wisconsin down there one year. It was viciously hot, even though the time was early December. Deer didn't move at all in daylight.

He said, "I'm going to take a walk on the ridges and jump a buck from its bed."

I admonished him to walk in the sunny spots because rattlesnakes are plentiful and in this warmth would be active, but always lying in shade. I also said, "I hate to discourage you, but you'll be hunting the wrong place."

This country is rolling. Some ridges are fairly high. Creek bottoms— really dry washes except when it rains—meander between ridges here and there. The heaviest, tallest vegetation grows along these because the most of the meager water always runs here. The ridges do not offer deer enough shade. Thus, in the heat, they invariably get into the more dense creek bottoms. Here there may be less breeze but there is much more shade. Some of the biggest bucks down there are taken every year by hunters prowling these dense creek bottoms, ready for a quick, short shot.

After this long discussion I'm sure you will begin to realize how entangled and overlapping all of these influences are that cause deer to move from place to place. In the beginning we spoke of terrain, but actually we have covered it in discussing weather and food and cover. The terrain does have an overwhelming importance to how you will hunt, and on where the deer will be, as we have seen. Think back to the chapters on whitetail and mule deer personalities, on differences in habits between bucks and does, and even to the habits and ranges of the individual species and subspecies in the first chapter, and you will understand by putting it all together how terrain bears on the deer and your hunt. The one item I keep repeating because it is so important is that if you are going to change hunting grounds from a familiar one to a strange one, terrain will influence where the deer are, where the food and water and cover will be, and how you must hunt. You have to train yourself to read it all quickly and to put the puzzle together effectively whether you are in heavy forests of the North, hardwood bottoms or swamps of the South, mountains of the West, or deserts of the Southwest.

Still the food, weather, cover, and water formula will always be intermeshed. During an unusually balmy fall, a hunter goes to Utah after a mule deer. The downward migrations, he knows, take place annually at about the same time. But not this fall. The unseasonably warm weather at timberline keeps the bulk of the deer out of his reach and his hunt perhaps is ruined. He could have saved that hunt by checking the weather and planning for later. However, is this instance attributable to weather, or terrain? Really it is a combination of both.

Let us say that rain begins as deer season opens. The drizzle is horribly uncomfortable. But is it to deer? Check the temperature. Fat deer with plentiful food forage along unconcerned on a drizzly, chill day. This weather is really a *break* for a hunter. He may shiver and get soaked but he can also move quietly.

What about the moon influence? I suppose this has to be classed under "weather" for lack of a better category. Some hunters scoff, some swear the moon influences deer hunting. I'll go with the latter. I am positive that during bright nights deer feed more avidly than on dark ones. They can see little better at night than you can. They depend on their ears and nose. But on moonlit nights they move around without inhibition. This makes for poor dawn and dusk hunting. Much depends, of course, on when the moon rises and when it sets. But by and large the dark of the moon and the small slivers of moon furnish the best hunting.

I have some regard also for the Solunar Tables of John Alden Knight, now deceased. These are based on the pull of the moon, the tides. Tidal effect is as great inland as at the seashore, except you cannot observe it. Knight firmly believed that the pull influenced activities of wildlife—and perhaps people also. I have fished trout by the Tables often. Given normal conditions of weather, barometer, stream, etc., I am convinced the major and minor feeding periods Knight worked out are applicable, and that they have some use for deer hunters. The annual updated booklet, indicating corrections for your longitude, is available from book stores and on magazine stands. As I write this, *Field & Stream* magazine publishes the tables for each month. I used to check on deer activity when I was driving into the woods to go trout fishing. If I saw deer up and feeding or moving at two p.m., and a major feeding period for trout was indicated to begin then, I'd bet the trout would be active. Usually they were.

Switches in temperature may launch deer movements. But this also may be dependent upon terrain. On a warm day with deer bushed up, a sudden cooling and overcast may have them all out and feeding within the hour, even at midday. Or the effect may be only at higher altitudes. That's usually where the biggest deer will be anyway, in any terrain. On those rare and not wholly explainable days when deer move all day under leaden skies, great hunting is at hand. The more deer move, the better your odds, because opportunities soar.

It is possible that the barometer may have some bearing. I am constantly on the verge of letting myself be convinced that in any hilly to mountainous country the barometer not only influences deer activity but also the level where they will be found, i.e. in the valleys or on the ridge tops. You should not discard these theories. They may be difficult to prove, but the wildlife student with the open mind is the one attuned to learning. When I was a kid people were saying the automobile wouldn't last. I was thrilled seeing my first ones, in the somewhat isolated country where we lived. I thought they were here to stay and it wouldn't surprise me if I was proved right!

It is amusing to note that fisheries biologists have done studies that "prove" barometric pressure has no effect whatever on quality of fishing. And meanwhile others have done similar studies that prove that it does. Fishing quality, remember, is based only on *feeding* activity. I had the idea one time to see what correlation there might be when fishing my own small lakes for bass, between what I caught and how many deer I saw moving around. Then I got thinking about the old saying, "Wind from the east—fish bite the least." Such a wind is usually indicative of a sliding barometer or one at a steady low, and it means a storm may be on the way.

Deer feed heavily many times before a hard storm. But—and this is important—there seemed to be a direct correlation between a slow downward slide of the mercury and little activity of either bass or deer, and just as direct a correlation between a plunging barometer and high fish and deer activity. The subject, for curious deer hunters, may be worth pursuing. On a high, steady barometer, or a low, steady one, look for only modest movement of deer to forage. On a slow rise or slow fall, ditto. On a swift rise or fall, look for heightened activity. Normal movement will occur on a medium high or low that holds steady. I'm not going to guarantee these statements—but I intend to keep checking further at every opportunity. There are very definitely days when deer are all up top on ridges or hills, others when they are in valleys. Is this a barometric influence? No one is certain. But on a day when you find good bucks down low, hunt there, and vice versa.

A few basic rules of deer movements are as follows. Most deer, of either variety, move up—if there is any "up"—when they are jumped. There are some interesting variations. A muley jumped in a deep coulee with steeply eroded sides will go up the slope like a squirrel. There may be open flat for 300 yards on top and then a steep shale butte. The deer will have its sights set on that butte as "safety" and will race all the way across spang in the open to reach it. A whitetail jumped from the same location will dodge around several bends, running on the bottom of the coulee. It may go up then, or it may not.

In habitat where whitetails and muleys live in the same or comparable cover, they will act about the same when jumped. Edges and stream courses will contain them, but the whitetail will invariably be more adamant about putting long distance between it and the hunter before it stops, and of never leaving the cover. Any saddle in a ridge large or small is an absolutely natural passageway for deer. I remember a fine whitetail I killed in the northwoods one fall by standing in such a passageway above a stream course. This saddle was not fifteen feet wide and the ridge was not over ten feet above it. Interesting is the fact that I heard the deer splash across the river. It came to the ridge. But it did not cross. It turned and came

In many parts of Western deer range it pays to work eroded gullies, either on foot or mounted.

down the ridge to the saddle and then crossed! I shot it at exactly seven feet.

If there are openings on either or both sides of a ridge but timber on top, deer will use the timber as a runway, curving around through it, whether spooked or not. One of the greatest experiences a deer hunter can have is to get to know a piece of deer range intimately—as the deer do—every tree, stick and stone. On our ranch I know *exactly* the traditional movements of deer, that is, the courses they take. Breeze will make a difference, of course. But the point is, you can watch these deer travel along and there are places they always use—and places they *never* use. I am not sure in every instance why. But I can tell you that if you know the places deer travel naturally—I don't necessarily mean beaten trails, but cover-to-cover spots—you can take anybody's money on where they will run when frightened. The routes will be exactly alike, direction differing with breeze or your direction.

There can be exceptions when you jump a deer at close range and it is panicked. But at nominal fright ranges this is almost an iron-clad rule. It is valuable to the hunter who has learned his territory. When a deer runs, you can predict precisely where it is going to go! Seldom have I met a hunter who was aware of this.

So—this is a moral concerning terrain. Learn thoroughly the terrain where you hunt most. In addition, train yourself to be able to relate the basics of deer movements to any new terrain in which you find yourself. And interpret the term "movement" broadly. I use it here to encompass not only physical movements to feed, water, comfort, and safety, but to include the nonmovement of resting deer.

CHAPTER NINE

How to Look for Deer

Finding a deer that you wish to try to bag is a many-faceted art. You must be schooled in the several traditional methods of deer hunting. You must recognize deer sign and by it be able to judge if deer are scarce or plentiful. But perhaps most important of all, you must be able to *see* deer. That may sound very elementary, but it is surprising how many hunters look right at deer and never see them. Many times this is because they are looking for a *whole* deer when most of the time only a part of a deer is visible and even then difficult to recognize unless you know what to look for.

Perhaps we should begin with signs, because these are what any hunter seeks first the moment he gets into the woods. We have already covered in detail, in Chapter Seven, the rubs and scrapes of bucks. These are of vital importance to the buck hunter. But other basic signs tell you whether or not deer are present and how abundant they are. These are tracks, droppings, flattened places where deer have bedded, and indications of feeding.

In areas where there are domestic animals, deer beds and calf or sheep or goat beds can be confused. However, bed spots are worth noting for two reasons. They can tell you where deer are habitually bedding down, and hint at their sizes and sex. I have seen thickets where grass was underneath that had dozens of flattened patches that were quite obviously deer lie-ups. The trouble here is that you can't tell much about which deer made them, bucks or does. If you discover three together and two seem to be smaller than the third, this will probably be a bedding sign made by a doe and twin fawns. Check out carefully all the spots that seem perfect to you for buck bedding places—related to material we have already gone over. If you find several flattened spots at the head of a draw, or maybe only one that seems well used, it may be that a big buck habitually rests here.

In a dry swamp where tall grass grows with some shade overhead there may be numerous bed spots. Probably this indicates that a number of mostly antlerless deer and small bucks use the place. It can serve as a good stand. Get into it or near it well before dawn, before the deer go in to lie up. Or take a stand near it late in the day when they should be coming out. Or on days when prowling is possible make a sneak here in midday.

Look for bedding places in dirt or hollows in rock formations along ledges or rimrocks. They will at least tell you deer have been here. But always try to check more thoroughly than just a cursory glance. I remember one time in the Arizona desert finding a place in brush where at first glance deer beds appeared to be numerous. Sifting some dirt from them through my fingers, however, showed me javelina bristles. It thus pays to make sure no other animals, wild or domestic, are leading you astray.

Tracks are certainly a good indication of deer. No tracks, no deer. Varying mediums—snow, mud, dust, shale—record tracks with varying degrees of clarity. These same mediums also can give you an idea of the age of tracks—or lie to you. For example, tracks in thick dust under a rock ledge out of the wind could be a year old and still plain. In certain soils, tracks made after a rain in soft earth will bake into perfect receptacles when the sun comes out. Morning dew may fool you by making them appear moist and fresh when they are a month or more old.

It does not take many deer to leave a lot of tracks. There is a place on our ranch where an exceedingly steep canyon comes to a head with

In desert soils, age of a track is difficult to judge. But one should be able to distinguish between small deer, left, and javelina, right. Javelina tracks are more rounded.

a straight drop too long for deer to use. So all deer in this area that wish to go from one side to the other move in a half-circle on level ground around the canyon header. There is seepage here. Thus, tracks in moist to wet earth show plainly. The spot is cut to pieces with tracks. It might appear that a hundred deer walk here. Probably ten or twelve do.

At water holes in country where watering locations are scarce, the earth will be similarly cut up. If there is a large enough expanse, you can learn much from a place like this because you can separate all the small tracks from the large ones. Large tracks obviously are made by large deer and one of them may be one you want. Be careful, however, not to misread some of the tracks. Once I had a friend strange to arid country tell me excitedly that the fawn crop must have been tremendous. He had been checking a waterhole—and misreading javelina tracks for small deer tracks. Javelina tracks are unmistakable; the toes are blunt and rounded.

The track of a walking deer. Don't waste time trying to determine if it's a buck or doe.

In foothill country where antelope are found along with deer, their tracks are sometimes easy to confuse with deer tracks. Most are chopped off at the rear, but some cannot be differentiated. So are the tracks of domestic sheep and goats, although usually the inner curve of the toe is more abruptly concave and the outsides not as smoothly rounded. Cattle tracks, of course, are no problem, although if you are after deer and elk both a tyro can mistake calf tracks for elk tracks.

One seldom has need to try to distinguish between whitetail and mule deer tracks or between mule deer and Columbian blacktail, even where two of the species live on the same range. And it is a good thing. It cannot be done reliably. An Easterner used to seeing the trim tracks of a whitetail might believe he was making the distinction in mule deer country. But it is only that the recording medium and the terrain in which the deer move are so different. Mule deer tracks in rocky country may appear toe-rounded and rough and splayed. The hoofs are worn from the rock. Whitetail tracks in the same country will look the same.

You can distinguish between the tracks of running whitetails and running mule deer, if the imprints are in proper material. The galloping whitetail going all out places the hind feet at each jump *ahead of* the tracks left by the forefeet. The fore dew claws are closer to the hoof than the rear ones, and if they show (as in light snow or mud) it is easy to tell which feet left which tracks. Mule deer running tracks show all four feet close together but the front feet ahead.

A great many hunters like to believe they can tell a buck track from a doe track. Some fair guesses can be made, but there is no way to be absolutely certain. A buck, some say, drags its feet. Well, in snow or soft earth even a fawn drags its feet. The buck track, some claim, is larger and more rounded. A better way to say it is that *some* buck tracks are larger, and *some* are more rounded. A buck, the legend goes, being heavier, sinks down farther. Maybe. In mud. One time in northern Michigan I saw two deer weighed, an old doe that was 135 pounds, and an excellently antlered buck that was 150. Just out of curiosity a friend and I closely compared the feet. Cut off, you could not tell which came from which. I doubt if the minor extra poundage would embed tracks with enough difference to allow distinction. A hunter might make a right *guess* two out of three, or three out of three, or none out of three.

Certainly a lone deer with an extra-large track that left a plain impression may well be a buck. And two tracks, one large and one medium, during the rut may mean a buck and doe traveling together. An apparently huge track in melting snow can fool you. It may have been so-so, but the melt enlarged it. In my opinion the greatest value of tracks when one is looking for deer are as signs that they are present or have been present, and to tell you if does and fawns and small bucks made them all or if possibly a big mature buck was also present.

I once knew a man from Minnesota who claimed he could get on a buck track and "walk the deer down." I do not disbelieve this. But I hate to think of the labor involved. Even this gentleman spotted his buck first and then took its track. He knew better than to pick up a track from scratch, imagine it was a buck track, and follow it. For one thing, the wandering deer might have meandered several miles from where the track was intercepted.

I've never tried walking a buck down. A number of hunters have, and some, at least as they tell it, have been successful. The scheme is to jump a buck, take its track, and walk steadily after it. This has to be done in snow because no other medium will hold a track well enough to allow steady pursuit. Presently the buck is jumped again. After several times, it realizes the hunter is doggedly on its trail. It begins evasive action, circles back around behind for a look perhaps. Presently there is the hunter again, still on the trail. In due time, if the hunter is tough enough, he gets close enough for a shot. The deer makes an error, or becomes weary itself. Interesting, I'm sure, but a difficult way to look for deer.

Tracks are invaluable signs when attempting to follow a wounded deer. In snow they show plainly enough, but in dry country each one must be picked out. Even a mortally wounded animal, depending on where it is hit, may not bleed much. Always when working out such a track, mark a spot where a drop of blood is found so you can go back if need be to start over. I always carry a big wad of toilet paper or facial tissue in hunting coat pocket anyway, and it doubles for trail marking. Note well that in strange country it is a good idea to hang such markers over or near a

Where waterholes are scarce, a check of tracks will tell you much about how many deer and what sizes are using the spot.

gutted deer if you have to come back for it. Markers should be high enough and in a place where they are easily seen from some distance.

I want to interject here a few notes about a rather distasteful subject, but one important to a hunter. This concerns blood sign on the trail of a wounded deer. Examine very closely the blood or material left along the trail and often you can deduce rather accurately where the deer is hit and how it will react. If there is paunch material, the case is a bad one. Don't crowd this deer. Let it lie down an hour or more. It can go for miles. If blood has light-colored frothy bits in it, probably the lungs are harmed and the deer won't last long. One of the worst signs, after a shot at a standing deer, is to find that the tracks where it stood look as if the forefeet had slid sideways at bullet impact and there is a small amount of dark lines of blood obviously mixed with saliva on the ground. This deer in all likelihood has been shot in the jaw and will be very difficult to get, but it will most certainly die.

In some places in my part of the country, ranchers train dogs especially to run down wounded deer. A friend picked up a huge jaw-shot buck just that way a few years ago. One man I know of had an old, burly cow dog trained to run down wounded deer, and it would get to the deer and lie down beside it and stay there, baying occasionally until the owner came. It might be a good idea if dogs were legal for following wounded deer in every state.

If there are bone chips in material where the deer was hit or they appear soon after on the trail, probably it has been hit in a leg. This is not infallible, of course. But if little blood shows it is fairly certain to be a leg wound. If you shoot at a deer running straight away—a really bad idea anyway unless it is a trophy you desperately want—don't be too hasty about giving up. Not a drop of blood may show, yet the deer may be lying dead within a hundred yards.

I recall one time hunting in snow in the North with a friend, prowling a dense cedar swamp at the end of a hard storm. We jumped a good buck and my partner shot at it impulsively. It did not appear hit. There was no blood. Since we were going that way anyway, we followed along on the track. Seventy yards or so farther on we saw a single drop of blood on the snow and were puzzled. The deer lay within thirty feet of us, stone dead. It had been hit straight in the rear. The bullet went on forward into the lungs. The deer bled internally and left no trail except that single drop.

It seems to me that deer droppings are often a better indication of deer abundance than are tracks. Walk along through forest or on an open slope and the soil or ground cover may be such that tracks do not show readily. Droppings will. I recall a hunt I made a few years ago in the West in a place that had been highly touted to me. The first day out I walked all day and never saw a single pile of deer dung. I told the others that I felt the deer population was exceedingly low. In four days of hunting not one of five hunters even saw a deer.

Droppings quickly tell you a lot about deer. Perhaps you find a spot under or in cover of a type that might form a good bedding area. There are droppings all over the place. When deer bed down for a period of hours, they get up and move at intervals, and during these "stretching" periods the bowels are usually activated. In a few minutes the deer lies down again. If a great many of the droppings are small, and a few larger, you can bet that does and fawns use this spot. A place where droppings are numerous and all of a size may well be the lie-up of a big, secretive buck.

It may interest you to know that in some scientific studies biologists make deer population surveys through droppings. A friend of mine in New Mexico whom we kidded a lot about his job was supervisor of a crew doing just that one year. Each man carried a spray can of yellow paint. Each had a plot of range to cover systematically. Every time he found a pile of droppings, he sprayed it. When existing piles had been sprayed, they started in counting fresh ones. They knew approximately how many piles per twenty-four hours each deer would leave. By continued spraying they had down rather pat the number of deer using this range. We told the supervisor that his job classification was "Deer Dung Painter Supervisor," a new category in bureaucratic pyramids!

On ranges where domestic sheep or goats are present, one must be careful to identify properly. It isn't always easy. Also, in checking ranges where deer spend the winters, if different from summer ranges, care must be taken not to misread. Best idea is to look when the range is dry, as at midday during dry weather. The reason is that when moist, as from dew, deer pellets may appear at a glance to be fresh but may not be.

I remember a hunter in Colorado who became very excited one fall because he had found a place simply littered with deer pellets. But he hadn't seen any deer and he was perplexed. I went with him for a look. The first sign I saw were two discarded antlers, weathered and white. They had been dropped on this range the winter previous. This was a wintering range, and the deer were not down from the higher elevations yet. The pellets he had found were from the winter past. When dry they looked it, too.

When deer are on soft feed, the pellets are not individually formed. They are in a somewhat formless, soft lump. Such droppings usually indicate that they were left in summer. Not always, however; deer eating apples or comparable feed in fall may leave this sign. However, in most instances winter pellets will be just that, hard and individually formed. The deer are on dry forage. I go over all these little items because, as I have said several times, you cannot have too many facts about your quarry, and you may find great use for such knowledge in individual instances.

Browsing signs sometimes are valuable. In the North where poplar shoots may be abundant on a certain range, a keen observer will note places where they have been snipped off by foraging deer. If the cuts are fresh, undoubtedly deer are using the patches daily. The most striking illustration of browsing signs occurs where biologists have experimentally fenced off patches so that deer cannot get at them. Inside the high net wire, willow or poplar or other browse grows thick and high. Outside it is pared down. When you are scouting early for a place to hunt deer on their winter range later in season, always watch for browsing sign left from the previous year. New growth will have come on, but if many bushes edible by deer show signs of having branches snipped off, undoubtedly this is a concentration point in winter.

I stated in an earlier chapter that deer, particularly mule deer, feed heavily on lechuguilla in some desert situations. This is a tough-leaved, low-growing plant that appears in large colonies on rocky slopes. The deer work at the spiny leaves, getting them out of the way so they can eat the center of the plant and some of the leaf bases. Be sure to draw proper conclusions from feeding signs, however. Prickly pear pads, for instance, that show small scallops where some animal has eaten on them probably have been chewed either by pack rats or rabbits. Shredded pads strewn about have been ripped by the dog teeth of javelina.

So much for signs. How do you go about looking for and seeing the deer itself? First you have to learn that a deer is by no means as large standing up as the average hunter thinks it is or often imagines it to be. If you want to try a startling little experiment, go into any brushy cover and measure it. Walk through and see if it comes up even with your shoulders. An average man is under six feet, probably around five-seven to five-nine. This means that standing erect he will be 56 or 57 inches from ground to top of his shoulder. Brush this tall would be considered almost anywhere modestly low cover. Yet even a good-sized whitetail buck with its head up will be completely out of sight in it, and many mule deer will be also.

Mule deer foraging on lechuguilla. Know the foods, wherever you hunt.

A tremendous record-book trophy about to be collected in South Texas. To hunt low cover properly, you have to be well informed about how high a deer stands.

To this day, having looked at hundreds of deer with naked eye, binocular, scope, and long camera lens, my mind still keeps telling me they are *big*. And I have to keep reminding myself they aren't *that* big. Many small whitetails are no more than *30 inches* at the shoulder. Place a yardstick beside your leg and measure off 30 inches. If you are average height it won't even reach to your hip joint. A large whitetail may stand as much as ten inches taller at the shoulder. That's about to your belt line. Most mule deer are somewhat taller than average whitetails, but not all. Many will stand no more than a yard high at the shoulder, or a bit less. Big mulies will be from 40 to 42 inches at the shoulder. Granted, they *do* look big, and they *are* big. But they don't *stand as tall* as your mind's eye usually places them. If you stood up beside a mature muley buck its shoulder height would be just above your belt line, assuming you are of average build.

Now suppose that you are looking, with eye only, no glass, off there 200 yards or more. An animal 30 to 42 inches high at the shoulder won't look very large, will it? Yet many deer seekers are looking for that *big* deer way off yonder. In fact, looking distantly, while valuable, should be tempered. I've hunted with people in open areas particularly who were always looking way off and missing deer standing stock still and staring from fifty yards. Deer-looking should be like fly-casting for trout. Comb the nearby water first so as not to spook those close-in fish while trying for the long-cast trout!

It is astonishing how a deer that stands immobile spang in the open can be passed over by the human eye. Much depends upon the background, of course. Deer are not conscious of contrasts. That is, an animal does not select a place to stand so it will blend. It may happen to, and it may not. But the human eye, like that of the deer, sees motion quicker than mild color contrasts. Running whitetails seen distantly are spotted because their waving white flags call attention. Mule deer, which have whitish areas around the rump and tail, can be picked up moving or standing at great distance even with the naked eye, once you know what you are looking for. Because they are gregarious, invariably one or more of a group will be turned tail on or partially so. These pale spots show plainly. The alert mulie hunter is constantly seeking pale spots on distant slopes. Maybe they turn out to be rocks, but they are always worth glassing.

Of course, nine out of ten deer spotted by hunters are not seen as *whole deer*. The difference between a truly astute deer hunter and the so-so deer hunter, I have long maintained, is that the former never even looks for a whole deer, assuming he will recognize a whole one if he can see part of one. But what should one look for? Examples are all but limitless. In snowless country where it may be mild to warm, deer are commonly bothered by insects as they stand or lie in their beds. They flick their ears to drive insects away. I have glassed many a mockingbird as it flitted in brush because I caught a flicker out the tail of my eye. And I have also spotted a number of ear-flicking deer that I thought at first were mockingbirds!

One of my own boys taught me some years ago about the value of looking for deer legs. When Terry was about small-deer high he was following me around on a deer hunt and I was trying to teach him to prowl slowly and quietly. He tugged my arm and pointed. I saw nothing. Then I realized he was much lower than I was and bending down at that and looking under the cover. I slowly hunkered down to his height. As he pointed, sure enough I could see four deer legs. I could not see anything else. But by mentally computing where antlers, if any, should be, I found with my glass a tip of one. Further careful maneuvering picked up the ear of the deer and it became venison.

Deer legs are a giveaway because there is hardly any cover on the continent in which saplings of deer-leg size grow in twos or fours that straight, and that symmetrically. But here again you have to know how high you are looking. On a big deer the distance from ground to brisket may be as little as 22 inches—under two feet. You have to get down low to spot deer legs in cover.

Antlers are often a giveaway too, but again you have to know what you are looking for. Antler shapes are not at all like branch shapes, even though both can fool any of us. Anytime you see a branch, through your glass or otherwise, that appears curved, have a closer look. In other words, don't be embarrassed in front of other hunters to be wrong. One year in Ontario I hunted moose with an excellent guide who kept chiding me because I incessantly glassed uprooted trees—dark blobs far off on a lake-shore—from our canoe, wondering if they were moose. Then one day I saw this distant blowdown and he agreed it was and I said I'd glass it anyway—and it was a moose. That was the moose I collected, the only one seen on the trip!

There is an old saying among experienced hunters that most shapes in the woods—meaning trees and vegetation—are vertical. The bulk of a broadside deer even screened by vegetation is a horizontal outline that cries out to be examined. That is not all. The rounded rump of a deer looks like nothing else in the forest. The neck line ditto. A listening deer,

The sharp-eyed hunter seeks blocky horizontal shapes in cover that is chiefly vertical.

immobile with ears cocked, shows an inverted cone shape at the head that insists you examine it. A whitetail staring straight at you through a screen of cover still shows that white or light-gray circle at tip of lower jaw and the patch underneath it and at the throat. Any sharp deer hunter will instantly recognize this. True, rocks or stumps can fool you with any of these shapes. So—glass 'em anyway!

Deer antlers shine in the sun, and the more vigorous the deer and the better shape the antlers are in, the more evident the reflection. Sometimes you can spot the glint of sun on antlers at surprising distances. A deer standing in brush, let's say, has the antlers above the cover. As it turns its head, sun picks out the polished tines. When deer are in good condition, with coats smooth and healthy, there is a distinct shine on the body or rump, too. A deer in sunlight at the edge of a woods a long rifle

Always be alert to a situation like this, where low afternoon light makes hide and antlers shine.

shot distant really glistens, drawing instant attention of the observant hunter.

A phenomenon I have had the good fortune to photograph is the curious reddish glow in the low light of evening or oncoming dawn, as weak, yellowish illumination touches, especially by sidelighting, the curve of a deer's body. A couple of years ago I followed a buck with a camera and 300mm telephoto and shot pictures until close to full dark. Where the light touched the curve of the rump, or along the backbone, or even the legs, hair on the deer's outer coat stood up just enough to draw a brown-orange line of illumination. From about a hundred yards this was visible to the unaided eye. A hunter who knew what to look for could easily have spotted it. Then a scope (or in this instance the camera lens, which is comparable to a 6 × glass) could have picked up the animal in full relief.

On several occasions I have sat at evening where I could watch a pond or lake shore as the sun went down. With the sun at the side or partly backlighting, water will look leaden but reflect light well after the sun has dropped behind the timber. A deer feeding or drinking or moving along will be totally silhouetted against the pale hue of the water. This is a trick used to advantage to wring out the best possibilities for the last of the shooting light at evening.

On dull days deer are difficult to see, whole or in part. Most terrain on overcast days will have a drab overall gray-green hue. The gray cast of deer blends perfectly. On such days you must learn to glass far more carefully, and *slowly,* because it is easy to pass over even a whole deer. On such days, in fact, it is a good trick to look hardest just for "pieces of deer"—that throat and lower jaw patch, whitish insides of ears cocked toward you, the pale rumps of mule deer.

Always when there are light problems—very bright or somewhat dull—try your best to relate conditions to how best you can see what you are looking for. We've touched on keeping bright sun in the eyes of the deer when possible. But when the sun gets high and deer may lie or stand

A deer silhouetted against water at evening.

in cover there is another trick to utilize. Light from above or behind filtering down among large trees will tend to partially silhouette shaded deer against any background paler than they are. There are scores of times when by looking with or without your glass through fairly dense timber cover you will perceive that the grass or small brush of the floor is very pale, even tan. A deer standing in shadow will be outlined beautifully against this lighter hue. Always search such places carefully. The curve of an antler, the back line—some part of a deer may suddenly seem to leap out at you.

When deer are bedded they are usually the most difficult to see simply because they are so low. If I am buck hunting, I always think "antlers." A buck lying in tall grass may not realize that one of its tines or several tips show plainly. In addition to parts of antlers, the nose of a deer is often the "piece" that gives the whole deer away. A bedded deer will usually stay immobile, as we've discussed, hoping danger will pass. When it is aware of danger it will be looking in that direction—this means toward the hunter. The nose of a deer is wet. The more arid the terrain or hot and dry the day, the more the animal licks its nose. One year I thought I saw what could be the curve of an antler, then decided I was wrong, and just then I caught a subdued shine. The spot was rounded. It was also in the proper place, so in relation to what I'd thought was an antler it could be a deer's nose. Very careful examination with my binocular proved there was a nice buck bedded here.

Probably the classic example of shiny noses giving deer away can be seen in warmer climes where mule deer bed down in fairly open places. One deer season in Wyoming I was working a series of hills that were rather barren but dotted here and there by low, gnarled junipers. The day was hot. The sun was so bright that in this light-colored country shade from the small junipers was utterly black in contrast.

With me was a Wyoming native who had hunted in the area many years. Pointing off across a canyon as we rested, he said, "There are four old discarded light bulbs under that small bunch of junipers yonder."

What an apt description! I'd never thought of it just that way. Suppose you were to toss a burned-out light bulb under a tree in deep shade where the sun was extra-bright above. It will pick up at least some reflection and seem to glow. That's exactly the way those four shiny spots looked— discarded light bulbs. Oddly, even with a binocular it was difficult to make out the deer. But we did. I've been looking for light bulbs ever since. Deer lying on a ledge overlooking a valley can be spotted from below in this same manner. The more they lick the nose, the more it shines.

Which of the basic hunting methods you use while looking for deer—stalking, standing, driving—will depend on several factors. One is weather. When the woods are tinder-dry and leaves are down, prowling after deer is a precarious undertaking unless wind is high. Wet weather welcomes the stalker. So does snow, if it is soft and loose. Another factor is the time of day. That is, early and late will be good sitting times, because deer are most likely to be moving then. The bulk of the day when deer are bedded is good stalking or driving time.

Incidentally, I have long disliked the term "still-hunting" because I discovered some years ago that numerous beginning deer hunters are confused by it. "Still-hunting" *could* refer, even though it doesn't in "book" usage, to either moving very quietly, i.e. "still," or sitting quietly. To avoid any possible confusion I have used "prowling" or "stalking" to mean moving about. Technically, stalking should mean moving into rifle range on a deer already spotted. The terms "sitting" or "standing" I have used to mean just that—taking a stand of some sort and watching for moving deer within range.

Obviously combinations of these methods are not only possible but often a good idea. A couple of years ago I was on a stand, hidden in brush, when I spotted what might be a good buck much too far away to shoot at. I crawled through some brush to get a ridge as cover and made a sneak to within range. As it turned out I decided not to shoot. But I could have taken the animal easily. Of course, meanwhile I probably messed up my original stand, for I spooked several nearby deer. However, those are the breaks.

Some hunters are adamant stand hunters. Some simply cannot abide sitting on a stand more than a few minutes. I'm quite certain there is no way to prove which is the better method. The best one is the one used on a certain day when you collect a deer that makes you happy! I said earlier in this book that the old rehash about stalking, standing, and driving and which is best becomes less and less consequential as you gather more and more *knowledge about deer.* You simply fit the method to the situation at hand. If deer are not moving around it is pretty darned silly to sit behind a bush waiting for one, unless you just like to sit behind a bush better than you like to hunt a deer. If they need to be located in their resting places, then there are two ways to do this, by prowling, or by driving to chouse them out.

It is impossible to tell anyone precisely where to sit, or stand, to kill a deer. Odd as it may seem, thousands of hunters simply pick a spot that as they say "looks good." Does it "look good" for some specific reason related to deer sign, such as a scrape or a lot of rubs or because much movement of deer is indicated here by sign or because there is an especially desirable variety of forage here? Or does it "look good" because you can see a long way and it's comfortable? In our foregoing chapters you have all the bits and pieces of the jigsaw, which can be fitted together to add up to what is or is not a good stand. Even then, however, if a spot adds up perfectly but you deduce that for one reason or another deer are not likely to move much (bright moon period), then you probably should forego sitting and take off on the prowl.

One point about stands really does concern comfort. I do not mean that your own comfort should be unduly considered just for its own sake. Any deer hunter has to learn to suffer heat, cold, rocks, thorns gracefully! But when you have selected the general spot from which you are convinced you can waylay a deer, then select your standing or sitting place with all the comfort you can find at that place. A sharp small rock under your backside will keep you hitching around. Twigs in the way of vision will have you moving, too. The more comfortable and content you are, where you can see well and not be seen, the less you will move during the tedious hours of staying on a stand, and thus the less chance that you will be discovered by a deer.

In the part of Texas where I live presently, deer blinds are common. I've described them earlier. Some are very high—twenty feet or more— fashioned like small buildings on stilts, with sliding windows, comfortable chairs, the works. I was in a deer blind one time on a certain ranch that had a gas heater, a urinal, and a telephone for calling the other blinds or the headquarters! This is sort of comic-opera deer hunting. However, in brushy cover and in mixed cover where a hunter must get above the lower story to see much at all, tree seats, available in easily portable form, are common nowadays. They are not legal in all states, and in some the legal height above ground is specified. For brush country such as South Texas has, the permanently placed seat is now marketed by several firms. This is usually some form of a tall steel tripod with a comfortable swivel seat and foot rest perched at the top. Some of these even have little cubicles to protect the hunter from the weather and to hold in his scent better and shroud his movements.

A stand of this sort looks out over a large area. Some stand hunters like to pick such a spot at random in rolling or hilly woodland or mountains, a place not especially selected because of nearby deer sign but simply one that covers a lot of territory. A lot of deer are killed by this somewhat

Elaborate blinds like this are used in some states, especially Texas.

hit-and-miss method. But having a *reason* for a certain stand selection kills more. There are lots of acres which deer seldom move across and only a few corridors they habitually follow. The pinpoint method based on knowledge beats shotgunning it, in my opinion.

It seems to me the most important admonition I can make regarding hunting methods is that you should not become stereotyped. Always remain flexible so far as approach is concerned.

You may drive along a back trail, for example, or ride horseback in wild country and constantly glass for deer, then get down and make a stalk when you see something you like. That entire method might be called "stalking" I suppose. Don't plan, incidentally, on sneaking up on deer too handily while on horseback. Some hunters believe deer aren't spooked by horses. Don't you believe it! They'll run first and wonder what made the sounds later! Even wilderness deer are disturbed far more by horsebackers than by a vehicle, curious as that may seem.

If you are riding or driving and don't see deer, then make up your mind to switch to trying to move them. As I said earlier in the book, one of my favorite methods is sneaking very quietly, rather than forcibly moving deer by driving them from cover. The satisfaction of a good buck collected in its bed is great. But you *must* learn in this instance how to make such sneaks. Of course in open country you may have glassed and spotted the deer, then laid a plan for the stalk, keeping yourself covered and with the wind right until you are close enough. But chiefly when I think of prowling I mean just starting out in good country and finding a deer. This requires some *walking* knowledge that is seldom used elsewhere. Basically it requires the patience to take one step at a time, checking where each boot will be placed to make no sound. Then another, and another, incessantly listening and staring.

You may take an hour to move a quarter-mile or less, or a half-mile. You may take sixty careful steps, then with "that certain feeling" slowly ease down, hunkering to listen and peer for ten minutes. Any small pocket that may hold a deer must be combed thoroughly with a binocular.

Never use your rifle scope as a binocular. This is a ridiculous practice of some hunters. It requires raising and lowering the rifle. Awkward! Deer-alerting! Carry your glasses on a short strap so they lie on the middle of your chest, not dangling and floppy on your paunch. I use a length of elastic with hook and eye at the ends. Loop it around the center post on the binocular, run the ends around under your arms and snap the elastic in back. This holds the glass flat against you, yet allows raising it easily to look through. Today you can buy copies of this idea for as high as ten bucks. I was using the simple elastic twenty years ago and in fact wrote of the idea at the time in several magazines. A deer hunter wearing his binoculars flopping on his belly tells much about his prowess.

At any rate, a binocular banging around and whacking brush as you sneak is abominable. And believe me, for this sort of "thrill hunt" you will need to bend and crawl and duck under limbs.

Just keep telling yourself when prowling that there is *no hurry*. If you have done your homework properly according to our preceding chapters, you already know where you are going to look, and why, and when, and for what. Obey all the rules for remaining unseen yourself. Imagine you are a mountain lion trying to grab a buck in its bed. If you happen to make some untoward sound—a clink of rock or snap of stick—

freeze right there. Listen and look and don't move for ten minutes. I've observed how deer that were unseen yet in easy range would lie for that long after such a disturbance, then carefully ease up into view on all fours and silently start to fade out. A hunter may feel that he has really blown it when he makes a noise, and so he goes right on making more, saying, "The hell with it." Don't do it! Wait and let the woods settle down. The wait can bring you a shot!

This sneaking approach, and rattling, are in my estimation the highest and most exhilarating arts in deer hunting. The drive can be, too, sometimes, if you plot everything so that success comes of it. However, I always approach writing about deer drives with some hesitation. Hunters must understand that unless properly planned and executed, deer drives can be exceedingly dangerous. A great many accidental shooting deaths have occurred on them.

Drives in flat country with dense cover, where a line of blockers awaits deer driven out by another line of oncoming hunters, are, to me, anathema. If one man gets out of line, ahead of the others, he can be endangered. Such drives are often made with a lot of noise. The shooters get on their stands, placed to intercept deer driven out of a river bottom, or a pine planting or a large thicket or woodlot. The drivers start on the other side, and shouting and beating on tree trunks, they come through. Unless drivers stay close together where they can watch each other, or use maps and signals, they seldom are able to keep a straight line. And sharp deer double back behind the line. The only safe way to handle such a drive is to make a rule that nobody in the driving line is to shoot in the direction of the drive, and none of the standers is to shoot until driven deer have passed them. The fact is, I cannot write of this type of drive with any enthusiasm because I dislike the whole idea and I think it is dangerous in some measure regardless of how well executed.

Drives in canyon country can be handled much better. As we've said, disturbed deer will usually go up. Thus, before a canyon drive is begun there are shooters put on strategic locations along either side of a canyon rim, or on narrow canyons just on one side. They are in position to shoot deer as they top out, or as the deer move below them. Meanwhile, drivers coming up the canyon from its mouth may have chances at deer moving ahead of them, and these offer safe shots as long as the drivers restrict shooting to the canyon floor.

The best way to make such a drive is to do it without any shouting or undue racket. Two or three hunters moving quietly upcanyon through cover, prowling just as quietly as they can move at a fair pace, will shove

One hunter can sneak along the bottom of a rough canyon like this, driving deer toward the end of the canyon where another hunter is stationed on top.

deer out not in a panic but slipping ahead and listening behind. They make proper targets for those up on top, and though some deer may try to double back, most will trot ahead and slanting up the canyonside trails.

The type of drive I enjoy most is the one in which few hunters are involved. I explained earlier how John Finegan uses his slingshot to roust whitetails out of steep, narrow canyons. This type of "drive" is completely safe. A couple of hunters, usually together, stand up on top watching. Without the slingshot, a single hunter prowling around in comparable small canyons can shove deer out and up to others on top. And both can shoot safely as long as they abide by the rule to "shoot flat." That is, the man in the bottom shoots only on his level or slightly above, those on top shoot at deer topping out or near to the top. On most such drives the single hunter in the bottom—or two hunters—can easily be kept in sight all the time by the others.

Extremely sporty drives of this sort can be made in open mulie country that is treeless or nearly so and cut by deep gullies and erosions. A single man walking the bottom can often bag himself a deer on his level, while shoving others up the sides to a hunter or hunters on top. Most such eroded places are narrow enough so the range across the top is not far. Thus hunters, if there are several, should all stay on the same side, to avoid any remote chance of danger to each other. They stay some distance ahead of the man in the bottom, and he whistles occasionally to pinpoint his location.

Lakeshores, where land rises rather sharply, make good places to drive. The deer will go up at an angle ahead of the drive. And there is obviously only one way to go. A hunter or hunters atop the lakeside ridge can be placed to intercept. Steep cliffs in mountain country with rock jumbles and juniper near the bases and with occasional escape routes upward where trails cut them offer much the same type of opportunity. If the terrain is open outward from the face, the deer will move along the base and up the escape routes to the top.

On our ranch we have one drive we make each season at least a couple of times. It is an example of a wholly safe driving operation. There is a steep hill and ridge heavily covered with mature cedar that runs for possibly a quarter-mile. We discovered that the cedars atop this east-west ridge are a favorite bedding place. At the east end this ridge drops off steeply down to a small open field. On its south side the ridge drops away quite steeply over the entire length and into a couple of small canyons. The mouth is off our property.

We locate a single shooter down on the edge of the small east-end field. Then we park a vehicle on the south side of the ridge in such a position that almost any deer trying to come off that way will see it and be discouraged. Then two of us simply walk the ridge toward the field.

Usually it is my two boys and I who do this. The two of us on top have a no-shooting agreement. The only one who is to take any shots is the one by the small lower field. And he is to shoot only on his level as deer, if any, come off the steep ridge and down to him. We who walk the ridge do no shouting. We drift the deer off the ridge. Some escape, getting off on the south. And after we've made this drive once or twice it won't work again. The deer get wise to us. But on the first time we have put as many as twenty-nine deer past the one in the field. Mike, my older son, winding up a long "dry" season, took two good deer one noon late in the season as Terry and I pushed them down to him.

On drives, wind direction doesn't always make much difference, except in flat country. Then drivers must move with the wind, else the deer would scent the blockers quickly. With hunters on stands high above, as in canyon drives, the moving hunters in the bottom can move with or against any breeze. In most instances it is better to move downwind. That way the deer get the drivers scent, know where they are, and are not quite so inclined to double back behind where they would lose contact.

There are mule deer drives that can be made in full safety and with uncanny success potential. Here is a good illustration of what I have in mind. As any mountain hunter knows, a large mesa may have numerous side canyons that are broad at the bottom perhaps but narrow as they reach the rim of the mesa. One year in Utah I was riding a horse and Bid Clark, a supervisor for the game department and on vacation, was in his pickup. We were in the Dixie Forest. We dropped the horse trailer off at the bottom of a huge mountain atop which meadows and aspens covered an undulating mesa. I mounted and Bid told me which big draws would probably be best. He then left and drove far back around, heading up a trail to the top of the mountain.

Up on top, as he knew, there was a place where two of those huge draws "topped out." But where they reached the top neither was more than a crease on the slope and both came out almost together. By taking a stand in aspens a short distance back, he could watch the "swags" or saddles where each draw came to the mesa. Mule deer that are not especially frightened will nonetheless keep moving on up once they are disturbed below and continue to hear a disturbance. In mountain country, the sound of a man on a horse can carry a long way.

High in the Dixie Forest in Utah. The deer, disturbed on the mountainside, came up a draw and "topped out."

I rode off toward the base of the mountain, and when I figured Bid had had time to get situated, I simply began hunting. Along with heavy timber there was a good bit of brush. I crisscrossed back and forth, trying to jump a buck in a spot where I'd have enough room to bail off, haul my rifle from the scabbard, and fire. The horse was used to shooting. No problem on that score—but if you are riding a strange one, don't bet on what it will do when you fire!

At any rate, I suppose I moved a number of deer on the mountainside. As it happened I did not get a shot, although I saw several deer. But Clark, far out of my hearing up on top, picked off a beautiful big buck that I started up to him. It came trotting out of one draw, pausing to listen behind it to pick up my brush-popping mount.

If you are an any-deer hunter, undoubtedly by selecting your observation post properly you can collect a deer more quickly sitting than by any other method. But again, when deer aren't moving, you should know how to go after them. A windy day that makes deer jumpy nonetheless covers some of your prowling sounds. The drive, plainly, is for use when deer are moving little or not at all. The drive can be effective. And sometimes, as in dense coastal blacktail cover, it is about the only way to operate. But *outwitting* a deer either by taking a proper stand and waylaying it, or sneaking up on it, will always offer the greater satisfaction.

CHAPTER TEN

Equipment and Making the Kill

Up to this point we have concentrated on learning every fact about deer that can possibly relate to hunting. Now we come to the point where we must talk about equipment and how to use it. Probably it sounds anticlimactic to say it, but if you have done your homework properly, regardless of present-day fantasies and advertising agonistics about those "must" guns, loads, boots, underwear, knives, underarm deodorant to use while deer hunting, and shaving lotion and bourbon needed after, choice of equipment as such makes only a minor amount of difference. How you use it makes a lot!

Consider the early-day deer hunter. He had a muzzleloader, no scope, no binocular. His boots were of the roughest sort, or perhaps he wore moccasins. Special clothing would have seemed preposterous to him. He took to the woods in buckskin or homespun, usually well worn and ragged and no doubt often odorous. He could not shoot very far, nor with the accuracy of modern rifles. Thus his main chores were to outwit the deer and place his shot properly. These he did—or went hungry.

Certainly there are among all items of our modern hunting equipment some types that are better suited than others to the purpose. But for decade after decade now we have been deluged with voluminous inane make-problem chatter: which gun and which load are supreme, whether or not an extra grain of XC6Y4 powder and primer Z will do the job better, especially with a thumb-holed monkeywood gunstock and a Gewgaw brand trigger guard . . . so on and on to utter confusion and downright foolishness.

It is a fine thing to be an avid gun bug. Or a glassy-eyed handloader immersed in that hobby. But none of this has much to do, really, with successful deer hunting, any more than golf and chess do. I believe it is valid to say that it really doesn't matter very much what gun you use, as long as it falls within the law. In other words, translating that, I'm saying that it is best to keep your varied hobbies separated. Hunting is one. The others are adjuncts. What *is* important is how ready you are *at the crucial moment* with whatever gun you happen to have at hand, and how cool you keep and *how proficiently you use the particular tools at your command.* There are Indian guides in northern Canada who have never used any rifle except a .30/30 to kill moose, and have never shot one except in the ear. Thousands of deer have been killed—a good many still are annually, unfortunately—by poachers using .22 shorts.

This is not to say I recommend the .22 short for deer or the .30/30 for moose. It is simply an illustration to show you that the *man* is the important part of the equation. Any gun off the rack will shoot better than 95 percent of hunters can hold. That poacher with the .22 is quick and accurate with it; he doesn't fire indiscriminately, but only at ranges measured usually in mere feet and only when he has a chance at the ear or middle of the forehead. This is a matter of personal discipline. The pioneer did the same. He could not reload quickly. He got close, waited for the shot *he wanted,* and then was mighty deadly.

Over past years I have bagged a great many deer. In some years when doing magazine assignments and traveling into several states in a single fall, the score has been run up as high as eight in a season. One comes to have a rather practical outlook after all that, and this is what I intend to communicate here in this chapter. So if you are anticipating a batch of intricate statistics, stop here.

Many modern hunters go really laughably overgunned for deer. I've seen them carry enormous magnums out after small whitetails here in the hill country where I live. They want to be sure "to anchor 'em"—and undoubtedly gut 'em simultaneously. Others do likewise when after mule deer. It just isn't necessary. Conversely, some others are light-caliber worshippers, and are as bad. The beautifully accurate little .222, for example, has been touted in some places as a perfect deer rifle. It isn't. Sure it will kill deer regularly—in the hands of a hunter with experience and judgment. Others less wise do a lot of wounding with it.

In the world of guns, new calibers constantly appear. Many persons are interested in guns, and it is necessary for manufacturers to keep new items coming onto the market as a spur to business. Some caliber innovations have been valuable, some not. Spurred by media advertising and gun writing, hunters constantly take up new fads in deer rifles and then quickly drop them for some newcomer. But I believe we may best arrive at what may be considered a basis of adequacy by considering some of the older, standard calibers.

The long-popular .30/30 and the standard and properly renowned .30/06 and .270 are undoubtedly classic examples of good deer rifles. I personally have never been a .30/30 fan for the simple reason that I feel some other calibers offer the shooter a better and wider-ranging performance. There is no doubt, however, that for shots of average range the .30/30 shooting a 150- or 170-grain softpoint bullet is an excellent collector of venison. The .30/06 shooting a 150- or 180-grain bullet is one of the finest ever concocted, regardless of its age. The .270 with 130 or 150 grains is as good. If you will base a choice of caliber on these—that is, relate the ballistics of all others to them—you cannot go wrong.

For example, the .30/30 150-grain bullet leaves the muzzle at slightly above 2400 feet per second and carrying well above 1900 foot-pounds of energy. Out at 100 yards, sighted in for that, it will have a midrange trajectory slightly less than an inch high, and it will hit at 100 yards with 1360 foot-pounds of energy. The 170-grain bullet will leave about 200 feet per second slower, raise a bit higher en route, and carry a little less energy out at 100 yards. Past 100 yards the .30/30 begins to lose energy and velocity fairly rapidly, and to get a pretty big loop in its trajectory, which makes careful shooting and pinpoint placement at up to 200 and between that and 300 yards precarious, and energy in my opinion is comparably low. However, this old weapon that has been with us a great many years and undoubtedly will be for many more is a good short-shot deer rifle, preferably up to 100 yards or a bit more.

The .30/06 is quite a different proposition. The fact is, with the variety of loadings available for it, the '06 can efficiently take any species of North American big game, and has, even to the largest of the bears. Ditto for the .270. For big mule deer the 180-grain bullet in the '06 does a fine job. This is not an especially high-velocity rifle, but it is powerful. The 180-grain bullet leaves at around 2700 f.p.s., but with an energy of above 2900 foot-pounds. Depending on the type of bullet—and in this chapter I'm talking about standard average factory loadings in regard to all loads—it still lays down a wallop at 300 yards, moving along at from 1700-plus to above 2000 f.p.s. and with foot-pound energy ranging from above 1200 to around 1650 or more. Further, even way out here the loop at midrange is not bad, around 7 or 8 inches. Sighted at 200 yards it's about 3 inches high at midrange, which means you could hold easily on a mule deer's ribs anywhere in between without a quibble. The 150-grain bullet moves somewhat faster, packs a little less punch, but shaves the path down in flatness. For both big whitetails and big mule deer I prefer the 180.

Basic factory loads for the .270 have bullets of 100, 130, and 150 grains. The 130-grain has been an extremely popular load and is typical of what the .270 can accomplish. Muzzle velocity is around 3140 f.p.s. Clear out at 300 yards it is still moving at about 2400, and carrying 1660 foot-pounds of energy. At 200 yards, a long shot for most deer hunters, energy is 2000. Also at 200 yards, midrange trajectory is only slightly more than 2 inches, and with 300-yard sighting it is 5.3 inches. This is excellent performance.

Now it may seem odd to many readers that in a modern book about deer hunting I start off talking about deer rifles by using the .30/30, .30/06 and .270 as examples when so many newer ones are available. But for beginners and even some old hands rifles can be utterly confusing. What we need to arrive at is the answer to one question: What rifles, in the hands of a cross section of deer hunters, are *adequate* and have proved it with tens of thousands of successfully concluded hunts? Those oldies certainly answer well. With that basis, you know what is needed, and can go on from there by comparisons.

Beginning, for example, in the .22-calibers, I am personally a great fan of the .243 Winchester and its companion 6mm from Remington. The arms companies believe these are among the most accurate calibers ever conceived. I have killed many deer, both whitetails and mule deer, with the .243, using both 80-grain and 100-grain factory ammo and a number of 85- and 90-grain handloads. I have even at times considered the 80 (or 85) better than the 100 for absolute deadliness. The small bullet has a muzzle velocity around 3500 f.p.s., muzzle energy of almost 2200 foot-pounds. It is still traveling at over 2400 f.p.s. out at 300 yards and still carries over 1000 foot-pounds of energy out there. Further, it is a flat-shooter's dream, with a midrange of less than 2 inches at 200 yards, less than 5 at 300 yards.

I have killed Desert mule deer with an 85-grain handload in the .243 at an honest 375 paces, and made a dozen or more instant kills at 200 to 300. On whitetails it is just as lethal. Friends of mine use the 6mm on Rocky Mountain mule deer every year. I have killed black bear with the 100-grain bullet in .243, and friends have killed elk. I don't say this is an elk and bear gun. There may be times—and in hands of certain hunters—when it isn't even proper for big mule deer.

As a matter of fact, one thing I wish to emphasize here is that I do not intend to state what is the "perfect deer rifle." Or even which is "best." All of them do all right depending on how each is used and by whom, and there is no accounting for tastes. The .257 Roberts has been popular in some places. It has lost popularity recently. The .264 magnum, with which I had much experience a few years ago, is certainly an excellent rifle for long range and for large deer of either variety.

I see little need for using the several magnums in .300 caliber for deer. They sure do the job, but these are too much gun, in my opinion, more than is needed. They carry heavy recoil, and are all-round poor choices for average hunters. The .308 is fine. I've used one a great deal, with 150- and 180-grain loads. This, of course, is the NATO cartridge made available to hunters in the mid-1950s, closely comparable to the .30/06. The .35 Remington with its big 200-grain bullet was at one time highly touted as a great brush gun. More on brush guns later, but I'd just say that the heyday of the .35 is probably past. Some hunters like the .44 magnum with its big old plunker 240-grain bullet. I shoot one occasionally, but I can't get very enthused about such calibers. There is not much they can do that something smaller and more refined can't do better.

That scattering of calibers will give you a basic idea of what to found your choice on. Again, if you use as a measure the .30/06, the .270, and the old .30/30 you will get a heavy cross section of the bullet weights and ballistics that kill deer by hundreds of thousands throughout the entire continent every year. Then if you want to try a concoction of your own, or some other caliber, you know where to start. As one illustration, the

In dense brush shots can be tricky and often have to be fast—but a special "brush gun" isn't going to do the job unless the hunter is alert and ready.

.25/06 that has become popular and standard recently, although it started years ago as a wildcat, is a tremendously hot-shooting, lethal weapon for deer of all sizes and at long ranges when you need to reach out.

Arguments over "best" will never be settled. For what it may be worth to hear my general opinion, however, after having hunted from Maine out across the Great Lakes and Canada, the Midwest, South, West, and Southwest, I'll simply say that calibers giving you fairly high to extremely high muzzle velocity have immense advantages. Velocity combined with moderate bullet weight means a flat trajectory. That is important not just for extremely long shots. The real advantage is that you can sight in at from 200 to as much as 300 yards and still not have to worry unduly about any range in between or even past. With a slow, heavy bullet that describes a big looping course, you are in fair condition at short range but have little idea when things are moving fast and with excitement where to hold farther out. Shocking power also is high with fast bullets. No bullet, remember, large or small, "knocks deer down." The shock of the impact unhinges nerve ends and the animal falls down. "Knock-down power" is a term that shouldn't even be in hunter vocabularies.

Now let's look briefly at those so-called "brush guns." It is unfortunate the term ever evolved. The vision it conjures is of a rifle that fires a bullet true to aim through brush. Nice, of course, in theory, only it doesn't work very well in practice. Certainly a slow, large, round-nosed bullet like, say, the .35 Remington or the .44 magnum rips through brush in fair shape. But not once in ten times will such a bullet rip through *to point of aim* if the target is very far from the first twig struck. Many hunters, I'm sure, have been amazed to fire through a sapling, cutting it off and killing the deer standing twenty paces farther on. If you are sharp you won't interpret this performance to mean anything, least of all that you can do it every time. All bullets are deflected in varying degrees by anything they strike while in flight. A blade of grass can send a .22 short off point of aim. A pencil-sized twig can foul up the flight of a 240-grain .44-magnum slug.

Granted, the faster the bullet, undoubtedly the more easily it is deflected. But no experiments ever conducted have shown that there is any means whatever to deduce what a bullet—any bullet—will do consistently after it hits *anything* while in flight—grass, twigs, saplings, brush. And so the sometimes highly touted "brush calibers" may not exist in reality. The more you get depending on "shooting through brush" to get a deer, the poorer rifleman and hunter you become. And maybe also the more impulsive and dangerous.

You see, it is only one step from here to shooting at flickers of movement unidentified in cover, or at sounds, the good Lord forbid! What you might better do is forget the brush-rifle nonsense and grab the handle of the razor instead of the blade! You may not be willing to believe it until you try, but you can kill just as many deer with a .243 or a .270, scoped, in the Maine forest—and maybe more if you'll train yourself to be a real deer *hunter*—than you can with that so-called brush rifle, unscoped and short-barreled, that you shoot impulsively at the slightest quiver of deer hair through a screen of cover!

As a matter of fact, I have long thought that the worst hoax ever foisted upon the hunting fraternity many years ago was that ancient wheeze about the dense cover of the East requiring a brush gun, while in the West shots are long and wide open and a flat-shooting rifle is required. It would be interesting to know who concocted this pat little half-truth theory, which is plain garbage. It belongs in the category with the Southern myth about their cover being so thick they must use dogs. And the Texas hunters who claim in their dense cover they have to use stilt blinds and in some cases bait deer or they'd never kill one.

Eastern woodland cover is comparable to Great Lakes woodland cover. Neither is as thick, for example, as numerous stretches of coastal blacktail range on the Pacific coast. Deep South deer cover is in some places dense, granted. But the reason dogs have long been used and still are in some places is that this was a tradition. This was how early residents hunted deer. And they enjoyed it. And then when pressed they made excuses in order to keep their sport. I'll say personally that I can readily understand how exciting a dog chase is. I'm not discussing sportsmanship or morals. Who will judge? The deer is as dead stalked as run by dogs. As long as the herd is not overhunted I doubt it makes much difference how. It should, however, make a difference in the minds of individual hunters, and does. The Texas hunter who has never shot a deer except from a blind and over corn thinks he is a deer hunter and is happy, and maybe it is as well to have him tied down and not in the way. The landowner sets up such hunts because he doesn't want hunters walking around. The main point to be made is that cover actually makes little difference as to which gun you select—except possibly in length of barrel.

As an example, I have killed deer in heavy forest in northern Michigan with a .308, and used the same rifle in wide-open mule deer country in Wyoming and Montana during the early years of this caliber. You do not need, believe me, any special rifle (or separate ones) for Minnesota, or for Maine, for Arkansas, Louisiana, Arizona, or Idaho. A widely experienced deer hunter can tote the same gun from coast to coast, border to border, and be successful in all places. I really believe modern hunters are learning this. You definitely do *not* need one type for the East, one for the West. Do you know why this has been said for years? Somebody started it. Others took it up, repeated it, and embellished it. After a while it became "fact."

To illustrate how preposterous this old hokum is, consider that today ads and TV programs tout the short-barreled, lever-action "saddle carbine" as the gun of the Westerner who put the U.S. together and ate off the land. Meanwhile the gun magazines are still getting into ecstasies over this same gun as the only practical item for the "dense cover of the East." The saddle carbine was, and is, used to a great extent in the West. But one year my good friend Gage Holland, previously mentioned, and I had a shooting match between his tried-and-true saddle gun and my well-scoped .264. We had a good laugh. You can easily guess which was most effective. Mine. Indeed, the saddle gun was a rifle tuned to a time and a need, to stick in a short scabbard under your stirrup strap. It and the Eastern "lever thutty-thutty" were both born of need and what was known and available. Mostly they became popular in both places simply because they were economical and for no reason whatever of super appropriateness to the terrain. Today's Southern deer hunters hunt more and more with scoped rifles as dogs are outlawed on game management areas. And thousands use the same rifles in Vermont that they take to Colorado.

Thus, my theme is this: Select the rifle you want and like and shoot well, but choose wisely as to how you will use it. Pay no attention whatever to that old malarky about short, unscoped guns East, long, big-scoped guns West. Any well-built rifle that fits you and that you can shoot well and that is adequate for the chore will bag deer anywhere on the continent. But, the flat-shooting ones capable of long *or* short range will do it best, everywhere!

As an example, the longest range at which I have ever killed a deer where I could be absolutely sure of the distance was 456 paces, using a .264. This was a big whitetail, in the South Texas brush. One of the shortest shots I ever took was with the same gun, in the same terrain! I killed that one, too. In Western mountain muley hunting I have jumped deer at fifteen paces, and taken shots at several hundred yards. In the Great Lakes region I have seen situations where deer could be scoped at 300 yards—and others where they burst out at ten feet.

The only norm, therefore, that can possibly be conceived would be to say that very generally shots east of the Mississippi *may be* shorter than those west of it, but are not always, and that shots presented in the Pacific Coast Ranges closely approximate what *may* happen in the East. However, what has never to my knowledge been said is that a rifle efficient for the West can be just as efficient in the East, but a rifle that, as the old wives' tale has it, is suitable only for the East is by no means as suitable in the West. Therefore, select a rifle with all-round, all-terrain, all longitude and latitude capabilities, learn to shoot it—and you can hunt with confidence anywhere on the continent, and in general for other big game as well as for deer. This, mind you, now begins to eliminate to some extent the popular old .30/30 because it has its limitations. By and large, if you will take the .30/06 and the .270 as a main basis of comparison on which to found your choice of deer rifle, you need take no further advice from anyone. You are on the proper track, and you will be able to hunt for deer with confidence and success anywhere in North America.

So we come to rifle actions. There are four—the lever, bolt, slide, and auto. It is at least reasonably accurate to say that the best actions are those that have proved over many years the most popular. After all, a hunter has to like using a certain action or he would change it. The lever and the bolt are far and away most popular. Slide-action big-game rifles have never proved very popular, and for logical reasons. They are inclined to be heavy in front and a bit unwieldy. And accuracy has never been as high as in others. Currently a number of autoloaders are on the market, and a number of hunters carry them. The lever has had great popularity chiefly because a number of early rifles used this action.

Arms makers, the expert riflemen, very nearly unanimously claim the highest accuracy with the bolt action. It is also probably the most foolproof and strongest. Although I don't believe that there are any very black-and-white pros and cons about rifle actions, I personally would always choose the bolt. It is simple, easy to keep clean, and awesomely sturdy. And it is fast enough.

That last statement needs brief discussion. You can take bets with anybody that the hunter who selects a particular action because he can "work it fast and get off several quick shots" will be one of the poorest hunters and inexpert shots in the woods. Speed of shooting is a poor criterion for rifle choice. Fact is, the rifle is a weapon for pinpoint shooting, not spraying. The first shot is the one that always should count. If you handle that first one properly you won't need more. If you do need more, how *fast* you get them flying is in almost all cases inconsequential. Few if any hunters can shoot several fast shots with any accuracy at all. An old adage is, "If you don't have time to work the action and resight carefully, you don't have time, period." Therefore speed of action among those available should not figure importantly in your choice.

The sight or sights you use are a crucial part of the equation. It is a curious fact that even in today's modern hunting world there are hold-outs about scope sights. Here and there a hunter will claim scopes are just no good, or that he cannot learn to use one. Anyone can easily learn to use a scope. And in this age of advanced equipment the use of iron sights instead of a scope is the equivalent of using a horse and buggy instead of an automobile. There certainly are instances where iron sights can be handy—as for example when a scope is broken. But scopes of today are sturdy indeed, the "bugs" have been meticulously worked out over many years, and it is possible to state unequivocally that anything iron sights can do a scope can do better.

In the first place, front and rear sights on a rifle barrel require the bringing into line of three points: the two sights and the point of aim. A scope eliminates the tough part of that alignment. All one needs is to place the reticle center—crosshair or dot—on aiming point. One of the most ridiculous fallacies about using a scope is that it "makes you wobble." A hunter may say he uses a low-power scope because he "wobbles too much with higher power." He wobbles just as much whether he uses open sights or a high-powered scope. Only, the higher the magnification, the more he is aware of the "wobble." In fact, a good method of practice for super-accurate holding is to use a scope of 6× to 9× and to keep attempting to cut down unsteadiness.

Another and more important fallacy about use of a scope is that in thick cover a scope is useless whereas in open country it is not. If you will learn how to use a scope in heavy cover you will never hunt any other way. A scope, let's say, of 2½× will pick out small holes in brush or

This photograph was taken with a 300mm lens—comparable to a 6X scope. Exact openings for a shot are plain to see, but without a scope the shot would be very risky.

forest through which you can shoot. With open sights you would never see twigs that may deflect your bullet, whereas with the scope you do. To be sure, shots at deer running in heavy cover are somewhat tricky with a scope. It all depends on how expert you get in picking up moving targets. As one who is very skeptical of running shots anyway, I'm not sure there is a scope argument here. "Throwing" a shot through cover at a running deer is a rather inept gambler's game anyway.

Some of the late-model variable scopes are beautiful instruments for all kinds of deer hunting. One I use, for example, is a 1×-4×. With the ring turned down to 1× what you see is the same sight picture, only more clearly and with simple point of aim, that you would see with open sights. At 2× in heavy cover you can still aid your eye without high magnification. And with the 4× you can make 300-yard shots easily if you take a rest. In more open hunting I use a 3×-9×, and I have a habit of taking a careful rest, picking up my long-range target at 3× or 4×, then cranking up to as high as 9×. This may show you how much you "wobble," but it also shows your aim point very precisely even at 300 yards.

Because the variable scopes are so versatile, I would suggest to any deer hunter that he use one. The Pennsylvania hunter may claim that his 2½× or 4× fixed-power is all he needs. But if he travels some year to some other state where the shots may be longer and the country more open, he may wish he had variation. The 1×-4× is a good all-round bet. Some brands offer 1½×-4×. There are also combinations such as 1¾×-5×, 2×-7×, 2½×-8×, and several others. Scopes in the 2×-4× or similar class offer a compact sight. The 3×-9× types are in general somewhat larger. It is questionable that anything above 9× in a variable is practical for deer hunting. It should be noted that a scope is excellent for persons with various eye defects, because you can focus the eyepiece so that with glasses on or off, if you wear them, you have a clear, crisp view.

This is a good place to point out that any deer hunter should "get the rest habit." Very few riflemen are capable of holding accurately off-hand. Once in a while it may be necessary to shoot without a rest. But not often, if you use some imagination and ingenuity. Once as an example I lay flat on an open, rolling plain and used my belt knife in its sheath to form a rest. I gripped it snugly with point down on the ground, laid the rifle barrel across the top of my hand at grip point, while resting my elbow on the ground. I contrived a quite stable rest that way.

A rest can always be contrived somehow. The old-fashioned crossed-sticks method works fine, and a Western-style hat or a belt knife and sheath will do the job too.

There is almost always a limb or a stump, a sapling to grip, a rock, a cutbank—something on which to stabilize your gun barrel. You can even gently lay it through the crease in a Western-style hat placed on the ground. Always, of course, pad the barrel or fore-end beneath. Otherwise your rifle may not shoot accurately. I have trained myself so thoroughly about the rest habit that I seldom even accept a shot nowadays unless I can find a rest. I recall with some amusement an incident of several years ago when I was hunting rather open country. I saw a big buck come up atop the small dam of a cattle tank. There was not a chance I could see anywhere of taking a rest. But the shot was long and I knew instinctively that I should not try it offhand. For one reason, if I wounded the buck it had only to drop off the dam in one bound and be into brush where I'd perhaps never find it.

The more I glassed the deer, the better it looked. I ducked low and trotted through some brush fifty yards to where a wire fence crossed this large ranch pasture. I knew there was a good chance the deer would see me, or just wander off regardless. But when I made it to the fence the buck was still there. I rose carefully and slowly up behind a skinny post and laid my upturned left palm atop the post and then my rifle across it. The deer now stood three-quartering rear to me. A carefully placed shot would hit the ribs and range on forward. But the slightest error might mean a gutshot buck.

I said to myself, "If you walk off in that direction, you're home free. If you turn broadside, I'll give it a try."

The deer turned broadside. I decided just for the heck of it to try the neck. At the shot the deer fell instantly. I paced the distance at 186 paces. While it was a pretty fair shot, it was not one that any competent hunter couldn't make. The rifle was well sighted, and the rest on that post was what really made the clean kill possible.

This is as good a place as any to discuss which shots to accept and which ones to turn down. To some readers it may seem inconceivable that any shot would be rejected. However, the surest sign of an inadequate deer hunter is too much eagerness just to shoot, regardless of the situation. I feel that many hunters have the priorities exactly backward. They go out hunting desperately hoping some deer will give them an opportunity for a shot—any kind of shot. What you should carry afield with you is a firm decision as to what shot or shots *you will accept.* This type of hunter is in control, instead of letting the deer have control.

Look at it this way. Of the hundreds of thousands of deer killed annually, only a small number are trophies, and a few more may be "brag-

A deer that is still unaware of the hunter often offers an excellent shot. But if he spooks and runs away, it is a good idea to hold fire; all you have is a rear-end shot.

ging deer." Most are so-so animals. I can understand any hunter rather desperately wanting to collect a true trophy buck, and perhaps accepting an unwanted type of shot to get it. But I can't understand any reason for taking long-shot gambles on running forkhorns or does or spikes or any so-so deer. Filling a tag has become altogether too important. Connecting with a "fancy" running shot may make you feel good, but you know very well it is plain lucky in nine cases out of ten. Why take chances on wounding deer? A great many are wounded each season and never retrieved.

There is certainly no reason to be ashamed of taking a doe or a small buck. My point is that you should go hunting with a firm idea in mind of what sort of animal you will settle for. If you see a big buck, fine. If not and you are agreeable to taking a doe, fine. But whichever you have decided to accept, whichever deer you *want,* have in mind that you do want it and are not just shooting because you are kill-status conscious. Then, accept only the type of shot you want. Don't be hesitant to turn down others that are precarious. Look around a locker plant sometime where scores of deer are brought in. You'll see gutshot forkhorns, ham-shot spikes, does shot in the rear end and all but decimated. These kills are certainly not much credit to a hunter and they are less on the table. Why shoot? Why not let deer hunting be a true craft in which you control situations and turn down moves, just as in a chess game, that you don't wish to make? If you are trophy hunting, go home empty unless you see what you want and have a surefire cinch shot at it. "Take a rest or pass up the chance" is a good way to think. Accept only the shot *angle* that *you* want, not just those that so-so deer happen to offer.

What shots should you accept? This is one of the most important matters in deer hunting. It is the climax and conclusion of the hunt. What you do with the bullet is that climax. The best way to state what you should do is to look back at the old meat hunters. Some years ago I wrote a piece for one of the outdoor magazines stating that though it is now fashionable to low-rate the so-called meat hunter, not only the market hunter of old but also today's meat hunter, actually every hunter should be one. The article created quite a stir. And it drove home to readers the simple fact that meat hunters follow two ironclad rules: shoot as little as possible; ruin as little meat as possible. When you ponder this, you begin to realize that the meat hunter is really the most expert deer hunter of all!

Consider some of the facts. Meat hunters want a sure thing. That means no chancy running shots. Oldtime market hunters wasted no cartridges. Those were expensive, and shooting to no avail brought in neither money nor food. The first shot was the one to count on. That meant outwitting the deer, and placing the shot so the "money meat" was untouched. And the plain fact is, every "meat-hunter shot" not only leaves all of the best venison unmarred by the bullet, but *these shots are the most deadly and positive.* There are several of them: the ear, the forehead, the neck, the ribs, the heart. Among them is the shot you should accept, on any given occasion.

What you want in a deer will make some difference as to which you accept. A forehead shot on a big buck can split the antler base apart. So can an ear shot. There are also fairly good reasons for being wary of these placements. Unless the range is short and you are extremely accurate, you may break a jaw or cut off an antler.

The neck shot is better. If the animal faces you, sight very carefully for the throat below the chin. This shot will mean either a clean miss or an instantly dead deer. If the deer is broadside or the neck turned for a broadside shot, my practice is to place the shot quite far back on the neck, about where it joins the body. This avoids possible foul-up of a broken lower jaw, shattered antlers, or worse yet putting a bullet through the soft windpipe part of the neck, a bullet that may not upset properly. It can and does happen, not often, but occasionally. Most modern loads, however, will upset even so, and a neck-shot deer will go down instantly.

Of all shots presented that are positively lethal, the rib-cage-area shot is undoubtedly best and easiest for all hunters at any range. But there are considerations here, too, and reaction knowledge you should have. When a deer faces you, a dead-center shot squarely in the brisket drops it. But be very careful about placement here, and especially on small deer which offer a small area or on any deer at long range. A shot that drifts off center can simply break a leg or shoulder and do little else. Or it can break a shoulder and crease the ribs.

A broadside stance of a deer gives you the best chance to make slight errors of placement and still make a quick, clean kill. However, I have never been hasty to recommend heart shots. Many hunters in fact do not really know where the heart lies. It is so low that it is almost between the front legs. A deliberate attempt to heartshoot a deer may result, with error, in only breaking one or both front legs. In any case, most heart-shot deer will run. Some will run a surprising distance. If you shoot for the shoulder, a placement I dislike, you will put the deer down, you may damage the heart and lungs, but you shatter much bone and ruin shoulder

End of the trail for a heart-shot buck that ran.

meat, usually on both shoulders. Many hunters hold for just behind the shoulder, and low. This usually results in heart damage and lung damage, but error here, again, will mess up the shoulders.

A shot I learned to accept some years ago when I had to appear in a number of hunting films, and had to make certain to put the deer on the ground instantly, is a placement *high in the ribs.* Look at photos of deer, or at dead deer, carefully and you will see that there is a fairly large area here, below the backbone far enough so you won't shoot over, and above and behind the actual shoulder blade. It is also far enough removed from the paunch so that chances of error on that score are slight. For some reason a deer shot squarely in this area usually falls as if lightning struck. It is a through-the-lungs placement and yet sends tremendous shock through the ribs and backbone. This is one of the best choices for average as well as expert hunters. Occasionally a deer shot at long range, where the bullet shock power has fallen off some, will kick its rear legs like a kicking horse when hit here. This sign almost without fail means the deer has been lung-shot.

I do not like the tricky backbone shot. It invariably ruins part of the backstrap, and there is danger both of overshooting and of paunch shooting. However, a shot I have already mentioned, at the base of the neck, is a good selection. This gets the bullet above and ahead of the top of the shoulder blades, breaks the neck where it joins the back, does little meat damage, and leaves almost no chance for error. Unless you have a deer close to you or are very sure of your ability, be wary of shots from a rear angle. I noted a few pages back that a deer standing three-quarter rear to you can be shot at the back edge of the rib cage. But it doesn't take much error to paunch-shoot this animal. Bear in mind that a deer not aware of you may well move into a position to offer the shot you want. Always give it a chance. If it moves off—so, that's one you didn't bag. Forget it and go look for another. You'll be a better hunter for the discipline!

Now go back a moment to other related equipment and rifle types. There may be some differences of opinion, of course, but I'd personally feel that carrying a rifle without a sling is about like going to a party half-dressed. The sling serves time after time as a steadying influence even when you have a rest. It also avoids the need to stand your rifle against a tree or bush or rock. I get so used to having a sling looped over my shoulder that I seldom put my rifle down, even when resting. Further, when you have to drag a deer, carrying a slung rifle certainly beats toting it by hand.

The general type of rifle you can carry comfortably will always be related to how and where you hunt. Regardless, I see little point in rifles with extra-long barrels. One of the reasons I lost interest in the .264 I shot for several seasons was that it was equipped with a 26-inch barrel. That's an exaggerated instance. Few deer rifles have a barrel that long. A 22-inch barrel is usual. Such a rifle carries easily and is efficiently handled in cover. One reason some of the older lever rifles were so popular is ...at they were (and are) equipped with 20-inch barrel. Any deer rifle that will be carried on long jaunts should be as light as you can get without having recoil difficulties. I have one featherweight-type rifle that I've used

If you have to do any climbing, you'll appreciate a light rifle with a sling.

a lot, and it is fine when I'm shooting at a deer. But when I shoot it at a target I am conscious of the recoil. Some shooters have more recoil tolerance than others. Be sure you are comfortable shooting a rifle before you go all-out for it. If you are skittish of recoil, even subconsciously, it may unhinge your holding ability.

A few states, and portions of some states, nowadays require that shotguns only be used for deer. Stipulations may be for single ball only, that is, the rifled slug, or in some cases buckshot may be used. Because of these restrictions, a number of gun manufacturers now make special "deer shotguns." In general these shotguns have a 22-inch barrel, specially bored for slugs, and are equipped with ramp front sight and adjustable rear, just as for rifle shooting. There are even helper sights on the market

This Michigan hunter uses shotgun and slugs for close-in, quick shots at jumped deer in snow and heavy cover.

(Slug Sight, for example) to assist in aiming shotgun slugs. Some of these deer guns come equipped with swivels and sling also.

If you happen to have to hunt where shotguns only are allowed, it is important to know about what you can expect of present-day equipment. Buckshot, though deadly at short ranges, is tricky in pattern and can be a wounding load unless properly handled. Unless law demands buckshot, one might better stick to the rifled slug. These have been engineered to high efficiency. It is best to use one of the new deer shotguns especially made for the purpose. However, rifled slugs, contrary to opinion here and there, do not harm your gun barrel. But they should not be used in double-barreled shotguns, for they are never as accurate shot from twin-barreled guns.

Although a slug will shoot a long distance, it is accurate at the most up to 100 yards and preferably shots should not be more than 50 to 75. Properly sighted, you should get groups of not more than 4 inches at 50 yards and 8 inches at 75. Accuracy is better in open rather than snug chokes. Although slugs are made for the smaller gauges, the 12-gauge is recommended. This slug packs quite a wallop: at 25 yards over 1800 foot-pounds, 1340 at 50 yards, 1050 at 75 yards. The trajectory is also surprisingly flat. If you sight in for 75 yards you'll be only about 1½ inches high at midrange.

In my opinion there is little reason to hunt with a shotgun for deer unless you are required to do so by law. Keep in mind that the slug is a mighty big projectile and its wound pattern is large. Incidentally, you can even outfit with a "no-power" scope adapted to shotgun, and this can be of much assistance in sighting.

Regardless of where or how or with what gun a hunter goes after deer, one of his most important items of equipment is a good binocular. Some hunters still try to get along without a glass. They handicap themselves, and will never realize how much until they use a binocular for a few hunts. Having depended on glassing for so many years, I would feel practically naked and very frustrated without one. A good binocular lets you see accurately at long distances, and lets you see "into the woods" where the naked eye stops at the boundary. It collects light and shows you deer at dawn and dusk that you would otherwise miss. And it allows you to decide what a deer intends to do and if it is one you wish to try for.

I suggest a *quality* glass. There are a lot of cheap binoculars on the market today that are worse than none at all. A well-made binocular is fairly expensive. But it will also be a lifetime proposition. Probably the best all-round size for hunting anywhere on the continent is the 7×35, preferably in a lightweight model. Mountain and plains hunters sometimes use a 9×35, and I have seen some hunters carry a 10×50. Both the latter are somewhat heavy and unwieldy and generally unnecessary or not suited to average deer hunting. The 6×30 is a little too small. There are wide-angle glasses available in sizes such as 8×35, some with screw-in caps that allow wearers of glasses to use them more efficiently. I like the double-focus binocular better than center focus. The double type allows each eye to be separately focused. There are markings plus and minus on each eyepiece. Thus, when you find proper focus for each eye you may have, say, a minus 1 on the left and a plus 2 on the right. Memorize this

Glassing a distant ridge in high mountains, Wyoming.

and if someone changes the focus for their use, or it inadvertently gets turned, you can instantly set both eye pieces for proper focus.

An abominable habit of certain hunters who scoff at using a binocular is using their scope to scan for deer. I have got so I make excuses that allow me to get out of hunting with these. Using a scope as a kind of binocular has two faults: you cannot see as well with one eye as with two; you have to raise the gun to look, which may spook what you are looking for and also may swing the barrel all over creation so it points accidentally at another hunter. A rifle scope is a device for helping you *kill* a deer, not study it or try to find it!

We touched earlier in this book on how to glass for deer. To repeat a bit, take your time. Glass cover with exceeding care, looking for any part of a deer that may show. Where there are deep shadows a glass is illimitably helpful. You can probe deep into thickets this way because of the light-gathering powers of a good binocular. When glassing big sweeps of country, do it slowly. You will often be surprised to find a number of deer you had no idea were there, and the hunter who makes a quick sweep with his glass will miss many of them. Always when using a glass train yourself to raise and lower it slowly and unobtrusively so that a deer close to you of which you are unaware will not pick up the movement.

Remember that your glass is not only for finding deer but for judging them. Here again, don't be hasty. It is surprisingly easy to make errors in judgment about how many points on a rack or how large the rack, depending on the angle at which you are looking. A good quick way to make a fair stab at guessing whitetail points, when antlers are typical, is to assume there are brow tines, and then simply check number of points seen along the main beam. If there are three, this is probably a ten-pointer, for of course the end of the beam is a point. Mule deer can't be judged quite that way. But a quick shot at it can be taken by looking to see if each side has two forks. This would almost certainly be a ten-pointer— unless you get fooled and there are no brow tines. All told, however, if a deer is not disturbed, take your time glassing. Study it a long time. It's better to turn one down than to shoot a poor specimen, if you are looking for a "good one."

If you become a true trophy hunter, possibly you will want a spotting scope. The only problem here is that in most whitetail terrain there is seldom much opportunity to use one to advantage. A good binocular will check out whitetails, in almost all instances, really better than a spotting scope can, simply because you seldom are able to see and study a deer at more than 300 yards. In open-country mule deer hunting, if I was out for a real record-book deer, I would certainly carry a spotting scope and use it. There are numerous times in mountains when a deer can be seen at extreme range, and a binocular will not allow a close enough check. For the average deer hunter, a spotting scope is not a mandatory piece of equipment.

We discussed earlier the use of camouflage clothing as a help in deer hunting. Reams have been written lately about how the deer hunter should dress. Much of it is confusing to the fellow who wants to try deer hunting and is trying to find out what he needs. There are some very simple rules regarding clothing and boots for deer hunting. Aside from the use of camo, basic clothing should be selected first of all for your own comfort. If you will sit and it is cold, down underclothing is great, and down coats are, too. However, you should select soft wool for outer garments or layer if you possibly can. This will apply chiefly in whitetail or close-cover hunting where you may frighten deer because your clothing is "noisy."

Poplin or any hard outer material scratches in brush and also makes noise as you move arms and legs. Avoid it. But temper clothing selection with good sense. I have hunted mule deer, for example, in situations where it made no difference what you wore. No hunter was ever close enough to a deer for it to pick up clothing noise. In other words, just use a little common sense. Wear shades of outer clothing that will match the terrain and cover fairly well in *intensity or shade*. Wear soft, quiet outergarments, and drab, nonshiny materials. Of course if the law calls for blaze orange, that's that. For rainy weather you should use camo rain gear. Most of it, unfortunately, has handicaps for close work. It is noisy nylon. Some years ago I used soft, heavy wool when hunting in drizzle or wet snow. This material is somewhat waterproof, particularly if from wool without the lanolin removed. You may suffer some after a few hours, but you probably will live.

Hunting boots should be well chosen, for nowadays there are so many to choose from. Numerous bootmakers presently tout those "mountain climber" soles. Maybe. But most of the gents who write the ads have never been farther outdoors than Central Park in New York City. Some sole patterns are excellent, some poor. One season I tried a new pair of boots, beautifully made, expensive, with the then-new "self-cleaning ripple soles." Try walking a mountainside in high-country Colorado after snow and rain with these. There is grass and mud. The mud cakes, laced with grass. The soles truly were self-cleaning. The gobs of "adobe" squished out on all sides so that after a few steps each boot had an enormous pancake on the bottom. I might as well have used snowshoes. In such going, a plain old ordinary nonskid cushion sole would have been far better.

Insulated boots do very well even in warm weather. They keep cool as well as warm inside. In desert or arid terrain, where there may be cactus and thorns, wear boots with thick soles and uppers. Mesquite, for example, can in some varieties go right through the sole of a boot. There are several makes of boots on the market, leather boots, that are waterproof. These are excellent for any deer hunting, because they are also tough in dry, rocky terrain.

There really is not much more to be said that is of any value about clothing and footwear for deer hunting. I presume I am akin to the colonists in some respects. You put on what you've got, keep it quiet and unobtrusive, and hope for all the comfort you can get. But you cannot be a hunter and expect not to suffer some, too. Just learn to suffer with grace!

My feeling of practicality carries over into such items as knives. Today you can read literally volumes about knives for dressing out deer and other game. Knives as a hobby are one thing. As a necessary piece of deer hunting equipment they are something else. I have quit carrying a long "hunting knife" and just carry a good-quality folding jack knife, one that is rugged and with husky blades of quality steel. This is not the "perfect" deer knife. It is a compromise. The huge-bladed knives often sold as "hunting knives" are not very well-conceived tools for handling deer. Neither are the thin, long blades presently popular to some extent that look more like fillet knives.

What is needed in a deer knife is one that can cut the abdomen skin easily, one husky enough to be gripped two-handed if need be to slash up through the rib cage, and one with a blade long enough to cut around the rectum and ream out the cavity in which the bladder lies. A heavy jack knife, I have found after much experimentation, can do all of these chores with fair proficiency, and it can be carried more easily than a belt knife, and with a great deal more safety. Big hunting knives have wounded a lot of hunters, while carried and in use. Jack knives can sometimes save a careless hunter from his own ineptness.

This covers the basic items you need for deer hunting. There are all sorts of gadgets and gimmicks on the market that certain hunters may wish to take along—deer scent, hand warmer, a pocket-sized hoist, a deer call, a portable tree stand, plastic gloves for wear while gutting a deer, plastic sack for carrying out liver and heart, wet-pack towels for cleaning the hands after dressing a deer. There are dozens of such odds and ends of equipment available, most of it not vital yet with appeal to individual hunters.

There are much more necessary odds and ends that many hunters should consider, if they will hunt in wild country. It is very easy for a hunter to get lost in deer woods. When I lived in northern Michigan I helped hunt about as many lost hunters as I did deer. They came from cities, were not used to "big woods" situations, and a good many started off just for a short circle from the car and didn't get back until a couple days later. New England, the Great Lakes region, portions of the South, and large expanses of Western mountains require caution to avoid becoming lost or getting into other difficulties. But along with caution it is an excellent idea to make up a basic kit that you carry along. A very small rucksack carried on your back will hold all you'll need for most terrain. A larger one may be a good idea for long treks into totally wild country. In any woods situation where expanses are large and population low or nil, it is a good idea, particularly if you are a total stranger to the area, to have with you items that will keep you alive and reasonably comfortable for at least one night in the woods.

Basic to the selection will be a good compass and topographic map, and thorough knowledge of how to use both. A light, compact first-aid kit is next, with a first-aid booklet enclosed in it. These kits, fully and carefully supplied, can be purchased already made up and in pliable cases. In any area where insects such as mosquitoes may be a problem, a squeeze bottle of insect repellent cream—very small, potent ones are available— should be in your kit. So should a snakebite kit, in any hunting area where temperature may be above 50 degrees.

Two items I always carry in country where there is spiny vegetation, such as cactus, are tweezers and a small magnifying glass. The glass can double as an assist in starting a fire if necessary. In big areas where search parties may have to help find you, a whistle and a regulation signaling mirror are standard survival-pack items. Suggestions for clothing that serve all sorts of weather-change or overnight needs are as follows: a light down underwear jacket; a nylon rain suit; a bright-colored (blaze orange) nylon windbreaker shell; extra socks; extra gloves or mittens; two large bandannas.

A small flashlight and extra batteries are good items to have along. So are an extra jack knife, several leather thongs plus the nylon rope, a roll of small-diameter copper wire, a spool of heavy fishline (monofil), and some hooks. Matches in a waterproof container are a must item, and wise hunters include a packet of fire-starter cubes. On numerous back-in trips I also have carried a couple of short, fat candles.

If you are afraid that you might have to spend a night or two, basic needs will be a nylon tarp, which is very light and compact and a heavy plastic sheet. A small hatchet or small folding saw completes camp gear. For eating, always have salt. Those paper packets restaurants have, snugged in a moisture-proof plastic bag, pack nicely. Tea bags ditto. Heavy foil folded flat will serve to fashion makeshift cooking containers. Or in a fair-sized pack you can stow a basic mess kit made up of two containers that nest, and a spoon. A few packets of freeze-dried foods, a water canteen, and some halazone tablets for purifying water wind it up.

Obviously this seems like a lot of gear for a day of deer hunting. And it is. You can cull out some of it, depending on where you are intending to hunt. The reason I list these materials here is that with them, plus at least fundamental knowledge of survival techniques such as how to build a temporary shelter and how best to build fires, you could actually get along quite well for several days on your own in the wilderness. And

Sometimes ingenuity helps in getting your deer out. Here my son Mike lowers a whitetail down a bluff with a rope and I take it into the boat.

the entire pack will weigh less than ten pounds. Any hunter should be able to select from this list what he will surely need, or may need.

Tyro deer hunters should have at least some idea about how they will get a deer out of the woods if they cannot drive to it or pack it out on a horse. Beware of the utterly ridiculous photos and writing here and there about carrying deer and dragging deer. I have been appalled to see photos showing a man purportedly throwing a 190-pound Rocky Mountain mule deer over his back and getting set to carry it over or down a mountain. This is a chore for a weightlifter. It is dangerous from a health standpoint and you also may get shot. But besides that, an average hunter can't even get a deer of that size onto his back, let alone carry it.

It is possible to carry out small deer, but it's a bloody job and dangerous in heavily hunted country. I've helped carry a deer tied to a pole. This is a preposterous idea. The deer swings back and forth and is at the least impractical to carry in this manner even though light enough. Dragging deer has been illustrated in every unbelievable detail. On snow or dry leaves a buck can be dragged most easily by first forcing the forefeet up behind the antlers, then attaching pull ropes to the antlers or simply seizing the antlers and hauling away. Not long ago I saw a photo in a magazine

A difficult way of carrying a deer—but dragging it over cactus and thorns is worse.

of two hunters supposedly hauling a big mule deer off a mountain by tying ropes to its hind legs. If you want to find out what is wrong with this operation, besides leaving most of the meat on one side of the mountain— try it. Deer can be dragged short distances on dry or rocky ground. It takes only a hundred yards to remove all the hair from the down side. The next hundred begins to gouge the flesh.

There are three ways to get big deer out of back-in situations. Maybe four. Perhaps you can fly them out, but if so most have to be cut up and carted to the plane. On horseback hunts deer can be loaded on horses. Whole. But you darned well better be sure the horse has had experience! Some horses absolutely won't hold still for loading a whole deer on them. In a great many cases nowadays hunters are able to get a vehicle—four-wheel-drive or otherwise—close enough to drag deer to it, or else drive right to the kill. One year friends of mine used a four-wheel-drive with a winch and even hauled dead deer out of canyons in this manner. They were then loaded into the vehicle. The fourth way is to drag, or carry, and as I have said much written about this is silly.

The very best way to bring a really big deer out of an impossible spot is to butcher it, have net bags ready, place the quarters in the bags, and load them on behind saddles or carry them on your back, and the antlers likewise. A few years ago the Burnham brothers and I were in

A fine way to bring out the venison—if you have have a trained pack animal.

It won't take long to wear the hide off this muley. Dragging a deer is never easy, even downhill.

Colorado on a hunt. I contracted some bug and had to stay in the tent to recuperate. They climbed a mountain, killed two bucks, and quartered them, and carried out part on that trip and part the next day. So, what I am saying basically is: forget the nonsense of carrying a big deer on your shoulders several miles, or dragging the meat off it ditto. Just try dragging a 150-pound mule deer up and over one small mountain a distance of one mile and you will quit believing all the weightlifter junk you read!

So of course this gets us to the part of this book I have dreaded from the beginning: how to gut a deer. Perhaps it is because we live in such a ridiculously computerized and educated age. I'm uncertain. When I was a boy nobody taught me how to clean a raccoon (which we ate often) or later a pheasant. The guts were inside and you just took them out, one way or another. As recently as two years ago a gentleman who was on his first deer hunt said to me, "Now I've killed a deer, what do I do?"

"Gut it," I said.

He said, "Where are the guts and how do I remove them?"

I was thinking that we must somehow have fouled up our whole age. But I was so disgusted I said, pointing to the belly, "They're in there and if you can't get 'em out somehow then you shouldn't be deer hunting." And I turned and left him. He did clean the deer, but not very well.

So. You have a dead deer. Take out your knife. If the deer is a buck and the metatarsal glands on the hind legs are wet and smelly, slice them off skin and all to avoid getting scent on the meat. Turn the deer onto its back. A buck will lie well if the antlers are flat down on the tips. If necessary, block up the hams, side to side, with rocks or chunks of wood so it will lie on its back. If this is a buck, grab the testicles and cut them off. If you follow these embarrassingly simplified instructions for a buck you can dress a doe easily.

Now seize the buck's penis in your left hand (if you are right-handed) and cut the skin ahead of it. Then cut beside it back toward the pelvis, on each side progressively. You will discover that it goes back almost to the rectum. Go ahead and cut skin on either side until you have it cut right back to where it seems to disappear inside the pelvis. This will be far to the rear. Now continue to cut gently on each side. This will bring it down until you can see where it enters the rear bone cavity. Cut very gingerly ahead of it. This loosens the penis and tubes. You can now see where these run inside the protected cavity inside the pelvis.

Now leave this operation. Cut very carefully through the thin, tough muscle over the belly of the animal just forward of where you started to loosen the penis. Seize the muscle if you can between thumb and forefinger of your left hand and make a tiny cut or slice. This opens the cavity of the entrails and paunch. Now place the first two fingers of your left hand (if you are right-handed) inside the small cut. Put the blade in, cutting side up, and cut very carefully toward the fore end of the animal, pressing down with the left hand to keep the ever-bulging paunch low. By careful cutting; you will come soon, cutting hide and muscle, to the diaphragm. If you intend to have the head mounted, cut just up past the diaphragm. Do likewise if you must drag or load the deer for a long haul. Otherwise, stand spraddle-legged over the animal, on its back and you facing toward the head. Get hold of the knife solidly with both hands. Cut and rip upward at the right edge of the sternum if you are right-handed, left edge otherwise. Cut with two or three heaving, solid strokes upward so that the ribs are severed from their connection with the sternum. This cut should continue right on up to the throat.

Now tilt the deer toward one side or the other, depending on how it lies with land angle. Always in hilly country you should start with the deer's head uphill. Roll the paunch out onto the ground. Roll all the entrails you can outside also. Now cut the diaphragm along the rib cage. Pull heart and lungs out. Reach far up in the throat and cut the windpipe. Haul all of this out onto the ground on the same side as the paunch. Cut remainder, if any, of the diaphragm free and pull out. Cut cords to kidneys loose and haul these out. Liver and all will now be beside the deer, on the ground.

Now you have two choices. You are either a "reamer" or a "splitter." This means you either split the pelvis by pressing the hips apart and cutting the soft bone just offside of mid-pelvis; or you ream out the rectum and bladder. I am of the latter school. If you have a partner along, have him draw the hind legs forward and wide. If not, you have to play it the best you can. Cut down around the rectum from the rear, holding the tail down. When the rectum is free, run the knife blade in very carefully around the edges of the rectal opening and cut the tissue free. Be very careful not to puncture the bladder. When properly "reamed" you will have the rectum and some skin around it, the bladder, penis, and main gut all cut loose. All can be pulled through into the body cavity gingerly (so as not to break the bladder) or it can be pulled out the rear. If that is done, the gut is cut off. The hole through inside the meeting of the pelvic bones is now open and clean. Raise the deer up by the antlers or head and all blood flushes out this opening.

That's it. If you are in a camp, or near one, get the deer moved and hung up *by the head* as soon as possible. Deer hung by the hind legs are just waiting to spoil in the front. Hang bucks by a rope around the

Dressing out deer is easy but a little messy. In cactus country I wash blood from my hands with saladillo—a spineless plant full of salty water.

antlers, does by the neck. When the deer is hung tail-end down, high enough to get it off the ground, place a sharpened, long stick from gambrel to gambrel of the hind legs to spread them. Place a shorter stick in the rib cage, pulling it forcibly open and spreading it wide. If you have cut only to the rib cage because you needed to drag the deer and didn't want to get dirt inside, or because you wanted to mount the head, get the head off and the cape if necessary and spread the chest open with another stick. Be sure to remove the windpipe as far up as you can reach. In warm weather, leaving it in may sour part of the upper meat.

Don't wash the body cavity with water. Wipe it with a cloth, paper, or grass. In high mountain country a crust will quickly form on the drying meat. In fly country you have to cover the deer, plug the nostrils with paper, and be wary of blowflies. Dry crusty deer meat will keep some days. Moist meat will sour. If you are in country that is cool at night, leave the deer out. Then by day if weather is warm take it down and cover it with tarps or whatever to hold the coolness in.

For some years I have had my own method of handling deer after the drying-out period. I skin them from the neck down. Then I cut the fore knee joints and twist the fore joints of the legs and cut them off. I slit the hind gambrels, cut the hind knee joints, and cut these off. Now I lift the shoulder blades and with one long slash on each cut the entire shoulders free. This exposes all of the backstraps. These I bone out from high on the neck down to the ham as the deer hangs rear down. Now each entire ham is cut off, whole. If the deer is large, these can be sliced in two later. After that the inside tenders are removed. This leaves nothing of value but the neck and ribs. If you have a big, fat deer and wish to cook or barbecue the ribs, saw them out. If you like neck roasts, remove and trim.

This is a fine method for small deer especially. For large mule deer, if you want everything, and have a locker, then cut up as you'd cut a beef. Cut steaks, chops, etc. We are roast and tenderloin fillet and deer-burger addicts so we seldom do this, but obviously each to his own.

There are many other ways to handle all these chores. I don't intend to try to give all, or argue over which is best. Nor do I intend this as a cookbook, with recipes. I will just say that the more the tyro cook tries to "disguise" venison, the worse the mess. My wife has become something of an expert on wild-game cookery. But not with involved recipes. She roasts a whole venison ham with no tricks. It tastes, if the deer was prime, like venison. She does not try to make it taste like something else. She broils backstrap fillets and they are sinfully delicious. They do not taste like beef. They are better! Thus the only advice I intend here is to say, don't take the tack of trying to disguise what you are eating. If you do, why not try to make sirloin of beef taste like aged venison?

The important points to be made in winding up the how-to portion of this book are fairly simple. There are many ways to kill a deer, many guns to accomplish that end, many concoctions for cooking the result of the hunt. But I would like the effect of this book to be that it just possibly will give readers a better understanding of their quarry, hopefully much greater respect for it, hopefully also an enlightened disregard for all the pseudo-facts and legends that have for many decades surrounded the wonderfully exciting sport of deer hunting. Let's make it in future years a true art and craft based on carefully researched knowledge, even right down to the end product, the venison on the table. I would feel vindicated for this effort if I thought at least a few readers went out better prepared psychologically to take on the challenge, artfully, regardless of success, and fewer went out vowing to fill their tags regardless!

CHAPTER ELEVEN

Deer Management, Hope for the Future

The subject of deer management is intricate and extremely broad. Scientists have been researching deer and how best to manage them for over half a century now in the United States. A tremendous literature has accumulated, and today's deer biologists have all of it to draw on, plus endlessly continuing studies and experiments in virtually every state.

Thus federal and state wildlife biologists have come to know a very great deal, indeed, about deer management. I think offhand of one study for which a number of whitetail fawns were bottle-raised so that they were quite tame. As they grew, each was taken out to feeding grounds on deer range nearby, and a researcher with clipboard and pencil walked beside each deer, making notes on plant species of every single bite of food. I recall another study in which hundreds of highway-killed deer were checked, and the does opened during pre-fawning months to see what fawn ratio was in progress not only generally but as related to specific ranges.

Scores of disease studies and predation studies and movement studies have been accomplished. In one movement study every deer on a platt was equipped with an electronic collar signaling device and monitored constantly for full twenty-four hour periods several times a week from a central control tower. Hundreds of such projects have been concluded.

These are just random examples of the intensity with which scientists in the wildlife field constantly try to learn more and more about our deer. But what is immensely disturbing is that a great number of hunters are inclined to scoff at scientific efforts and to underestimate the value of them. Many an average hunter has an innate suspicion of "college kids and their experiments." The fact is, few nowadays are "college kids" and some who are fresh out of college have had a vast exposure to the literature of deer management, drawing upon what would add up literally to tens of thousands of hours of deer study by full-time professionals. Some of the individual deer management specialists with game departments have been working with and studying deer and deer habitats within their own states for as long as forty years.

It is well known today among game men that deer *must* be carefully and expertly managed in the future if we are to continue to have them in abundance. It is pleasant perhaps to quote the "balance of nature" bit, and indeed many of the unlettered instant ecologists of the present scene talk about that balance as if we should just let nature take its course, "without our interference." The fallacy is that we have already interfered, long ago, by injecting the human element into what was a wilderness with only a few humans. The awesomely devastating and continually growing influences of man upon nature have made it necessary in our age to manage all wildlife almost as we manage domestic animals.

Because so many hunters are so little exposed to what deer management is all about, and so many suspect it or underrate its importance, I have elected to attempt in this last chapter to give at least brief space to fundamentals of deer management, its meaning, and its great necessity.

Habitat destruction by man is one of the most severe influences that makes management ever more important. For example, the encroachment of cities into the countryside everywhere, plus the lands destroyed as wildlife habitat in order to build highways, have for some time been totaling over 3000 acres every day, which adds up to well over a million acres each year. Further, there are scores of locations on this continent where once deer roamed that are today clean-farmed right to every fence row. Hardwood bottomlands are progressively destroyed in the South so more

A most unusual photograph. It was taken with a telephoto lens from above; the whitetail buck is not lying in an open field, but in a small opening in dense thicket.

soybeans may be raised. Pine plantings of little food value leaving no room for understory cover millions of acres of once-prime deer range. Stream channelization and wetland drainage remove cover and food and hiding places.

Meanwhile, as actual habitat is cut down drastically, whitetail deer have learned to cope with civilization and so overpopulate many places in which once perhaps they would not have survived. If they are not cropped annually by proper management, they eventually ruin their ranges. There are no new ranges into which to spread and colonize. Ranges may be brought back, but it takes years, and in some instances it never can be successful. Meanwhile the more naive and less adaptable mule deer of the West loses habitat but cannot cope as well. Yet on some ranges it, too, overpopulates and must be managed and cropped with care and expertness.

To many hunters all of this is too often all black and all white. I used to hear them say, when deer yarded up and were starving in the North in winter, "Why doesn't the state carry hay to them? Or grain?" In the first place it would be impossible to get food to many of the concentrations, and in the second place domestic feeds are not generally suitable. One of the most ridiculous suggestions is often made nowadays by the bushy-haired, anti-hunting stir-once-lightly ecologists who have probably not even seen a deer in the wild. "If there are too many deer in one place, move them to where there aren't so many." Obviously the cost of such movements would be prohibitive in most cases. But regardless of that, to where should they be moved? Most suitable ranges over the entire United States now sustain full deer populations. Some have more than they can properly sustain. So there is no place to which to move surplus deer. Or should they be moved onto private lands? Ha! Most landowners with suitable deer-range lands would not want them. They have enough, or need the land for domestic animals. No, deer management is not that simple. It is not possible to crowd two pounds into a one-pound bag!

In a number of states hunters constantly grumble because there are not as many deer as there once were. Their hunting, they claim, grows poorer. But these same hunters fail to realize that there are always very good reasons why in certain places there are less deer for each hunter. One reason is that in many instances there are more hunters. I noted earlier that Michigan has been selling around 600,000 deer licenses some years, a preposterous sale, and taking around 90,000 to 100,000 deer. They were taking about the same number back when only 300,000 licenses were sold. Obviously, success percentage has fallen, even though total kill remains stable.

In this same state there was a time early in the century when, following intensive lumbering, the climax forest had been removed and second growth began to come up. With it deer thrived and multiplied. But thirty or forty years later that second growth was becoming mature forest itself. The suitable range was fast diminishing at a time when deer numbers were still rising. Something had to give. And the first part of the equation always to "give" is the fragile habitat. It was being destroyed. Deer management people deduced, and rightly, that deer numbers had to be tailored to available forage and optimum habitat. This cropping obviously had to include does and fawns. It brought on violent criticism, and still does. Hunting *is* poorer. It is poorer because optimum habitat is less abundant, and if deer are not kept in line with it they either die off, destroy the best ranges they still have, or both.

A basic management problem is that deer are not evenly distributed. Various estimates have been made of the total national deer herd. Of the millions presently in existence, if we could give each animal a like amount of space it would probably have about fifty acres all to itself. The trouble is, deer like all wildlife do best where habitat conditions are optimum, and that means that in some places there are extreme concentrations and in others sparse herds. In some of the spots of heavy concentrations even liberal hunting laws fail to keep the animals in balance with available food and living room.

There are many examples of what can happen when no cropping influences of either man or predator are brought to bear upon deer. One

Two bucks fight while a doe looks on.

of the classics that has been related in many books concerns the great mule deer debacle of the Kaibab plateau in northern Arizona. Briefly, an especially excellent mule deer herd had been established there probably for centuries. There were ample numbers of predators—wolves, mountain lions, bobcats, and coyotes. This was also a prime seasonal hunting ground for Indians of several tribes. They came here annually to get hides and sinew and meat.

Undoubtedly a fair balance between attrition by predators and Indians and other natural attrition had been reached and held for a very long time. The deer were large and vigorous. They were also virtually trapped here because of the Grand Canyon on one side and desert lands surrounding the others. Early in this century the region was dedicated as a national game preserve by that great hunter, President Theodore Roosevelt. Unquestionably he thought he was doing a proper thing, and so did many others. Little was known of deer management at that time.

Previous to the dedication of the area as a preserve, there had been much grazing of sheep and cattle here, and stockmen had systematically decimated the predator population, Later professional hunters, thinking they were protecting the fine deer herd, went after the predators again, literally wiping them out. Stock had been removed, and all hunting by both white men and Indians was stopped. At this time there were thought to be 4000 or 5000 deer on the plateau. But within a dozen years there were 35,000 to 40,000.

This appeared, from what was then known, to be a wonderful occurrence. The deer were being "managed" and were responding. But already there *were* two pounds stuffed into this one-pound bag. In another five or six years there were estimated to be over 100,000 deer on the Kaibab. But not for long. Special hunts were held. Of course these barely scratched the surface. Shortly thereafter some 60,000 deer starved to death one winter, and 25,000 or more the next. Browse lines on the trees were uniformly at the height deer standing on hind legs could reach. The range, and the herd, was ruined.

There is more to that story. There was litigation between state and federal governments over hunts that were held. But the hunts, even by government hunters, removed few deer and hardly kept pace with production. There was even a comic-opera deer drive attempted, to push the deer off the plateau and down through and across the Grand Canyon. No one seemed to have considered that even if this had worked—and it didn't—it would solve nothing. At long last severe herd cropping was brought to the Kaibab and the herd was pared down and kept to a reasonable level. Today the northern Kaibab furnishes a substantial portion of the annual Arizona deer kill, and of the number taken a husky percentage is made up of does and fawns.

Illustrations such as that should help hunters to understand the continuing need for expert deer management. There are many others. One that intrigues me is a study done just out of curiosity by a rancher friend of mine, Bob Ramsey, who lives in the Texas hill country. A sight seen here, and nowhere else that I know of, is the so-called deerproof fence. A good many ranches here have them, fences of woven wire so high that deer cannot jump them. I have been told they originated, in this area where deer hunting is highly commercialized, so that "my deer couldn't get out of my pasture and over on yours."

There is a pasture on the Ramsey ranch that has a deerproof fence around it. The fence has been there for a number of years. State deer management personnel have estimated that the general carrying capacity of that area is about one deer to every ten acres. This is considered maximum. Because of the cover types in this pasture, and its shape and fencing, it is possible with a few people working at it to get a quite accurate count of the deer inside the fence. Each year two counts have been taken, by different parties, and they have always checked out quite well.

For some years the deer count ran just about as the biologists thought it should—one deer to every ten or twelve acres. But then one year unusually favorable conditions caused eruption in the fawn drop. The herd suddenly skyrocketed to a deer for every three acres. A hunter unschooled in nature's rather cruel methods of striking a balance might have thought that was just great. But it wasn't. A few bucks were taken off by hunters and these were tallied, and that next fall the herd was back down to about normal again. The extra deer that the range could not sustain had starved. And over the next several years there were fluctuations, apparently because of low fawn production.

Presently, however, there was another extra-good year and the herd shot up again. There was one deer for every seven acres. But the range and the herd could not get along at this ratio, and probably the other high years had done harm, too. Whatever the cause, only one fawn was found that fall, and each deer now had about eighteen acres. In later years the ratio of one deer to ten or twelve acres was reestablished.

Two important conclusions can be drawn from this interesting record. One is that even though there was a fair amount of hunting of bucks over those years, the modest hunter kill seemed to have no effect on the ups and downs, probably because the cropping was not severe enough. The other conclusion is that *some hundreds of days of recreation and some hundreds of pounds of venison were wasted by not balancing the herd to its pasture every season, rather than letting nature do it.*

Deer management experts know well that quota hunting can balance any given deer herd. True, a few mistakes are made now and then on the side of excessively high quotas—that is, overcropping on a given range and in a given season. But when such an error occurs it can be rectified. To illustrate how *flexible laws* (most important) and the findings of biologists can work together to keep the deer population tailored to the range, with a maximum number of animals on the range and a maximum number utilized for sport each year, as the deer drop dictates, consider findings in Maine in a recent season.

There had been a severe winter, and management people suspected a substantial loss of deer to starvation and related disease. In addition, severe winters with their attendant poor forage conditions usually mean a lowered fawn crop. Does either do not conceive, or their physical condition is such that fawns do not survive. In Maine all deer killed in season must by law be checked in with local wardens. There is some antlerless hunting. The previous season the ratio of fawns to does at check stations had been 98.8 fawns to 100 does. That showed an excellent fawn crop, and, particularly, high survival from the previous year. But during the fall following the severe winter, the ratio dropped by almost half. There were only 50 fawns checked in per 100 does.

Biologists had already predicted that this would probably happen. Also, in checking buck-doe kill ratios they found both the previous good year and this poor fawn crop year about the same, around 60 percent bucks, 40 percent does. By careful continued monitoring of the herd, they thus could adjust as needed, perhaps with a lower kill quota on does to compensate for the poor fawn crop that would influence the total deer numbers. By killing fewer does, given normal seasons they could up the fawn crop even if it was only a modest drop, and quickly build the total herd back up. This case illustrates one of the basic tools of deer herd management.

More complicated but extremely effective controls are illustrated in a historical briefing of Oregon deer, and in other Oregon deer studies reviewed in the *Oregon State Game Commission Bulletin* for January 1972. In early days of management in Oregon, when as elsewhere fewer facts were on hand, game managers were too good to their deer. Bucks-only laws and a refuge system brought an increase in mule deer until in some of their best ranges they were vastly overpopulated. Blacktail deer zoomed in population as logging on the coastal slopes opened new habitat for them. Finally the legislature gave the game department a free hand to study deer of both kinds and decide how many should be harvested and what levels of population they should strive for.

Soon hunters were allowed either buck or doe, and out of annual harvests averaging above 100,000 some 35,000 antlerless deer were being taken. Now deer management people were learning more and more, and they saw a new and crucial problem. This was in the late 1950s. The trouble with the system was that *hunters* were not properly distributed. Some areas were receiving tremendous hunter pressure near population centers or because of easy hunting, and some that needed more weren't getting it. Out of this grew the management unit program, one which is in use by numerous states and has been now for some time.

Probably some readers already know how this works. All of a state's deer range is split up into fairly small Units. Each Unit is composed,

A handsome whitetail buck, with a characteristic worried look.

wherever possible, of an overall type of habitat. Surveys can be made both on the ground and via kill statistics to keep a check on the number of deer in each Unit. As a Unit herd moves upward in population, a higher kill quota (number of permits) can be set. When it moves below the level considered a norm for that habitat, the quota can be cut. Kill statistics show year after year approximately what hunter success is in any given Unit. In some the terrain is more difficult for hunting than in others. With a fairly accurate forecast of what success will be, a quota can be set to compensate. For example, if a Unit usually brings 50 percent hunter success and the management people feel that 500 deer should be taken, the kill quota can be set at 1000. When necessary, quotas for both bucks and does can be set. In most instances, however, it is the antlerless permits that would be raised or limited. In other words, by using Units and kill quotas and average kill statistics and buck and doe limitations or nonlimitations all together, management can not only keep herds regionally balanced to their habitats but can distribute hunters in relation to the amount of cropping desired.

Systems of this general variety are extremely flexible. In Oregon, for example, one recent winter was unusually severe and a high deer loss was anticipated. In the following seasons the worst-hit parts of the state had no antlerless permits at all, and other portions only a few. In another instance in northeastern Oregon there was poor fawn production, and while the reasons may not have been entirely clear, the antlerless permits were slashed for the following season.

Oregon is high on the list of states that are exemplary in their meticulous studies of their deer herds. It is easy, for example, for critics to blame a low deer population on overshooting of bucks. But if biologists listen to these criticisms without attempting to get the facts, they would do the critics themselves a disservice. Oregon deer management people already knew that among Oregon mule deer the buck-doe ratio was a one-to-ten average and sometimes below that. Was this enough bucks? Did it really affect fawn production? They did studies on accidentally killed mule deer does and some collected from other sources, and found what would seem to be a very good average of 150 fetuses for every 100 does. Certainly there were enough bucks.

Biologists know that in many states winter is a deadly time for deer. This may even be true in warm climates. Texas has experienced high die-offs in the hill country in winters following a severe summer drought. In cold climates it can be worse. Another Oregon example concerns a group of seventy-seven blacktail deer that were held for study purposes in an enclosure of roughly a half-section. During a recent severe winter all the fawns and yearling bucks, two-thirds of adult bucks, and a substantial number of adult and yearling does were lost. Again, as in the Michigan starvation incident I noted in an earlier chapter, the drastic ups and downs caused by weather illustrate the desperate need for facts, and scientific management.

But regardless of how much new information scientists come up with, they can never rest on their laurels. Because of man primarily, but with other influences thrown in to confuse issues, relationships in nature are constantly changing. At the present time deer biologists in widely separated areas of the West, as an example, are disturbed over mule deer declines, and so far they have been unable to pinpoint precise reasons, at least not past the general supposition stage. Studies are in progress in Arizona, Colorado, Oregon, and elsewhere. Years ago no one would have considered it possible that predation was remotely a serious influence on deer numbers. This was like the old wheeze about how the foxes were eating up all the pheasants. During that big argument one Michigan scientist actually followed fox tracks, in pheasant country, for over a thousand miles all told, and found only a scattering of pheasant kills. However, today deer men are wondering about predation. In Arizona some are considering that it may well be a reason for deer decline, because they know that potential fawn production is high but that fawns are somehow being lost.

Oregon researchers also are wondering. Again drawing on material published in the *Oregon State Game Commission Bulletin,* there is as I write this a study in progress in the Steens Mountain area of southeastern Oregon. Fetus ratio here per 100 does has been found to be as high as 165. This indicates numerous twins. During the ten months that followed the fawn drop, 70 percent of that potential from fetus counts had disappeared. And all but a small percentage of this loss occurred apparently during the first six months. It is believed that coyotes, and other predators, may be at least partly responsible for this high mortality.

From a management point of view, fawn mortality is a *waste,* no matter what causes it. Certainly if all fawns survive there will be high deer populations and probably overpopulations. But proper hunter distribution and quotas can balance those out. Full hunter participation and recreation, an important commodity in our pressured age, plus the lesser consideration of meat on the table, are the ultimate goals. The more fawns that survive, the more deer the hunters can be allowed to bag and the higher success hunters will have. These are prime considerations of the deer manager in our complicated age, and the researchers, dedicated people, need all-out hunter support and hunter "sale" of their programs to the general public. Basically, the highest use of the resource commensurate with the good health and balance of the herds is what they are aiming for.

Today thousands of younger deer hunters take for granted excellent hunting in their home states, and do not realize that some years ago there was little or none, and that enlightened management is responsible for the improvement. In the early days of market and hide hunting, and later during times when game laws were few and not well enforced, in state after state whitetail deer were on the verge of extinction. Early in this century, deer in Virginia, for example, were only a remnant. North Carolina, with a herd creeping up toward half a million today, had very few fifty or sixty years ago. At the turn of the century West Virginia had probably less than a thousand whitetails.

In state after state the situation was similar. Kentucky whitetails were practically wiped out. Forty years ago Tennessee had only a scattering left. In the now-populous states of Ohio, Indiana, and Illinois deer were all but exterminated during the last century and early part of this one, yet today these states have at least fair and huntable numbers. Missouri in the 1920s was down to so few deer that conservationists predicted extinction. The story was the same in Arkansas and Louisiana.

In most instances the techniques used to rejuvenate the deer herds were closing of seasons or severely limiting them, and transplanting live-trapped deer to ranges where they might, with protection, reestablish themselves. The whitetail, as we have seen, is resilient and prolific and has been able to adapt to man's settlement. Transplants were made in the beginning to only the most secluded areas where habitat was prime. As soon as the deer, under protection, got a foothold, they spread out. During the early transplanting years much was learned about live-trapping and handling deer and bringing in new blood from other states, for best results and the least harm to the animals. Meanwhile much range research and research on the animals themselves was progressing. Game departments hired biologists who spent their entire time studying deer and their needs, and these scientists were recognized as worth their salaries many times over. It is to these people of early research days, to those who have followed, to the enforcement people who gave the transplants opportunity, and to patient sportsmen who were willing to hold their fire for some years that we owe most of the excellent deer hunting we have today.

Probably the most insidious current threat to the nation's deer is the disruption of scientific management by the ignorant and preposterously emotional anti-hunting crowd. Some of these people may be well-intentioned, but good intentions that ignore scientific fact are unlikely to have good results. And of course the hard-core anti-hunting people are really not interested in deer or other wildlife at all; they are simply fanatics with a fixation against the killing of any wild creature by man with gun or bow. Yet they eat beef, pork, and lamb. The danger from such people is great indeed. As an example, a small clique was recently able to block a hunt on an Eastern refuge. Hunting is rather commonly used on wildlife refuges as a tool for removing surplus animals. Such hunts are very carefully planned and controlled and supervised. In the instance mentioned, deer were badly overpopulated. A hunt was scheduled to remove the surplus, but the anti-hunting group was able to stymie it in the state legislature.

The refuge managers know well that over the next several years, as the deer population builds up, more and more habitat harm will occur. Eventually there will be a heavy die-off of deer. But whether habitat can keep pace as the herd builds again is questionable. And if the herd builds swiftly enough, there will simply be another period of starvation. In some instances it is possible to wipe out an entire herd in this manner. Certainly no deer will be shot by a hunter. Ignorant, bumble-thumbed legislators have seen to that. Unfortunately, a great many *more* deer than the hunters would have taken will die the much slower deaths of disease and starvation, to no good use whatever.

Mule deer does bedded in shade in dry wash.

The real danger is that if such an influence is allowed to spread and gain enough of a foothold nationally, everything that has been learned and accomplished over three-fourths of a century will go down the drain. With no herd management, and no habitat improvement—which is constantly going on in many places—there will in due time be few deer remaining, either for hunters or for nonhunting wildlife observers, or for silly anti-hunters to gloat over. The most exasperating side is that the virulent anti-hunter refuses even to *listen* to what schooled and experienced management people have to say; he remains wholly ignorant of the facts while letting his emotions run wild.

An isolated but important illustration concerns not deer but the small tule elk of California. It is worth noting here because this is the kind of influence deer hunters must battle, with quiet patience and with facts, while holding their own emotions in check against the arm-waving and often extremely vindictive "anti" crowd.

The tule elk is the smallest of North American elk. It was native to interior foothills and valleys of California. Settlement all but did it in. But some years ago a small herd was transplanted to the Owens Valley. Without the transplant, paid for by hunter money, these elk would now be extinct. There has never been room in the transplant area for more than a token herd, and game department plans had long been to hold numbers to three hundred or less. There is not range enough for more, and as the herd grows animals get onto private lands and there are damage complaints.

Thus, this small band of an endangered species could be kept indefinitely as a remnant, showcase herd. When it grew beyond what the range could sustain, small, closely regulated hunts were held. In years when the herd did not advance, no hunts were allowed. A short time ago, however, as a hunt was scheduled, several of the "new ecologists" of the "like, man, wow" variety convinced others who were undoubtedly sincere in their views that a "bloodbath" was about to be visited upon these endangered animals. And so they were able to stop the proposed hunt.

Unfortunately, the *lack* of cropping is what really is endangering this species. As this is written the latest news is that there are now too many elk. The state has been trying to give them away without success so far, and has even tried as far away as in Mexico. As damage complaints come in, obviously animals will have to be removed, alive or dead. Unless some way can be found to get rid of the surplus, the tule elk may well breed itself to extinction right there in the valley that could have been a permanent haven.

Whether over future years the number of deer hunters will grow or whether hunting may taper off as a mass-interest sport is difficult to predict. But it is interesting that deer managers in a number of areas have learned that they could be taking many *more* deer annually than are now being harvested. If hunter numbers grow, this argues affirmatively for supplying the demand. For example, in some prime habitats where severe winter die-offs do not periodically occur, it is thought that up to 40 percent of the total herd might be cropped annually without any ill effect. While that could not work everywhere and is a specialized situation, it is well known that in almost all habitats higher percentages could be bagged than are now being taken. In most states the harvest runs from an estimated 10 to 15 percent of the total herd. Yet on top of this there is a substantial amount of natural attrition. Deer removed in proportion to this attrition would have little effect, biologists know, on the total breeding stock left; the extra harvest simply reduces natural attrition.

On a quite different scale this may be likened to quail management. These are short-lived birds. Some 80 percent of the annual hatch succumbs to natural attrition before the next breeding season. And it makes little difference whether or not the birds are hunted. Studies on some high-yield ranges that go unhunted show that 60 percent of the quail population is already gone by end of the year, regardless. Thus, those birds might as well have gone into hunters' game vests.

One of the most astonishing and enlightening sets of figures on what might be done in harvesting deer comes nowadays out of Texas. This state is believed to contain around one-fifth of the total U.S. deer herd. The annual harvest nowadays hangs close to 300,000 animals, highest on the continent. Total deer numbers are estimated to be around 3.2 million, and there may be even more than that. Thus, the kill actually is less than 10 percent of the total deer herd. Management people feel that at least 25 percent of the herd could be taken every season—with exceptions occasionally when there is a drought.

Consider what that would mean—a total state kill of 800,000 deer! That's a half million more animals annually than are now harvested. It's also about 25 million pounds of venison that is not being eaten, and, because Texas deer hunting is almost totally commercialized, it is somewhere between $25 million and $50 million annually that landowners are not collecting, plus hundreds of thousands of man-days sport hunters are not getting. It has even been figured out how much food those half million deer eat that livestock might be eating—and that amounts to about $13.5 million that ranchers could be saving in feed bills.

Over recent seasons some 200,000 or more doe permits have been offered annually in Texas. The system here is to issue them to the landowner, who in turn can issue them to hunters on his property. But it is difficult to get that many permits used. Hunting for bucks is so good few wish to kill a doe. On our small ranch we get a few doe permits, but we simply cannot use them all ourselves or find hunters to take them even though we would make no charge. All of which illustrates that management in many ways is far ahead of demand, and in this odd instance is often stymied because of lack of demand.

The control of disease also has much bearing, in management, on deer numbers. Endless studies have been made of deer pests and diseases. But curiously, learning how to combat these occasionally results in complicating management problems. One of the classic examples concerns the screwworm fly. The maggots, or larvae, of this fly eat living flesh. In Florida and in the Southwest, the screwworm has for centuries been an extremely serious problem to stock owners. When a calf, lamb or goat, is born, the flies lay eggs in the bloody navel. Or when an animal gets a cut, the flies go after it and literally eat it alive, to an extent where it succumbs.

While protecting livestock was the impetus for attempts to control the screwworm fly, biologists have long known that the loss of deer to this pest is tremendous. It has been estimated that in screwworm range in some seasons fawn losses have been as high as 80 percent. Some years ago the Department of Agriculture experimented with artificially raising screwworm flies, feeding the maggots meat and blood kept at the body temperature of living stock. The male flies were then sterilized and released by millions from planes. These were to breed with wild females, to interrupt the cycle of reproduction.

The first tests were in Florida, and in due time the screwworm fly was literally wiped out there. This was one influence that speeded the growth of the Florida deer herd, which had had many difficulties. But growth was so fast in some places—notably Collier County—that some extreme die-offs occurred. In Texas, where billions of screwworm flies have been raised, sterilized, and released over past years, the screwworm has been brought under control, and now with cooperation from Mexico there may come a time when it can be brought to extinction across the Southwest, too. But this has skyrocketed fawn crops in some counties that were already at peak deer populations even with the presence of the screwworm, and thus thousands of deer die from starvation or other causes simply because there are too many.

It is often difficult for hunters to believe that thousands of deer die from natural attrition. Many have said to me, "If that many dead deer were around, we'd see them out in the woods." This is a popular fallacy. One recent fall I found a small deer hung in a fence it had tried to jump. It was barely alive and was in such bad shape that I shot it, removed it from the fence, slit it open, and left it there. Opening it entices meat-eating birds and animals more quickly. I was hunting the area and decided to see what happened to the deer.

There were buzzards and gray foxes, jays, a few ravens, and a scattering of small rodent species on this range. In exactly a week there was absolutely nothing to mark the spot except some hair and a stain on the ground. Everything had been eaten or dragged away. Remains of animals in any latitude do not take long finding their way back into the life chain and the soil.

It is my hope that this small insight into deer management may spark the interest of hunters. Though you may not become a professional deer manager, knowledge of management raises your understanding of your quarry and its requirements, and thus makes your hobby more interesting. Certainly, as I said in the beginning, management is an intricate affair. The study of deer requirements actually must begin with the soil. Which soils furnish the best forage, proper minerals for antler growth, and so on? What foods do deer prefer on any given range, and what is their daily requirement in forage relative to the size of the deer? Are the deer on a given range increasing, and if so are they harming their range by eating too much of the favorite plants, the first to be harmed under such conditions? If these favorite foods are overbrowsed, then the number of deer this range can sustain will be lowered swiftly.

How can it be established what the carrying capacity of a given range is? This is a prime problem for the deer manager. He *must* know the answer. Then he must attempt to strike a balance. His goal will be to keep the deer numbers at least slightly *below* maximum capacity of the range. That way upward fluctuations are not as likely to harm the habitat—which is the crucial factor. Tied in with all of the studies that must be made, the biologist must know not only what forage plants are available, which ones favorite, how much each deer will eat per day, and how much pressure the forage can accommodate, but he must also know thoroughly what deer require in actual *nutrition*, proteins, etc., and from what it will come. Working out the complicated equations carefully, a good manager can keep a herd at a level below what its range will sustain with two main

aims: to keep the range stable and continuing at a top level in nutrition value; and to raise the fawn production of the herd. The better the forage conditions, the higher the fawn crop from a given number of does.

Of course antler development must be considered, for heavy antlers appeal to the "consumer," the hunter. But meanwhile it is always the hope of the manager to get as many antlerless deer harvested annually as the herd can stand. For this, too, will have a direct bearing on antler growth, puzzling as that may sound at first reading. For example, on our ranch we have a difficult time collecting bucks with good antlers. We are quite sure we know why, but there is not much we can do about it unless we begin heavy commercial hunting, which we really don't want to do. We have too many bucks with small or spike antlers. And we know that a large percentage of these are not yearlings. They are older. This is because we have too many deer. The occurrence of numerous bucks with small or spike antlers almost always means there are too many deer for the amount of living room and forage.

Although a prodigious amount of information has accrued over past years, there is much still to be learned. It is well known that most of the best deer habitat on the continent came into being not by man's plans for deer, but because of other circumstances, such as lumbering. From here on more and more conscious attention must be paid to managing habitat deliberately. In high mountains, small spruce or other conifers intrude into the mountain meadow edges, crowding out young aspens. The spruce must be kept back. Conceivably the clear-cutting of forests, which is so controversial today, may be conducive to forming better future deer range. Fire has already been used to some extent. It is quite likely more use will be made of it in future to open clearings. It is even possible that fire control may be slackened to some extent in the future, both for the good of the forests, which may need "weeding out" at times, and for wildlife.

Indeed, wholly scientific and meticulously researched management of our deer herds and the ranges on which they thrive is the hunter's best hope for the future of his sport. All of us must realize that, and be willing to learn from those who have done the research. We must be willing to listen, and to help, rather than to attempt to stem progress in this direction simply because we do not understand the facts.

Index

Ontario, deer and hunting in, 50
"oozing" effect of scent, 122
Oregon, deer and hunting in, 27–28, 233, 234, 235
overcast days, seeing deer on, 181

Peninsula mule deer, 22
Pennsylvania, deer and hunting in, 42, 156
photographing live deer, 72, 73, 113, 127–28, 153, 180
physical condition of whitetails, typical, 57
piñon nuts as deer food, 148
placement of shots, 208–10
placid temperament of mule deer, 60, 72, 77–78, 82–83
planning for hunting success, 24–26
point counting, 102–4
population estimates of deer, 3–6, 24–27, 83–84, 174, 229
predators and deer, relationships of, 55–56, 116–17, 230
public lands, hunting on, 27–43 *passim,* 85

Quebec, deer and hunting in, 50
quota hunting, value of, 232, 235

rack: *see* antler spread
Ramsey, Bob, 231
ranges of deer in U.S., Canada, and northern Mexico, 27–51; of whitetail, 12, 13–19, 52–54; of mule deer, 19–22; of individual deer groups, 153
rattling antlers to attract deer, 126–33, 187; choosing antlers for, 136
recoil, problem of, 210–11
regulations, current hunting, 26, 32, 34, 35; in Mexico, 51
removing carcass from hunting site, 219–20
rests, rifle, 203–5
Rhode Island, deer and hunting in, 48
road-killed deer, 106
Roberts, Travis, 79–80
Rocky Mountain mule deer, 7, 10, 19, 28, 29, 31, 38, 49, 71, 81, 196
Roosevelt, Theodore, 230
rubs, buck, 133–35, 167, 184

rump patch, white, of mule deer, 20, 21, 22
rutting behavior of bucks, 128–32, 135
rutting period, 64–65, 132

Saskatchewan, deer and hunting in, 49–50
scent, human, deer reaction to, 116, 119–24, 131, 141, 190; minimizing, 122
scents used to attract deer, 126, 140–42
Schreiner, Charlie, 126
scope sights for deer guns, 201–3, 214
scrapes, buck, 67, 135–36, 184, 240
screwworm fly, 240
secretiveness as prominent trait in bucks, 87–88, 90–92
seeing deer, ability and ways for, 167, 177–82
sheep, bighorn, 2, 74; domestic, 55–56, 66, 174
shotguns, 211–13
signals, physical and vocal, used by whitetails, 62–67
signs for locating deer, 167–68 *ff.,* 184
sight, sense of in deer, 58, 105–9
sights: *see* scope sights
Sitka deer, 7, 8, 9, 19, 21, 49, 140
skull shape, 11, 13, 21, 103
skunk musk, 141
smell, sense of in deer, 106, 119–24
snorting signal in whitetails, 62–63, 64
Solunar Tables, 163
South Carolina, deer and hunting in, 44
South Dakota, deer and hunting in, 34
Southern mule deer, 22
spike bucks, 88, 90, 131, 132
spooking deer, 56 *ff.,* 64, 107, 115–16; by horses, 185–86
sport hunting, 6
squirrels, 52, 58, 125
stability in deer populations, 89, 98
stalking techniques, 110–24 *passim,* 133, 183, 185–87
stamping foot signal in whitetails, 62–63, 64, 112
stance of deer, as identifying point, 68
stand, hunting, 105, 122, 133, 183–85
"still-hunting," 183